Governance and Public Management

Series Editor

Paul Joyce, INLOGOV, University of Birmingham, Birmingham, UK

IIAS Series: Governance and Public Management

International Institute of Administrative Sciences (IIAS)—*Setting the Governance Agenda Worldwide*

Website: http://www.iias-iisa.org

Edited by Paul Joyce

The International Institute of Administrative Sciences was set up in 1930 by the International Congress of Administrative Sciences held in Madrid and is headquartered in Brussels. It is an association that has a scientific purpose. It provides forums and conferences for researchers, specialists in public law, and practitioners in governments and the wider public sector. IIAS, its main specialized association (IASIA), and its regional groups (AGPA, EGPA and LAGPA) together create a special "meeting place where knowledge and progress may be disseminated".

In its capacity as an international association with a scientific purpose, it has Advisory Status in the Economic and Social Council of the United Nations (1948), UNESCO (1962), and the International Labour Office (1987). As a scientific association it supports the pursuit of objectivity, privileging no particular ideology, experience, or system.

IIAS has fostered exceptional networks of researchers and practitioners who address the latest experiences and developments in the practice of public administration, public management, and public governance. Throughout its nearly 100 years of activity, it has continued to adapt to a world that is in continuous change.

Governance and Public Management Series

This book series is committed to advancing understanding of what is happening in public governance and public management, to searching for insights into causes and consequences, and to expanding expertise in making innovations, improvements, and reforms.

It is the intention of the series to include books that are forward-looking, emphasise theory and practice, are underpinned by data and facts, and offer ideas and prescriptions for improvements in public governance and public management.

The books in this series will offer intelligent points of view about the big challenges of the next decade and beyond. Challenges such as sustainable development, the climate crisis, poverty, social inclusion, public services, digital transformations, artificial intelligence (A.I.), open government, transparent and responsive governance, managing internal conflicts and violence within society, judicial systems, conflicts and wars between countries, and international cooperation and partnerships.

All books in the series are subject to Palgrave's rigorous peer review process: https://www.palgrave.com/gb/demystifying-peer-review/792492.

Juraj Nemec · Michal Plaček ·
Purshottama Sivanarain Reddy
Editors

Local Government and Fiscal Transfers

Enhancing or Weakening Democracy?

IIAS International Institute of Administrative Sciences
IISA Institut International des Sciences Administratives

palgrave
macmillan

Editors
Juraj Nemec
Department of Public Economics
Masaryk University
Brno, Czech Republic

Michal Plaček
Public and Social Policy
Charles University
Prague, Czech Republic

Purshottama Sivanarain Reddy
Governance, IT and Governance
University of KwaZulu-Natal
Durban, South Africa

ISSN 2524-728X ISSN 2524-7298 (electronic)
Governance and Public Management
ISBN 978-3-031-95673-7 ISBN 978-3-031-95674-4 (eBook)
https://doi.org/10.1007/978-3-031-95674-4

This work was supported by European Cooperation in Science and Technology.

This Palgrave Macmillan imprint is published by the registered company Springer Nature Switzerland AG
The registered company address is: Gewerbestrasse 11, 6330 Cham, Switzerland

If disposing of this product, please recycle the paper.

This publication is based upon work from COST Action IGCOORD, CA20123, supported by COST (European Cooperation in Science and Technology).

COST (European Cooperation in Science and Technology) is a funding agency for research and innovation networks. Our Actions help connect research initiatives across Europe and enable scientists to grow their ideas by sharing them with their peers. This boosts their research, career and innovation.

www.cost.eu

EUROPEAN COOPERATION IN SCIENCE & TECHNOLOGY

Funded by the European Union

Contents

Notes on Contributors

Amitava Basu holds a master's degree in commerce and bachelors in law from the University of Kolkata. Amitava is a Fellow of the Institute of Chartered Accountants of India. As Executive Director of PricewaterhouseCoopers, he worked with various government agencies in India and abroad in the public policy domain and reform strategies. He has also been teaching post-graduate students in leading business schools in India. Presently, he is a member of the Governing Council of the Centre for Environmental Management and Participatory Development, a research organization with pan-India network. Amitava is also a member of the Board of Management of International Association of Schools and Institutes of Administration (IASIA). He published book chapters in edited books with international publishers and articles in various national and international professional journals.

Tristan Canare is a Senior Researcher at the Bangko Sentral ng Pilipinas and a member of the Board of Trustees of the Philippine Economic Society. He was a Non-Resident Research Fellow at the School of Government and a Lecturer at the Department of Economics, Ateneo de Manila University. Previously, he was the Associate Director and Senior Economist at the Asian Institute of Management Policy Center and a Division Chief at the Economics Office of the Philippine Competition Commission. He also consulted for development organizations such as the World Bank and the Asian Development Bank, among others. He has journal publications on such fields as public economics, local public finance, decentralization, political economy, small and medium enterprises, and development

Amrie Firmansyah is a faculty member at Universitas Pembangunan Nasional Veteran Jakarta, where he holds the Head of the Accounting Department position. He possesses interdisciplinary academic qualifications in accounting, management, economics, and public administration. With a background in public service at the Ministry of Finance of the Republic of Indonesia, he brings valuable insights into fiscal policy and intergovernmental financial relations. His academic interests focus on sustainability accounting, financial reporting, taxation, and public sector governance. He has authored several books and contributed to numerous journal publications, and he is regularly invited to share his expertise at academic and professional events both domestically and internationally.

Satyabhama Andrea C. Gulapa was a research assistant at the Ateneo School of Government. She obtained her master's and bachelor's degree in Economics at the Department of Economics, Ateneo De Manila University. Her research interests include development economics, econometrics, and microeconomics of competitiveness. At present, she is a researcher at the Innovation Staff of the National Economic and Development Authority, the government central planning agency.

Janka Holíková is the doctoral student at the Faculty of Economics, Matej Bel University Banská Bystrica, Slovakia. Her research focuses on horizontal and vertical fiscal imbalance and its impact of municipal finance in Slovakia.

John-Mary Kauzya, Professor Extraordinary, School of Public Leadership, Stellenbosch University since January 2022, is a cerebrated and decorated Ugandan expert in public governance and public administration, who in 2022 retired from the UN after 22 years as Chief of Public Service Innovation Branch advising Governments on governance, Public Administration and Management and championing capacity development for innovation and transformational leadership in public sector institutions. In 2014 the International Association of Schools and Institutes of Administration (IASIA) gave him the O.P. Dwivedi Award for Outstanding Contribution to Public Administration and Public Policy in the World. In December 2022 the Africa Association for Public Administration and Management (AAPAM) awarded Dr. Kauzya with a Gold Medal marking his exceptional achievement that has made "significant contribution to the advancement of excellence in public administration and management in Africa".

Ondřej Kuba is a lecturer at the University of Pardubice, Faculty of Economics and Administration. He earned his Ph.D. in Public and Regional Economics, with his dissertation focusing on voter decision-making and the factors influencing electoral choices. His research interests include public economics, public policy, and well-being, with a particular focus on decision-making processes in the public sector. He has published his work in international conferences, book chapters, and peer-reviewed journals. In addition to his research activities, he participates in national and international projects.

Ajiv Maharaj is the Deputy Head of Economic Development and Investment Promotion at eThekwini Municipality and chairs the Economic Affairs Trade and Investment Forum at the Durban Chamber of Commerce and Industry. Prior to joining the eThekwini Metro he worked as a Development Consultant in the Province of KwaZulu-Natal, South Africa. In his current role within the eThekwini Metro he is responsible for economic research, policy, strategy and innovation and founded Innovate Durban which was the first city-led innovation agency in South Africa, as well as The Durban Edge, being the first city-led economic intelligence platform in South Africa. He has published several articles in international and domestic journals.

Ronald U. Mendoza is Under Secretary for Policy, Planning and M&E for the Department of Education of the Republic of the Philippines. He is a governance and institutional reforms specialist with over 25 years of experience in economic development policy and public administration reforms. Dr. Mendoza served as Dean and Professor of Economics with the Ateneo School of Government, from 2016 to 2022. From 2011 to 2015 he was the Executive Director of the AIM Rizalino S. Navarro Policy Center for Competitiveness. His research background includes work with UNICEF, UNDP, the Federal Reserve Bank of Boston, the Economist Intelligence Unit (EIU), and several Manila-based non-governmental organizations.

Beáta Mikušová Meričková is the full professor of Public Economics and Services at the Faculty of Economics Matej Bel University in Banská Bystrica, Slovakia. She focuses her research activities on the areas of public sector, public finances and new approaches to the provision of public services. These activities are documented by several monographs, many research studies and articles published in current academic journals and conference proceedings at home and abroad. Her research activities include cooperation in projects of international and national significance. She has the publications registered in Web of Science and SCOPUS, and book chapters with international publishers.

Nikoleta Jakuš Muthová is the assistant professor at the Faculty of Economics at the Department of Public Economy and Regional Development, Matej Bel University in Slovakia. Her research activities focus on the application of behavioural economics in the public sector, experimental economics, consumer preferences in the consumption of public goods and the use of innovation in the public sector. Her research activities include cooperation in projects of international and national significance.

Juraj Nemec is full time Professor of Public Finance and Public Management at the Faculty of Economics and Administration at Masaryk University in Brno, Czech Republic and part time Professor at the Faculty of Economics at Matej Bel University in Banska Bystrica, Slovakia, with more 40 years' experience in teaching on pre-graduate, graduate and doctoral levels. He served and serves in many positions in international organisations, also as the member of the Committee of Experts on Public Administration by the United Nations. In 2016 he received the DC Stone Award honouring a distinguished international scholar for advancing the well-being of IASIA and in 2023 the O.P. Dwiwedi Award for Outstanding Contribution to the Advancement of Public Administration and Public Policy Worldwide from the IASIA. He has published over 600 books and scientific articles in his field, including edited books published by well-known international publishers.

Tatsuro Niikawa is Professor Emeritus of Doshisha University. He is also Visiting Professor of Research Institute for Humanity and Nature. He was former Professor of Public Policy at Graduate School of Policy and Management of Doshisha University. His major fields of research are the study of government, governance, public administration, public policy analysis, intergovernmental relation, central subsidies and allocation to local government, citizen participation and social innovation. His publications and research articles focus on local government and governance, deliberative democracy and participatory decision making, social enterprise and business, civil society organization and citizen advocacy in Japan and comparison with other democratic countries.

Michal Plaček is professor of public policy at Charles University in Prague, Czech Republic, and global research affiliate at Sustainable Purchasing Research Initiative at Arizona State University. He has publications in high-ranking journals such as *Public Management Review*, *Waste Management*, *Public Money and Management*, *Journal of Comparative Policy Analysis*, *Journal of Public Procurement*, and Public Works Policy and Management. He won the award for the best comparative conference paper from the Journal of Comparative Policy Analysis in 2017. He was also awarded the Joint Seed grant scheme from University of St. Andrews and Charles University. He published several books with well know international publishers, including the book on local finance in the CEE region with Springer.

Andrius Puksas is the Doctor of Laws, legal practitioner (lawyer), data protection officer and affiliated researcher at Vytautas Magnus University (Lithuania). Currently he is a Vice-chairman at the Central Electoral Commission of the Republic of Lithuania, Senior Adviser to the Ombudsman for Academic Ethics and Procedures of the Republic of Lithuania, active member of Lithuanian Society of Lawyers and Lithuanian Scientific Society, honorable member ofLithuanian Society of Young Researchers.

Lucie Sedmihradská is an associate professor at the Department of Public Finance, University of Economics in Prague. Aside from teaching, she has been involved in several local and international research projects focusing on public budgets, local government finance, and intermunicipal cooperation. She has published approximately three dozen journal articles and book chapters and a monograph on the municipal budgetary process. She currently serves as an elected official in one of Prague's city districts and as a member of the Finance Commission of the Union of Towns and Municipalities of the Czech Republic.

Besa Shahini is a full professor in the Department of Statistics and Applied Informatics at the Faculty of Economy, University of Tirana. Her research interests include statistical methods, economic modelling, and various topics such as economic development, fiscal policies, market behaviour, the green economy, and political economy. She engages extensively in national and international roles that encompass the practical and strategic aspects of project execution and organizational consultancy.

Purshottama Sivanarain Reddy is an Emeritus Professor and local government specialist in the School of Management, IT and Governance at the University of Kwazulu Natal, in Durban, South Africa. He has served as the Vice—President: Programmes; member of the Board of Management and founding Project Director of the Working Group on Sub—national Governance and Development of the International Association of Schools and Institutes of Administration (IASIA) (Brussels). In 2014, he received the Donald Stone Award for being "A Distinguished International Scholar/Practitioner" and for his "Contribution Towards Advancing the Wellbeing of IASIA". Prof Reddy is currently the Vice–-Chairperson of the Policy and Programme Committee (PRAC) of the International Institute of Administrative Sciences (IIAS) (Brussels) and also serves on its Council of Administration. He has also served as a full/alternate board member of the Commonwealth Local Government Forum (CLGF) (London), representing universities and research organisations. He has published extensively nationally and internationally and is the editor/co—editor of twenty books and currently serves on the editorial/advisory committee of seven journals internationally.

Iwona Sobis is a retired associate professor at the School of Public Administration at the University of Gothenburg, Sweden. Before her retirement in 2022, she held the position of associate professor in public administration. Her main professional duties included conducting lectures and seminars for first-, second- and third-cycle students in the academic fields of sociology, social psychology and public administration, with particular emphasis on organization and leadership, methodology and public policy. In the years 1995–2010, her research focused on Western advice for Central and Eastern Europe in the period of transition from socialism to a market economy. Since 2011, he has been involved in comparative research in the field of public reforms, municipal development, local democracy, care for the elderly and internal migration in the EU. She is the author of 50 scientific articles, book chapters and books.

Philip Arnold P. Tuaño is Dean of the Ateneo School of Government, and Associate Professor, Economics Department, Ateneo de Manila University. He has written articles in scholarly journals and book chapters on a broad range of policy issues, including poverty and labor economics, human development, climate change, governance and international trade, political economy and public governance. He has also served as Director of the Macropolicy Unit of the National Anti-Poverty Commission of the Philippine government from 2001 to 2004, and also as development and governance consultant of various non-government and civil society networks.

Irwanda Wisnu Wardhana is a Senior Economic Researcher at Indonesia National Research and Innovation Agency (BRIN) and appointed as the Head of Research Center for Cooperative, Corporation, and People's Economy since 2022. He is a public policy professional with 22 years of substantial experience designing, leading, advocating, and implementing a broad range of policy initiatives in the public sector, corporations, and civil society organizations. His areas of specialization are political economy, business economics, and fiscal policy. He has outstanding achievements and experience at government agencies and state corporations. He is also frequently invited to be a speaker in nationwide and international events. To express views, articulate opinions, and advocate policy changes, he is publicizing findings and policy recommendations in the global and national reputable publication outlets as journal articles, book articles, books, op-editorial articles in more than 40 published materials.

List of Figures

List of Tables

CHAPTER 1

Introduction: Impact of Fiscal Transfers on Local Democracy

Juraj Nemec, Michal Plaček, and Purshottama Sivanarain Reddy

1.1 Introduction

As far as possible, grants to local authorities shall not be earmarked for the financing of specific projects. The provision of grants shall not remove the basic freedom of local authorities to exercise policy discretion within their own jurisdiction.

J. Nemec (✉)
Department of Public Economics, Masaryk University, Brno, Czech Republic
e-mail: juraj.nemec@umb.sk

M. Plaček
Department of Public and Social Policy, Charles University, Prague, Czech Republic
e-mail: michal.placek@fsv.cuni.cz; MichalPlacek@seznam.cz

P. Sivanarain Reddy
Governance, IT and Governance, University of KwaZulu-Natal, Durban, South Africa
e-mail: Reddyp1@ukzn.ac.za

J. Nemec et al. (eds.), *Local Government and Fiscal Transfers*, Governance and Public Management,
https://doi.org/10.1007/978-3-031-95674-4_1

European Charter of Local Self-Government

Over the years, we can observe a dynamic development of fiscal federalism theories. The original theories were concerned with the optimal distribution of revenues and expenditures between local and central governments. Contemporary theories focus not only on the problem of optimal resource allocation and provision of public services but also look at the broader social impact, e.g. on minorities, democracy, participation, and the like.

Ideally, local self-governments are expected to "pose adequate financial resources of their own, of which they may dispose freely within the framework of their powers. These resources shall be commensurate with the local self-government responsibilities provided for by the constitution and the law. Furthermore, a part (at least) of the financial resources of local authorities shall derive from local taxes and charges of which, within the limits of the statute, they have the power to determine the rate" (European Charter of Local Self-Government, p. 3).

However, there is no country in Europe where all the responsibilities of local self-governments (local governments, or if correct for the given country municipalities) are financed by their own resources, even if we accept that shared taxes, centrally collected and distributed as non-conditional grants based on a pre-defined formula, are their own resources.

Transfers from the central government to local governments are part of any system of fiscal federalism. These transfers can take several forms, have different purposes, and represent a critical part of local government revenues in all countries. As the general rule, we may distinguish between unconditional transfers (local governments have complete discretion to decide how to use them) and conditional transfers (local governments can only use the money received for policies specified by a higher level of government). Fiscal transfers can be a tool for reconciling differences between local governments. However, they can also be a means by which the central government enforces the obedience of local governments, supports pre-defined related local policies, or rewards some intentionally selected local governments, impacting local democracy.

The theories of fiscal federalism emphasise that intergovernmental transfers (and revenue sharing) should be determined by equity and efficiency considerations to support local governments in providing differentiated public goods to heterogeneous populations (Musgrave, 1959;

Oates, 1972). Thus, intergovernmental transfers and revenue sharing are the crucial components of fiscal federalism.

The existing standard literature (see, for example, the literature review article by Chandra Jha, 2015) defines primary economic rationales for intergovernmental transfers as follows: (a) vertical fiscal imbalance (it occurs invariably due to the expenditure and revenue assignment among different levels of government in a country), (b) horizontal fiscal imbalance. The horizontal fiscal imbalance may have several purposes, especially (a) some local governments may have better access to natural resources, better tax base, or other specific advantages which generate higher income levels compared to other local governments, (b) some local governments may have higher expenditure requirements (for example, because they may have a more significant size of poor, old, and young population, or specific environmental problems). Transfers are also used to address inter-jurisdictional spill-over effects.

All governments are expected to implement some form of fiscal equalisation, to reflect national specifics of vertical and horizontal fiscal imbalance. They should compensate (to the pre-defined level) local governments with a lower revenue base or higher expenditure needs (horizontal and vertical equalisation). This expectation is, for example, directly reflected by the European Charter of Local Self-Government (p. 3), as follows: "The protection of financially weaker local authorities calls for the institution of financial equalisation procedures or equivalent measures which are designed to correct the effects of the unequal distribution of potential sources of finance and of the financial burden they must support. Such procedures or measures shall not diminish local authorities' discretion within their sphere of responsibility".

The specific purpose of intergovernmental transfers is the delegated responsibilities. Local governments realise the delegated responsibilities on behalf of the state: the state delegates to the local level the execution of those decisions, which are ensured to be executed more effectively in this way than in the case of their execution from the central level. The European Charter of Local Self-Government principles expect the state to cover the full costs of delegated responsibilities. The national legislation typically defines the same principle. Suppose the state reimburses municipalities for the execution of delegated responsibilities. In that case, it is evident and standard that the resources allocated to finance delegated responsibilities are provided as conditional (targeted) transfers directly connected with executing a concrete delegated function.

1.2 Intergovernmental Transfers and Local Democracy

As we mentioned at the outset, contemporary theories of fiscal federalism are shifting from a technicist notion of finding the optimal transfer design to thinking about what broader social impacts transfers can have (Chandra Jha, 2015). One of the key issues is how transfers can affect local democracy—the theory and the recent academic literature highlight several possible positive and negative effects of fiscal transfers on local democracy. The fact is that both unconditional (shared taxes, formula-based equalisation grants, and the like) and conditional transfers come in various forms and create differentiated incentives and accountability mechanisms with potentially varying impacts on fiscal behaviours and local democracy. The academic theory deals in detail with the potential and materialised impacts of different forms of transfers and different techniques of how to deliver them (e.g. conditional input-based transfers of multiple designs, non-matching, closed-end matching, open-end matching, output-based transfers with accountability for results, tournament grants, or competition grants).

However, we do not want to provide such a detailed analysis in this book, so in the following text, we briefly highlight the main findings of existing research related to transfers to local governments and their impacts. The aim is not to be as comprehensive as possible but to demonstrate how complex the investigated issue is.

Empirical evidence frequently suggests that the distribution of transfers across local jurisdictions and their utilisation are heavily influenced by political incentives faced by both national and local policymakers (Akai, 2015). Politicians can frequently use transfers to build patronage networks, weaken opposition candidates, reward local governments supporting them, and punish local governments with leaders belonging to the opposition. This issue is probably the most frequently investigated concerning our topic—see, for example, De La O (2013), Finan and Schechter (2012), Jakli and Stenberg (2021), Jensenius and Chhibber (2023), and many others.

Fiscal and local financial management issues are also frequently investigated. Duan and Zhan (2011) state that in the context of China, it has been demonstrated that fiscal transfers from higher-level governments can lead to fiscally dependent local governments favouring the priorities of the higher-level government over local residents' needs. Moreover, an increased dependence on fiscal transfers can lead to fewer public goods being provided to local residents, as seen in Chinese villages where fiscal transfers resulted in more wages for village elites and stronger enforcement of higher-level government policies (Duan & Zhan, 2011). Intergovernmental transfers can potentially create local self-government fiscal dependency, leading to overreliance on central government support and undermining fiscal autonomy (Panao, 2021). The so-called "flypaper effect" is frequently analysed in the scientific literature. Courant et al. (1978) found that a grant from the federal government to the local government would raise the spending of that local government by a greater amount than an equivalent increase in local income.

The financial dependence of local governments and also on conditional transfers may result in local officials prioritising the interests of higher-level authorities over local residents, potentially compromising local accountability. It is well documented in many countries that politicians reflect their central interests when designing the transfer system, affecting local democracy (Lei, 2024). Khemani (2007) argues that the distribution of transfers across local jurisdictions and what local governments do with these transfers is heavily influenced by political incentives facing both national and local policymakers.

While fiscal transfers may deliver several pervasive effects and create dependencies and disincentives that may undermine local democracy, the literature also suggests that they can improve certain aspects of local governance and may serve as a tool that promotes local democracy, empowerment, and participation of local communities. For example, according to Dinh Thanh et al. (2023), fiscal transfers have enhanced transparency, control of corruption, and accountability in local governance in Vietnam.

The preceding paragraphs show that the effects of fiscal transfers on democracy are very context-dependent, and we still lack evidence of the key social mechanisms at work.

1.3 Methodology

This book documents different forms of how fiscal transfers to local self-governments impact local democracy. The authors of country chapters were invited to present the most critical (or most interesting from their point of view) ways in which transfers impact local democracy, not to deliver a comprehensive, detailed academic analysis. Such an approach has its specific advantages—the book provides a very interesting picture of what happens in different countries regarding the relationship between transfer and local democracy. In addition, the book delivers comparative data on the quality of local democracy in the annexes of all chapters.

We explore the effects of transfers by country case studies; this means that in a different institutional context. For example, we chose a highly decentralised country with strong institutions, such as Sweden, highly decentralised countries in Central Europe with low administrative capacity, facing the risk of populism, and emerging economies such as Indonesia. From the point of view of size, both large and small countries are included as the other selection factors. From the point of geography, we tried to cover the word as much as possible—the list of countries is as follows (alphabetically): Albania, the Czech Republic, India, Indonesia, Japan, Lithuania, the Philippines, Slovakia, South Africa, Sweden, and Uganda. One federal country is included—India, but the focus is on the relationships between the states and the local self-governments, which is possible as these relationships are almost uniform.

Table 1.1 characterises the countries included in our book from the viewpoint of the "quality" of local autonomy. We use three indicators in this table—Ladner et al. (2021) Synthetic Local Autonomy Index 2020 (LAI), Ladner et al. (2021) Financial Autonomy Index 2020 (FAI), and our synthetic index, calculated by the LoGICA methodology, described below. For some countries, the values of "Ladner indexes" are unavailable. Thus, only our calculations show the comparative position of the country (based on information in Tables 1 and 4 in annexes).

Such differentiated samples should provide a perfect base for investigating how central transfers function and whether there are any determining factors impacting their functioning. The selection of chapters provides an opportunity to conduct a unique, complex picture that

Table 1.1 The sample of countries

	ALB	*CZE*	*India*	*IND*	*JAP*	*LIT*	*PHI*	*SVK*	*RSA*	*SWE*	*UGA*
LAI	19.32	23.07	n/a	n/a	23.93	23.04	n/a	24.5	27.24	28.29	n/a
FAI	19.05	39.29	n/a	n/a	62.24	34.52	n/a	39.88	89.29	89.29	n/a
LoGICA	7	8	3.5	4.5	8.5	8	4	8.5	5	9	5

Source Authors

may advance the theory of fiscal federalism and especially enrich the documentation on how transfers work in different conditions.

To get a harmonised picture, we developed comprehensive guidelines to navigate authors of country chapters. To obtain a uniform picture related to the state of fiscal federalism in each included country, we decided to use Local Governance Comparative Assessment (LoGICA) as the basic tool for comparison. The Local Public Sector Alliance developed LoGICA, and its main objective is: "The Local Governance Institutions Comparative Assessment (LoGICA) Framework provides a diagnostic framework to evaluate the multilevel governance structure of a country and to assess the ability of subnational institutions to contribute to inclusive governance, effective public service delivery and sustainable, localised development" (Local Public Sector Alliance, 2022, p. 2). In response to the grand challenges faced by public sectors around the world, inclusive and effective multilevel governance systems—and empowered subnational governments—are needed to ensure that stakeholders at all levels of society can work together to solve these challenges collectively. Strong links exist between the list of characteristics expected of empowered local governments to possess and the chain of assumptions in the devolved "route of accountability" (Local Public Sector Alliance, 2022, p. 4).

This framework obtained by LoGICA mechanisms is always complemented by a single country case study that helps us identify selected national key mechanisms associated with transfers that may impact democracy in a given context. LoGICA data and the information obtained by the national case studies represent the base for the synthetic conclusions in the final chapter of this book.

The country chapters are prepared according to a standardised template to assure their comparability and ensure that all elementary information about the national system of financing local self-government is delivered.

The structure of the book has the standard character for the edited volume. The first chapter, written by the editors of this book, illustrates the topic and provides information about the methodology used by the book. Its aim is not to deliver a comprehensive literature review, taking into account the book's character and goal. The final chapter, written by the editors, summarises the results and delivers lessons learned. It provides a fascinating list of different forms of positive and negative impacts of transfers on local democracy, as they are visible in the countries included in our sample. The country chapters are delivered in alphabetical order.

The original aim of the editors was to try to cluster countries based on two dimensions—local autonomy and local financial autonomy. However, the differences between countries are so wide that any effective clustering is impossible.

Besa Shanini wrote the chapter on Albania, which states that local governments in Albania play a key role in local social, economic, and infrastructural development today by managing and executing local projects tailored to community needs. However, it also highlights that Albania's local government is too dependent on fiscal transfers and that the system of transfers includes several pervasive effects, especially the fact that transfers may favour local governments based on political orientation rather than objective needs.

Lucie Sedmihradská and Ondřej Kuba wrote the chapter on the Czech Republic. This chapter states that the Czech Republic is a decentralised country where local governments and regions have substantial autonomy regarding decision-making and budget spending patterns. The authors selected a particular topic to illustrate the impact of transfers on local democracy—their data suggest that low fiscal autonomy has a negative impact on electoral competition.

Amitava Basu wrote the chapter on India. India is a federal country. Thus, the relationships between the States and the local governments are investigated. The chapter documents several problems connected with the system of transfers in India. It concludes that for increased and more efficient funding for local government services in India, it is critical to build robust own-source revenue of the local governments, facilitate effective transfers from higher levels of government to the local governments, and ensure consistent guidelines from SFCs to support sustainable urban development.

Irwanda Wisnu Wardhana and Amrie Firmansyah wrote the chapter on Indonesia. It states that Indonesia's current governance system is rooted in its decentralisation reforms, which were introduced after 1999. As a result, local governments now play a critical role in public service delivery and regional development. However, the authors also stress that implementing fiscal decentralisation still suffers from significant gaps in institutional capacity, especially in less developed regions in Indonesia, and the fact that the current system of transfers does not sufficiently support equalisation.

Tatsuro Niikawa wrote the chapter on Japan. The author stresses that the Constitution of Japan guarantees a system of local self-government based on the principles of the right of resident autonomy and collective self-government. However, the author also stresses that local governments, which seem to have great fiscal authority, are caught in the middle of a separate and detailed local fiscal management statute frame. The local financial management is heavily distorted by fiscal management rules through the central government, specifically by fiscal transfers from the national government to the local governments.

Andrius Puksas wrote the chapter on Lithuania. Lithuania is a highly decentralised country where local governments are granted fairly extensive rights and freedoms. This financial independence enables local governments to address local priorities within the framework of available resources. However, balancing independent functions with state-delegated responsibilities and proper financing of delegated responsibilities remain significant problematic aspects of their governance.

Philip Tuano, Ronald U. Mendoza, Tristan Canare, and Satyabhama Gulap wrote the chapter on the Philippines. The authors state that the decentralisation and devolution of powers to local governments have been central features of governance reform in the Philippines, notably since the mid-1980s. However, emphasis on the continuing dependence of local governments on fiscal transfers raises critical questions about their effect on the quality of local democracy, even though the evidence collected by the authors suggests that transfers may also have positive impacts on local democracy.

Beáta Mikušová Meričková, Nikoleta Jakuš Muthová, and Janka Holíková wrote the chapter on Slovakia. The authors stress that a modern local self-government system was established in the country after 1990, and today, the Slovak local government is a legal entity with a comprehensive set of responsibilities and rights. Similarly to the Lithuanian chapter, the authors highlight the problem of financing delegated responsibilities and document the limited effectiveness of transfers to promote fiscal equalisation.

Ajiv Maharaj and Purshottama Reddy wrote the chapter on South Africa. The authors stress that the Constitution guarantees a high level of decentralisation in the country, where local governments are tasked with providing accountable/democratic government for local communities, ensuring sustainable service provision to local communities, promoting socio-economic development, a healthy/safe environment, and community involvement in matters of local government; however, this vision of a flourishing local democracy remains largely unrealised as the national/

provincial governmental spheres have primarily retained the functions/powers that are better served at local level. Local governments in South Africa heavily rely on the system of intergovernmental transfers, which do not sufficiently reflect the socio-economic realities and needs of South Africa and deliver different negative impacts on the local democracy.

Iwona Sobis wrote the chapter on Sweden. Sweden is one of the most decentralised countries in the world, where approximately 80% of local government revenues come from its own sources. The role of transfers in financing local government is, therefore, rather marginal, but certain pervasive effects also occur in Swedish conditions. Transfers complicate local financial management and create additional administrative burdens; moreover, transfers impact the decisions of local government on which services to deliver and create inequalities in service access.

John-Mary Kauzya wrote the chapter on Uganda. Uganda is the least decentralised country in our sample because local governments do not have adequate resources to cover their expected functions. Transfers in the past were instrumental in pushing forward the purpose of decentralisation; however, recently, there has been a trend of these transfers declining to the detriment of enhancing public and societal values pursued through local governments. Moreover, transfers are not well designed and, therefore, create several negative effects on local democracy.

1.4 Conclusions

The principles of the European Charter of Local Self-Government have legal power in all Council of Europe countries and serve as important benchmarks for all other countries. However, in some countries, only a few experts fully understand why the financial part of the Charter requires that local governments finance themselves based on their own revenues and why the percentage of transfers from higher levels should be as low as possible.

The goal of this book—to document different effects of transfers in different institutional settings—reflects the above limitation. Using the multiple case study method, we want to show as many different positive and negative effects of transfers as possible. Our aim is not a high-level academic study but a book to help us understand local public finance and the role of transfers versus local democracy. We hope that we managed to achieve this goal.

References

Akai, N. (2015). Fiscal consolidation and local public finances in Japan: Incentive problems associated with intergovernmental transfers and their political roles. *Advances in Japanese Business and Economics, 8*, 95–112. https://doi.org/10.1007/978-4-431-55127-0_4

Chandra Jha, P. (2015). Theory of fiscal federalism: An analysis. *Journal of Social and Economic Development, 17*(2), 241–259. https://doi.org/10.1007/s40847-015-0009-0

Courant, P., Gramlich, E. M., & Rubinfeld, D. (1978). The stimulative effects of intergovernmental grants: Or why money sticks where it hits. In P. Mieszkowski & W. H. Oakland (Eds.), *Fiscal federalism and grants-in-aid* (pp. 5–21). Urban Institute.

De La O, A. L. (2013). Do conditional cash transfers affect electoral behavior? Evidence from a randomized experiment in Mexico. *American Journal of Political Science, 57*(1), 1–14.

Dinh Thanh, S., Nguyen, C. P., Duy-Tung, B., Binh, N. Q., & Van, D. T. B. (2023). Spatial spillover effects of fiscal decentralization on governance and public administration quality. *Regional Studies, 57*(3), 478–496. https://doi.org/10.1080/00343404.2022.2078801

Duan, H., & Zhan, J. V. (2011). Fiscal transfer and local public expenditure in China: A case study of Shanxi Province. *China Review, 11*(1), 57–88.

European Charter of Local Self-Government. Strasbourg: Council of Europe.

Finan, F., & Schechter, L. (2012). Vote-buying and reciprocity. *Econometrica, 80*(2), 863–881.

Jakli, L., & Stenberg, M. (2021). Everyday illiberalism: How Hungarian subnational politics propel single-party dominance. *Governance, 34*(2), 315–334.

Jensenius, F. R., & Chhibber, P. (2023). Privileging one's own? Voting patterns and politicized spending in India. *Comparative Political Studies, 56*(4), 503–529.

Khemani, S. (2007). The political economy of equalization transfers. In J. Martinez-Vazquez & B. Searle (Eds.), *Fiscal equalization: Challenges in the design of intergovernmental transfers* (pp. 463–484). Springer. https://doi.org/10.1007/978-0-387-48988-9_19.

Ladner, A., Keuffer, N., & Bastianen, A. (2021). *Local autonomy index in the EU, Council of Europe and OECD countries (1990–2020)*. European Commission.

Lei, Z. (2024). The fiscal logic of responsiveness: Public finance, elections, and public goods provision in rural China. *Studies in Comparative International Development, 59*(1), 1–26. https://doi.org/10.1007/s12116-023-09383-2

Local Public Sector Alliance. (2022). *The Local Governance Institutions Comparative Assessment (LoGICA) framework*. Local Public Sector Alliance.

Musgrave, R. A. (1959). *The theory of public finance*. McGraw Hill.

Oates, W. E. (1972). *Fiscal federalism*. Harcourt Brace Jovanovich.

Panao, R. A. L. (2021). Beyond flypaper: Unconditional transfers and local revenue generation in the Philippines, 1992–2016. *International Journal of Public Administration, 44*(15), 1341–1354. https://doi.org/10.1080/01900692.2020.1759628

CHAPTER 2

Albania

Besa Shahini

2.1 Introduction

Albania is a small country in the southeast of Europe. The country's population is about 2.8 million, with a deep concentration in urban areas. Municipalities are the only form of the local government in Albania, and Tirana, the capital, is the most populous, with over 500,000 inhabitants. Other major municipalities are Durres, Vlora, and Shkodra, each serving as a major economic centre (World Population Review, 2024).

Local government in Albania has experienced important reforms to improve administrative efficiency and promote decentralisation. The most recent attempt—the Territorial and Administrative Reform of 2015 (Law No. 115/2014 "On the Administrative-Territorial Division of Local Government units in the Republic of Albania") reduced the number of municipalities from 384 to 61. Albania signed the European Charter for Local Self-Government in 1998 without reservations, with entry into force in 2002.

B. Shahini (✉)
Faculty of Economy, University of Tirana, Tirana, Albania
e-mail: besashahini@feut.edu.al

J. Nemec et al. (eds.), *Local Government and Fiscal Transfers*,
Governance and Public Management,
https://doi.org/10.1007/978-3-031-95674-4_2

Decentralisation in Albania aims to strengthen local government by transferring authority and resources from the central to local government to improve governance and service delivery. Local governments partly manage essential services such as education, health, infrastructure, and economic development, directly addressing local needs. This change increases accountability, promotes community engagement, and ensures efficient use of resources, fostering a more inclusive approach to governance.

Academic studies regarding the country suggest that Albania experiences asymmetric decentralisation (the different treatment of different units in different ways). Such a policy creates conflicts between the central and local governments or between different local units, especially those that generate high state budget revenues (Veliu, 2012).

In Albania, municipalities have different sizes and populations. According to the current administrative division, the municipality with the largest area is that of Kukës, which covers an area of 933 km^2 and has about 65,100 inhabitants. On the other hand, the municipality with the smallest area is Kamza, with a territory of 37.18 km^2 and a population of 125,632 inhabitants (Institute for Albanian Municipalities, 2024), making it the municipality with the highest population density in the country. These data illustrate the great diversity in size and population of Albanian municipalities.

2.2 Fiscal Federalism

The integration of fiscal federalism in Albania has been a gradual process driven by the country's transition to a democratic market economy. After the fall of communism in the early 1990s, Albania embarked on a path of decentralisation, diverting powers and resources to local authorities. This transfer of responsibilities sought to improve local governance, empower citizens, and improve the delivery of public services.

Fiscal federalism in Albania is also seen as an element that promotes economic development and social cohesion. Local governments are directly responsible for managing basic services such as education, health care, and infrastructure. This embrace of local needs allows for customised solutions specific to localities and a more efficient allocation of resources. The system, however, faces challenges in ensuring fiscal discipline, coordinating policies between levels of Government, and addressing changes in revenue generation and spending capacity.

In 2017, Albania adopted Law No. 68/2017, "On the Finances of Local Self-Government", which defines the rules and procedures for the financing of local governments. This law aims to strengthen the fiscal autonomy of local units, guaranteeing them the right to generate income independently and manage their finances following the principles of local autonomy enshrined in the Constitution of Albania and the European Charter for Local Self-Government.

2.2.1 *Local Government Revenues*

Albania's intergovernmental financial system relies on three main components: transfers from the State budget (general non-conditional and sectoral non-conditional/conditional), shared taxes, and own local government revenues.

The "general non-conditional transfer" is defined as a general budget fund distributed to the local government to fulfil and manage its functions. General non-conditional transfer funds are distributed through a formula, part of the Budget Law. The main variables determining the amount assigned to each municipality or administrative unit are population (the most important criterion), urban services, and area (which only applies to municipal units). The income from the non-conditional transfer is of essential importance to municipal budgets and redistributes some of the national resources towards municipalities with lower fiscal potential. Municipalities with lower incomes and/or small or rural municipalities benefit more on average income per capita from the unconditional transfer than large municipalities.

The "sectoral non-conditional transfer" refers to the amount transferred to local governance for the financing of responsibilities delegated to the local level. In accordance with local finance law, the unconditional transfer must maintain a level of 1% of GDP, thus also an important condition of the EU in the budgeting support program "EU for Good Governance" (EU4GG).

Shared taxes (which refer to the amount transferred to municipalities in accordance with their realisation of income from vehicle registration tax, personal income tax, etc.) and mining rents constitute a significant source of income as well.

Local revenues come mainly from three sources: local taxes, local fees, and other revenues. Borrowings are permitted, too. Local taxes, including property taxes, small business taxes, hotel taxes, and tax of

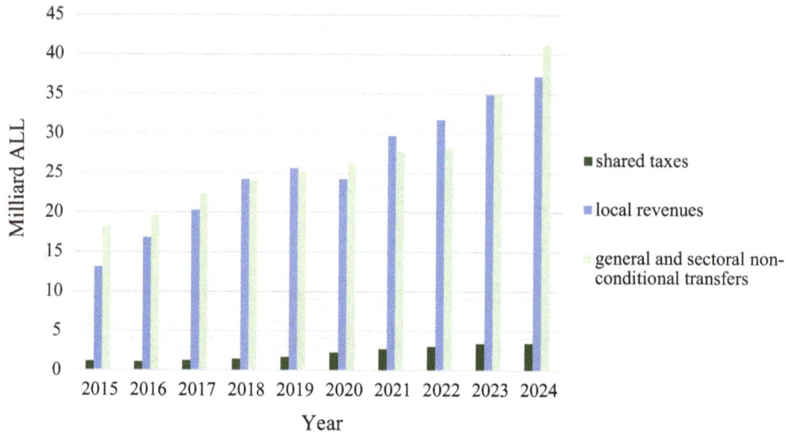

Fig. 2.1 Local government revenues: volume and structure (*Source* Author, based on data from the Ministry of Finances, Albania. https://financa.gov.al/raportime-statistika/)

real estate property transfer rights, make up a significant portion of local own revenues (around 60%). Revenues from local fees include those from local public service fees, revenues from utility tariffs for occupying public spaces, and revenues from fees for administrative and other services (100 ALL–1 EUR) (Fig. 2.1).

All three main revenue categories show a complementary growth model, which implies a well-balanced fiscal structure that supports the autonomy and strengthening of local government capacities. The high percentage of own revenues (Fig. 2.2) illustrates the progress towards financial self-sufficiency, while the stable growth of general and sectoral transfers emphasises the supporting role of central financing in ensuring balanced regional development.

2.2.2 *Local Government Expenditures*

Local government expenditures in Albania are classified according to their economic nature into the following main categories: personnel expenditures, operating expenditures, capital expenditures, and other current expenditures (Fig. 2.3).

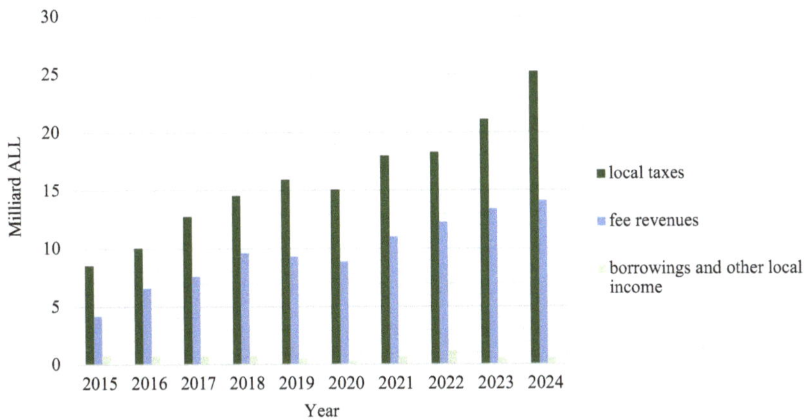

Fig. 2.2 Local own government revenues (*Source* Author, based on data from the Ministry of Finances, Albania. https://financa.gov.al/raportime-statistika/)

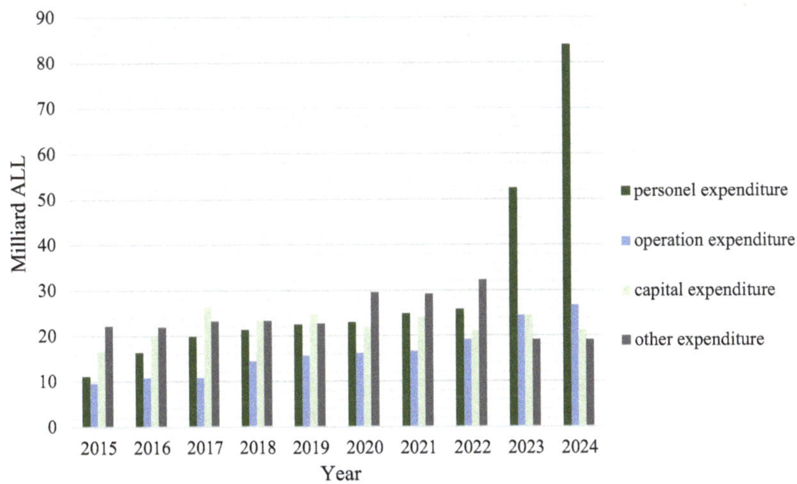

Fig. 2.3 Local government expenditures (*Source* Author, based on data from the Ministry of Finances, Albania. https://financa.gov.al/raportime-statistika/)

The chart highlights an overall rise in local government expenditures, driven by steady increases across all spending categories. The consistent upward trend in total expenditures reflects a stronger fiscal commitment to local governance, suggesting that local governments are increasingly well-resourced to meet community needs and foster sustainable development.

The significant increase in personnel expenditures in 2024 is probably a consequence of a government reform to increase salaries in the public sector, which aims to improve employee retention and the quality of public services.

2.2.3 *Transfers to Local Government*

In this part, we focus on sectoral grants, which are predominantly used to finance the competencies delegated by the central government to local self-government units. This transfer is regulated by Law no. 68/2017, "On the Finances of Local Self-Government", which determines that the functions or competencies transferred or delegated to local self-government units must always be accompanied by the necessary financial means and resources for their execution.

These delegated competencies (responsibilities) are financed mainly through conditional transfers from the state budget. These transfers are used only for the delegated function for which they were given and according to the relevant legislation or agreement provisions.

Non-conditional sectoral transfers are financial allocations from a central Government to local governments without restrictions or specific conditions on how the funds must be used. These transfers are intended to support the autonomy of local Governments by allowing them to allocate funds according to their priorities and local needs. The category of sectoral non-conditional transfer was introduced in 2019 to address specific needs arising from the decentralisation of certain public functions, such as pre-university education, rural road maintenance, and fire protection services. This new category aimed to separate and highlight the allocation of funds for specific decentralised functions within the overall unconditioned transfer framework. Local governments were given greater flexibility to allocate these funds according to their priorities within the designated sectors. These sectoral allocations ensured that local units had the means to fulfil newly decentralised responsibilities. For transferred functions, the law also provides for specific transfers, which finance local self-government units for a transitional period until a sustainable financing scheme is determined. The annual amount of these transfers must be at least as much as the annual average of the total expenses the central government has carried out for the same function in the last three years before the transfer.

The non-conditional sectoral transfer part covers the financing of new functions transferred to the local level and is calculated based on the specific costs of these functions. The rules of its allocation are updated yearly (Ministry of Finance: "Unconditional Transfer, Fund Allocation Formula, Criteria and Coefficients of the Year 2023"). The yearly document contains detailed information on calculating unconditional transfer, including the formula, criteria, and relevant coefficients for each local self-government unit. The calculations in the formula are based on the actual tax revenues divided between the central and local governments, which are collected and transferred wholly or partially to the municipalities by the central administration to ensure an effective horizontal equalisation of the unconditional transfer between local self-government units considering the different fiscal capacities between them. Fiscal equalisation is based on the actual income from the personal income tax, the annual tax on used vehicles, and the tax on the transfer of ownership rights for real estate, which are collected by the central agency and transferred to the local self-government units. In this way, the local self-government units ensure that the revenues they collect are not affected by the equalisation system, thus avoiding any disincentive in tax collection.

2.3 Case Studies

This part includes two case studies documenting the negative impacts of transfers on local democracy in Albania. The first focuses on the balance between the costs of delegated responsibilities and the number of transfers to cover them (vertical fiscal imbalance element). The second deals with the general and political aspects of central transfers.

2.3.1 Case 1: Financing of Delegated Responsibilities

In Albania, municipalities exercise functions and responsibilities delegated by the central government, which may or may not be mandatory. When allowed by law, central institutions authorise municipalities to perform certain functions, defining, when necessary, the procedures for performing and controlling their implementation. Delegated responsibilities are generally the same for all municipalities in Albania, as they are determined by the national legal framework, especially by Law no. 139/2015, "On Local Self-Government", which defines the rights and responsibilities of local self-government units. However, some differences may arise in practice for various reasons, as follows:

1. Institutional and financial capacities of municipalities: Not all municipalities have the same financial and human resources level to implement their responsibilities. For example, larger municipalities, such as Tirana or Durres, have larger budgets and staff, making them more capable of providing wider or better-quality services.
2. Local priorities: Each municipality has the right to determine its priorities within the framework of delegated responsibilities. For example, a rural municipality may focus more on agriculture and forestry, while an urban municipality may focus on public transport management and urbanisation.
3. Delegation contracts from the central Government: In some cases, the central Government may delegate specific additional functions to a given municipality due to special local needs or pilot projects.
4. Geographical and demographic characteristics: Municipalities may have different needs and priorities based on size, population, or geographic characteristics. For example, a coastal municipality like Vlora may have more responsibility in managing coastal tourism, while a mountain municipality may focus on road infrastructure and pastures.

A primary challenge for municipalities is accurately measuring the implementation costs of delegated responsibilities and determining financial needs. Various studies have highlighted the difficulties that municipalities face in this direction. For example, the Co-PLAN report (2021) points out that small municipalities face significant challenges in measuring costs and managing finances for delegated functions. Strengthening municipalities' financial and managerial capacities is necessary to address these challenges and create clear mechanisms for measuring costs and determining the necessary funding for delegated functions.

In Albania, municipalities face significant challenges in costing and financing some delegated responsibilities. The problems are mainly related to cost measurement, insufficient domestic sources of financing, and dependence on central government transfers, thus endangering the elements of local democracy.

Many municipalities, especially small ones, face limited technical and human capacities to calculate the real costs of delegated functions. According to the Co-PLAN report (2021), about 35% of municipalities do not have structured mechanisms for analysing and reporting expenditures, leading to underestimation or overestimation of costs for waste management and social services. For example, the municipality of Belsh has estimated that its internal capacity covers only 50% of the costs for waste management and the water supply network, a clear indicator of under capacity.

The inability to cover the costs of delegated functions creates dependence on the central government, limiting local autonomy to decide on local priorities.

2.3.2 *Case 2: Central Governmental Transfers and Their Impacts*

Figure 2.4 highlights local governments' excessive and growing dependence on central grants in Albania from year to year throughout 2015–2023. Dependence on central government transfers limits the real autonomy of municipalities.

The other issue is that several specific transfer mechanisms exist in Albania, especially the Arrears, the Regional Development Fund, and the Reconstruction Program after Earthquake. These specific instruments are often associated with a lack of transparency and risk of misuse, creating spaces for political preferences and use of funds for non-strategic purposes.

Arrears represent one of the biggest challenges of public finances at the local government level in Albania. These are unpaid debts to third parties, such as private companies, individuals, or institutions, that have gone beyond the repayment deadlines. In Albania, this problem directly affects the fiscal sustainability of municipalities and their ability to provide basic services to citizens.

Obligations mainly arise from a lack of proper budget planning, contracting projects that exceed actual financial capacities, lack of revenue collection from local sources (e.g. taxes and fees), and delayed transfer of funds from the central Government. According to the Ministry of Finance

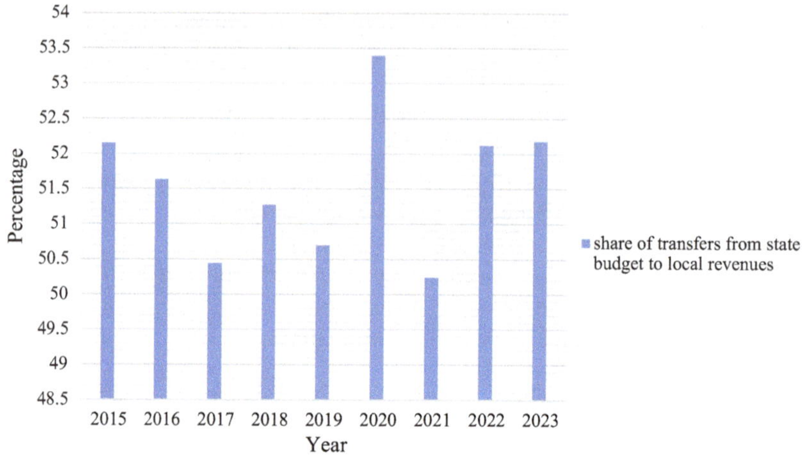

Fig. 2.4 Share of transfers from state budget to local revenues (*Source* Author, based on data from the Ministry of Finance, Albania [2023])

data, at the end of September 2021, the liabilities for unpaid investments were in the amount of approximately 41 million EUR, increasing by 4.15 million EUR, compared to the end of 2020. During election years, municipalities often initiate investment projects to show commitment to citizens, while there is concern that these expenditures may be used to influence electoral processes, including excessive recruitment in the public administration, as observed at the central level.

In some cases, the central Government has stepped in to help municipalities pay off their debts through additional financing or debt restructuring. These interventions have included allocating additional funds to ease the burden of debts accumulated by local self-government units. The concrete examples of interventions are as follows (Portavendore, 2022):

1. Kavajë Municipality: In 2021, Kavajë municipality had arrears of 11.3 million EUR. To help pay off these debts, the central government allocated 0.8 million EUR from the dedicated fund.
2. Tirana Municipality: In the same year, Tirana municipality reported arrears of 8.7 million EUR. The central government allocated 0.61 million EUR to help pay off these obligations.

3. Vorë Municipality: With arrears of 6.67 mil EUR, Vorë municipality benefited 0.47 mil EUR from the central government's debt settlement fund.

The central government's interventions in repaying municipalities' arrears have raised concerns regarding political influence in allocating funds. There have been cases, such as those mentioned above, where the distribution of funds has been perceived as favouring the municipalities run by the political party in power, raising questions about the transparency and objectivity of the fund allocation process. The funding allocation process must be based on transparent and objective criteria to address these concerns, avoiding political influence in decision-making.

The Albanian Development Fund is a public agency whose mission is to encourage sustainable, balanced, and cohesive socio-economic development at the local and regional levels. This agency distributes funds to local governments through competitive grants through the Regional Development Fund (RDF), created by the central government and donors' funding. RDF is often used as an instrument to channel conditional transfers to local governments, financing projects that match regional development objectives. In this context, the RDF acts as an important source of conditional funds, supporting infrastructural, social, and economic projects at the local level. The process of distribution of RDF conditional transfers includes several main steps as follows:

1. Identification of functions and projects: The central government determines the functions financed through conditional transfers, such as education, health, infrastructure, etc.
2. Determination of allocation criteria: Specific criteria are determined for the allocation of funds, which can be based on factors such as population, geographical area, level of economic development, and the community's specific needs.
3. Application and approval: Local governments apply for conditional funds by presenting projects or action plans that comply with the established criteria. After review, the central government approves the funds for the beneficiary units.
4. Monitoring and reporting: Once the funds have been allocated, local governments must use them according to the designated destination and report on their use. The central government monitors

implementation to ensure funds are used efficiently and transparently.

The allocation of funds from the central government via the RDF and the continuous increase in the pool of competitive grants reduce local fiscal autonomy and increase disparities. The distribution of funds from the RDF is neither predictable nor transparent, which leaves room for political intervention by giving more access to municipalities with mayors from the political force of most of the central Government. The lack of a clear and transparent methodology for identifying needs to be financed by the RDF (phased 1) creates disparities and negatively affects sustainable development.

The After the Earthquake Reconstruction Programme is another mechanism of transfers to municipalities from the central government. The information provided by Open Data Albania suggests that this fund's allocation is influenced by the political cycle. During the election campaigns in Albania (March–April 2021 for the parliamentary elections and April–May 2023 for the local elections), a significant increase in the distribution of individual grants for the reconstruction of housing damaged by the November 2019 earthquake was observed. On average, during the election campaign months, approx. 7 million EUR were distributed, compared to approximately 5 million EUR in the other months, showed an increase of 42% during election periods. This situation may raise questions about the transparency and fairness of the distribution of funds. One interpretation could be that the allocation of funds in election periods is related to a political strategy, using the Reconstruction Programme as a tool to gain electoral favour.

2.4 Conclusions

Albania's local governments play a key role in local social, economic, and infrastructural development by managing and executing local projects tailored to community needs. Their financial autonomy has been strengthened, allowing municipalities to generate and manage their revenues through local taxes and fees.

However, several issues connected with local government finance and the system of central grants still represent critical challenges. There are marked differences in the ability to generate income between different municipalities, which affects the quality and scope of services provided across regions. Smaller or rural municipalities are often faced with limited financial capacities, which affects their ability to fulfil delegated responsibilities effectively, having poor performance in the service offered to local citizens. The local government has significant dependencies on the transfer of the central government, especially for the municipalities with lower fiscal potential, undermining their financial autonomy.

Although the principles of fiscal federalism are established, their practical implementation varies significantly between municipalities due to their different administrative and financial capacities. Sometimes, there is a lack of effective coordination between different levels of government, leading to delays or uncertainties in service delivery. Ensuring fiscal discipline while promoting local autonomy remains a constant challenge, requiring continuous policy adjustments and capacity building.

Regarding the grant system, political influence sometimes affects the equitable distribution of funds, which may favour municipalities based on political orientation rather than objective needs. The influence of political dynamics is also seen in the allocation of resources during election periods, raising concerns about using public resources for electoral gains.

It is necessary to introduce more advanced financial management and planning tools to help municipalities better calculate costs and manage budgets effectively to reflect existing challenges. It is also necessary to guarantee the implementation of policies that minimise political interference in the distribution and use of funds, ensuring that allocations are made based on assessed needs and strategic importance. This will foster a culture of transparency and accountability, especially during election periods, to maintain public trust and the integrity of local government.

Annex: Country Profile: Albania

See Table 2.1.

The local self-government autonomy. According to Law no. 139/2015, "On Local Self-Government", municipalities have clearly defined powers but also have space to undertake initiatives that meet the specific needs of their communities. This autonomy was further consolidated with the adoption of the Intersectoral Strategy for Decentralisation and Local Governance 2023–2030, which aims to strengthen the capacities and increase the responsibilities of local units. However, their autonomy is limited by the legal framework and national policies, requiring that the

Table 2.1 Municipal political power structures

Criteria	*Results*
The level of autonomy of municipal governments over their functional mandates: the question of whether municipal governance institutions can only perform mandated tasks or can choose from a predefined scope of tasks Indicator: yes, partly, no	Partly
The level of freedom of municipal governments to decide their own political organisation and electoral system (can they, for example, determine their own electoral districts, number of seats, electoral system, etc.) Indicator: yes, partly, no	Partly
The constitutional or legal mechanisms to assert the autonomy of municipal governments. Examples of specific constitutional or legal mechanisms that allow municipal governments to assert their autonomy include (a) constitutional clauses or other statutory regulations protecting local self-government; (b) recourse to the judicial system through constitutional courts to settle disputes with higher authorities; or (c) other constitutional or legal protections of municipal autonomy exist (e.g. higher-level governments are prevented from forcing municipal governments to merge) Indicator: yes, partly, no	Yes
Municipal governments' right to use the legal system against higher-level government (de jure and de facto—do they use such right?) Indicator yes (both de jure and de facto), partly, no	Yes
The level to which decisions made by municipal governance institutions are subject to administrative supervision for their responsibilities and if higher-level approval is needed to act in their own matters Indicator yes, no	Partly
Does the higher-level have the right to remove local executives [or other local officials] without judicial intervention? Indicator yes, no	No

Source Author, based on own research (2025)

actions of the municipalities be in line with the legislation and strategies approved by the central government. For example, in local finance, municipalities have the power to collect local taxes and fees, but these are regulated by specific laws that define the limits and the relevant procedures.

Municipalities in Albania have no freedom to decide on their political organisation and electoral system. These aspects, including the definition of electoral zones, the number of seats in municipal councils and the electoral system, are regulated by national legislation, specifically the Electoral Code and other relevant laws. For example, according to the Central Election Commission (CEC), elections for local government bodies are held to elect 61 mayors and 1,603 members of municipal councils across the country, where mayors are elected through a majority system, while members of councils are chosen according to a proportional system with closed lists.

In 2024, Albania has constitutional and legal mechanisms that guarantee the autonomy of municipal governments. The Constitution of the Republic of Albania, in Article 13, determines that "Local Government in the Republic of Albania is established based on the principle of decentralisation of power and is exercised according to the principle of local autonomy".

Moreover, Law no. 139/2015 "On Local Self-Government" regulates the organisation and operation of local self-government units, defining their functions, powers, rights, and duties.

In case of disputes with the central authorities, the local self-government units have the right to turn to the courts to protect their autonomy. These provisions create a clear framework for protecting the autonomy of municipal governments in Albania.

In Albania, local self-government units have the legal (de jure) right to use the court system against the central government in case of disputes. This right is enshrined in Albanian legislation, enabling local units to protect their autonomy and interests through legal means. However, in practice (de facto), the use of this right is limited. Cases where local units have taken legal action against the central government are rare, and these may be related to factors such as lack of financial resources, limited legal capacity, or political dynamics that affect relations between different levels of government.

In Albania, local Government institutions enjoy a considerable level of autonomy in decision-making, but their actions are partly subject to administrative supervision by central authorities. According to Law no. 139/2015, "On local self-government", local self-government units have the right to make decisions within their competences without needing prior approval from the highest level. However, some specific decisions, especially those related to public finances, urban planning, and public property management, may require approval or supervision by central authorities to ensure compliance with national legislation and state policies.

Without judicial intervention, the central government cannot dismiss local executives like mayors. According to the Constitution of the Republic of Albania and the legislation on local self-government, mayors are directly elected by the citizens and have a legally defined mandate.

Their dismissal can only happen in cases where final court decisions prove serious legal or criminal violations on their part. This procedure protects local government autonomy and prevents arbitrary interventions by central authorities.

In Albania, electing mayors and councillors is regulated by the Electoral Code of the Republic of Albania and Law no. 139/2015 "On Local Self-Government". This system aims to ensure proportional representation and democratic governance at the local level. The mayor is elected through a one-round majority system. The candidate who receives the most votes (50%+1) is declared the winner. Voters can vote directly for their preferred candidate for this position. The role of the mayor is to direct the local Government and implement the policies approved by the municipal council (Legal reference: Article 10 and Article 109 of the Constitution of the Republic of Albania, as well as Article 162 of the Electoral Code) (Table 2.2).

Municipal councillors are elected through a proportional system with closed lists. Each political party, coalition, or group of citizens that competes in the elections presents a closed list of candidates for the municipal council. After the end of voting: (1) Counting of votes: The number of votes won by each electoral subject determines the number of

Table 2.2 Structure and quality of municipal electoral systems

Criteria	*Results*
How are municipal councillors elected? Indicator—election mode	Direct election, Majority Electoral Systems for mayors, Proportional for municipal councillors
For what term are municipal councils elected (years)? Indicator—years of mandate	4
What is the level of citizen participation in municipal elections? Indicator: Low—("Normal") voter turnout is below 35% of eligible (registered) voters Average—Voter turnout is between 35 and 60% of eligible (registered) voters High—Voter turnout is over 60% of eligible (registered) voters	Average

Source Author, based on own research (2025)

councillors' mandates. (2) Distribution of mandates: Distribution is done according to the d'Hondt method, favouring proportionality.

The number of councillors for each municipality depends on its population and is defined in Article 23 of Law No. 139/2015. For example, Tirana Municipality has a larger number of councillors compared to smaller municipalities. Legal reference: Article 162 and Article 163 of the Electoral Code. The electoral system for local government is:

1. Majority for mayors: This ensures clear leadership and stability in local government.
2. Proportional for municipal councillors: This system ensures fair representation of political and civic interests within the municipal council.

The system is designed to maintain a balance between representation and governing efficiency. While majority elections ensure strong leadership, the proportional system guarantees the broad involvement of political actors and citizens in local decision-making.

Local elections in Albania are held every four years. Citizens vote for the mayor and for lists of municipal councillors. The last elections were held on 14 May 2023. Both the mayor and the municipal councillors have a four-year term that starts from the date of their oath.

The trend of citizen participation in local elections in Albania shows a continuous decline since the 1990s, with some moments of slight growth, but still insufficient to reach the initial levels. The high turnout in the first years after the fall of the communist regime (over 70% in 1992) reflected citizen enthusiasm for democratic processes. However, after 2000, the level of participation stabilised in the 45–50% range, indicating moderate engagement. The peak of the decrease was reached in the 2019 local elections, where participation fell to 22.97%, mainly due to the opposition boycott and the lack of competitive alternatives. The 2023 elections showed a partial recovery (38.23%) (Open Data Albania, 2024), but this remains below the historical average, raising concerns about citizens' trust in electoral processes and their involvement in decision-making.

This trend reflects the challenges of Albanian democracy, where political polarisation and scepticism towards the system have negatively affected civic engagement. To improve this situation, reforms are required

Table 2.3 Nature of municipal political party systems

Criteria	*Results*
Which subjects can run in municipal elections? Indicator—define who can participate	Political parties, coalitions of political parties, independent candidates,
How are party candidates for municipal council elections selected? Indicator—selected by party, elected by party, self-nomination, other	Selected by party, self-nomination
Are there established rules for financing municipal political campaigns? Indicator—yes, no	Yes
Does the ruling national party have a dominant position in municipal elections? Indicator—yes, no	Partly

Source Author, based on own research (2025)

that increase the transparency and honesty of elections and the involvement of citizens in democratic processes (Table 2.3).

In Albania, entities that can compete include political parties and independent candidates. Political parties present candidates for mayors and multi-name lists for members of municipal councils. In some cases, political parties formed electoral coalitions to increase their chances. Independent candidates can run for both the post of mayor and member of the municipal council, following the relevant legal procedures. The selection of candidates for municipal councils by political parties is carried out through internal party processes, which may include proposals from local structures, internal votes, or decisions of the party leadership. These lists are closed, meaning that the party determines the order of candidates on the list, and voters cannot change this order during voting. The number of members of municipal councils is determined based on the municipality's population and varies from 15 to 61 mandates. Independent candidates for municipal council members must collect a certain number of signatures from the voters of the respective municipality, according to the requirements of the Electoral Code. After collecting the necessary signatures and completing the relevant documentation, they are registered with the Central Election Commission to participate in the elections. In the last local elections, those of 2023, some changes were made to the Electoral Code, including gender representation on the lists (at least 30% of the candidates had to be women).

Financing of political parties and electoral subjects is regulated by Law no. 10019, dated 29.12.2008, "Electoral Code of the Republic of Albania", as well as with Law no. 8580, dated 17.02.2000, "On Political Parties". The financing of election campaigns for local elections in Albania is supervised by the CEC and is based on public and non-public funds. Private donations are limited to 1 million ALL, while donors with public benefits above 10 million ALL are prohibited from financing. After the campaign, entities must report expenses. In the 2023 local elections, the CEC observed a lack of transparency, with many undeclared expenses, especially for media advertising, emphasising the need for better monitoring.

In the local elections of 14 May 2023 in Albania, the Socialist Party (SP) consolidated its dominant position at the local level, winning 52 out of 61 municipalities. The final report of the ODIHR Election Observation Mission (2023) states that the elections were well-managed and competitive but also evidences the use of state resources by the ruling parties, including numerous activities by the central Government and local administrations that ran afoul of electoral rules. These findings somehow show a dominance of the ruling party in the 2023 local elections, raising concerns about the use of public resources for electoral purposes and their impact on political competition at the local level. In the 14 local elections in May 2023 in Albania, the Socialist Party (SP) won 53 out of 61 municipalities, representing about 86.9% of the total. The opposition coalition "Together We Win" secured seven municipalities, or 11.5%, while the Greek Minority Party for the Future (MEGA) won the municipality of Finiq, which constitutes 1.6% of the municipalities.

In Albania, municipal council meetings are, as a rule, open to the public, ensuring transparency and citizen participation in decision-making processes. However, the law provides for specific cases when these meetings occur behind closed doors. According to Article 53 of Law no. 139/2015, "On Local Self-Government", municipal council meetings are open to the public. However, at the request of the mayor or one-fifth of the council members, and with the approval of no less than three-fifths of all members, its meetings may be closed to the public (Table 2.4).

In Albania, municipal documents and data are open to the public, following Law No. 119/2014 "On the Right to Information". This law guarantees citizens access to information produced or maintained by public authorities, including municipalities. According to this law, every person has the right to get to know the public information without

Table 2.4 P4 municipal political participation and accountability

Criteria	*Results*
Are all council meetings (required to be) open to the public? Indicator—yes, no	Yes
Are municipal records and documents (required to be) available to the public? Indicator—yes, no	Yes
Is the council (required to) engage in an open, participatory planning process? Indicator—yes, no	Yes
Are alternative participatory mechanisms, such as referendums or participatory budgeting, used? Indicator—yes, partly, no	Partly

Source Author, based on own research (2025)

being obliged to explain the reasons for the request. Public authorities are obliged to proactively publish information and provide access to relevant documents in case of specific requests. However, there are restrictions on information that contains personal data, trade secrets, or is related to national security.

In Albania, municipal councils must engage in open and participatory planning processes. Law no. 139/2015, "On Local Self-Government", and Law no. 107/2014, "On Territorial Planning and Development", define the obligation of local authorities to include the public and interest groups in planning and decision-making processes. These laws require municipalities to organise public consultations and ensure transparency in drafting local plans and development strategies.

In Albania, participatory mechanisms such as referendum and participatory budgeting are legally provided, but their implementation has been limited. The Constitution of Albania and the relevant legislation provide for the possibility of holding national and local referendums. However, so far, no local referendum has been held. The reasons for this include the lack of knowledge from citizens on the value of the local referendum, the low level of democratic culture, and the lack of interest from political subjects and local elected officials in promoting local referendum processes.

Participatory budgeting is a practice that aims to involve citizens in decision-making on allocating public financial resources. In Albania, several initiatives have been undertaken to promote this approach. Also, guidelines and training have been developed for the local government to implement this practice. However, the implementation of participatory budgeting remains limited and requires further efforts to ensure the effective involvement of citizens in financial decision-making processes.

References

Co-Plan. (2021). *Bashkitë e vogla dhe sfidat e decentralizimit: Manaxhimi financiar dhe Burimet Njerëzore*. https://www.co-plan.org/wp-content/uploads/2022/04/Raporti-final-Bashkite-e-vogla-dhe-sfidat-e-decentralizimit-3.pdf

Institute for Albanian Municipalities. (2024). *Qeverisja vendore ne Shqiperi - Raport mbi situaten aktuale*. https://iam.org.al/wp-content/uploads/2023/05/Raport-per-qeverisjen-vendore-2022-Shqip-OK.pdf#page=15.26

Law No. 115/2014. (2014). *The Administrative-Territorial Division of Local Government Units in the Republic of Albania*. https://www.prefektishkoder.gov.al/wp-content/uploads/2023/11/4.Ligji-115-2014-Per-ndarjen-administrativo-territoriale-te-NJVV-ne-RSH.pdf

Law No. 139/2015. (2015). *On local self-government*. https://shtetiweb.org/wp-content/uploads/2016/03/LIGJI_139_2015_PER_VETEQEVERISJEN_VENDORE1.pdf

Law No. 68/2017. (2017). *On the finances of local self-government*. https://financat-lokale.al/sq/node/118

Law No. 38/2019. (2019). *On local self-government, changed*. https://portavendore.al/wp-content/uploads/2019/11/Ligj-139-2015-i-ndryshuar.pdf

Ministry of Finances. (2023). *Unconditional transfer, fund allocation formula, criteria and coefficients*. https://financa.gov.al/raportime-statistika/

Ministry of Finances, Albania. (Live). *Raportime & Statistika*. https://financa.gov.al/raportime-statistika/

Open Data, Albania. (2024). *Open Data*. https://ndiqparate.al/?cat=1364&lang=en

Portavendore. (2022). *Bashkitë në vështirësi prej borxheve: Qeveria u fal 500 mln lekë*. https://portavendore.al/2022/02/06/bashkite-ne-veshtiresi-prej-borxheve-qeveria-u-fal-500-mln-leke/

Veliu, M. (2012). *The impact of decentralization processes in regional and social development*. https://worldpopulationreview.com/cities/albania

World Population Review. (2024).*Albania Population 2024 (Live)*. https://worldpopulationreview.com/countries/albania-population

CHAPTER 3

Czech Republic

Lucie Sedmihradská and Ondřej Kuba

3.1 Introduction

The Czech Republic is a unitary state with two tiers of subnational government—regions (14) and municipalities (6,250). Since 2004, it has been a member of the European Union. With over 6,250 municipalities and approximately 10.9 million inhabitants (as of March 31, 2024), Czechia is one of the most fragmented countries in Europe.

The current local government system in the Czech Republic emerged after major reforms in 1990 when the former system of national committees was replaced. Municipalities simultaneously exercise their independent responsibilities, exercised by the municipality and its elected bodies on its behalf, and delegated responsibilities, performed on behalf of the state. The state is legally responsible for the performance of the delegated power. The Czech Republic signed the European Charter of Local

L. Sedmihradská (✉)
Prague University of Economics and Business, Prague, Czech Republic
e-mail: sedmih@vse.cz

O. Kuba
Pardubice University, Pardubice, Czech Republic
e-mail: ondrej.kuba@upce.cz

J. Nemec et al. (eds.), *Local Government and Fiscal Transfers*,
Governance and Public Management,
https://doi.org/10.1007/978-3-031-95674-4_3

Self-Government in 1998, with entry into force in September 1999. It did not consider itself bound by Article 4, paragraph 5, Article 6, paragraph 2, Article 7, paragraph 2, Article 9, paragraph 3, paragraph 5, and paragraph 6, and this position remains the same today.

This chapter aims to present the current system of financing of Czech municipalities, to analyse the multilevel governance structure using the Local Governance Institutions Comparative Assessment (LoGICA) Framework (Local Public Sector Alliance, 2022) and the Local Autonomy Index data (Lysek, 2021), and to evaluate the relationship between fiscal autonomy (share of municipal expenditures financed from transfers) and local democracy by comparing the share of municipal expenditures financed from transfers in municipalities with and without electoral competition.

3.2 Fiscal Federalism

3.2.1 Local Government Revenues

Municipal revenues are specified in two laws: the Act on Budgetary Rules for Territorial Entities lists all municipal revenues, and the Law on Tax Assignment specifies the tax-sharing mechanism. According to the budget classification, the revenues are divided into four groups: tax revenues, non-tax revenues, capital revenues, and transfers.

Tax revenues are composed of shared taxes and local taxes, i.e. real estate tax and local fees. Since 2017, municipalities have received a share of the newly introduced gambling tax. Transfers include transfers for the execution of delegated tasks distributed based on a formula and earmarked current and capital subsidies from both national and EU budgets. Non-tax revenues are mostly rental incomes (Bečica, 2015), interests and capital revenues that come primarily from the sale of municipal property.

The tax-sharing system was introduced in 1993 and significantly changed in 1997 and 2001. The current system has been in place since 2001 and includes all three major taxes: personal income tax (PIT), corporate income tax (CIT), and value-added tax (VAT), as well as all three government tiers: state budget, regions, and municipalities (Sedmihradská, 2008).

The tax sharing is done in two stages: first, the shares of the individual government tiers are determined and second, when the shares of individual regions or municipalities are set. The first stage evolved gradually: regions' share grew from the initial 3.1% to 9.78%, and municipalities' share was between 19.93 and 25.84%. In the case of the regions, the second stage is fixed in the law and has not changed since 2001. Significant changes were made in the municipalities' cases in 2008, 2013, and 2017. Since 2017, the volume of municipal revenues from shared taxes has been based on a formula that does not consider the volume of revenue collected in the municipality's territory. The formula includes the number of inhabitants, number of pupils, area, and municipality size.

The individual municipalities cannot influence the volume of shared tax revenue they receive, so these revenues resemble more unconditional block grants than taxes (Blöchliger and Petzold, 2009) and, therefore, are shown separately in Fig. 3.1 (100 CZK=4 EUR). This Figure shows the development of the main municipal revenue sources since 1997. The share of municipal budgets in GDP fell from 9% in 1999 to 6% in 2012 due to changes in the assignment of tasks in elementary education and social assistance. It has oscillated around 6 and 6.5% of GDP ever since.

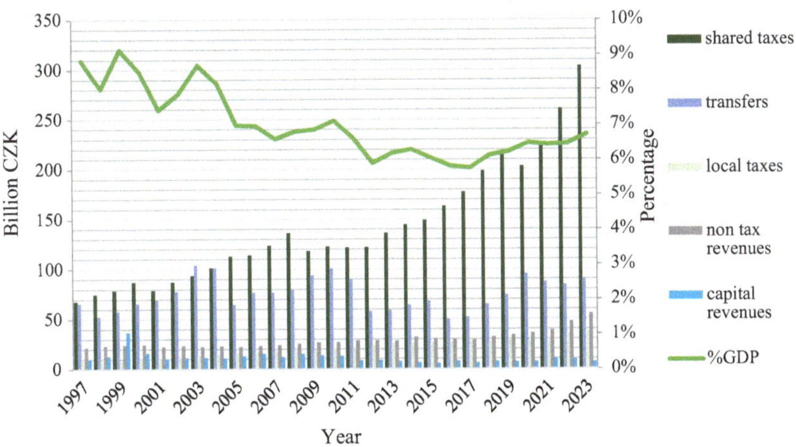

Fig. 3.1 Municipal revenues (*Source* Authors, based on Monitor data [2024])

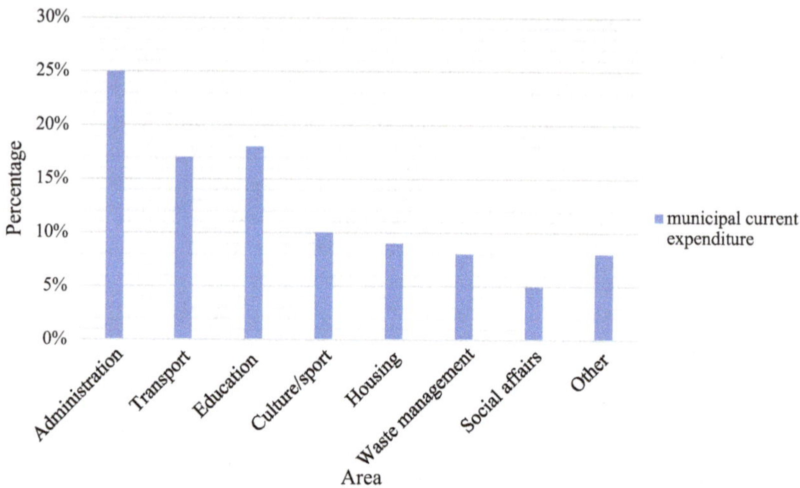

Fig. 3.2 Municipal current expenditure in 2023 (*Source* Authors, based on Monitor data [2024])

3.2.2 *Local Government Expenditures*

The current expenditure structure reflects the assigned competencies municipalities exercise: for instance, administration including delegated competencies, education, transport, local roads maintenance, and waste management (see Fig. 3.2).

The municipal capital spending structure has been relatively stable over time, and the total volume reflects, to some extent, the availability of EU funds grants in the different phases of the programming periods (see Fig. 3.3).

3.2.3 *Transfers to Local Governments*

In the Czech Republic, public administration is organised on the principle of a mixed model. A municipality manages its affairs independently, i.e. within its competence. In cases specified by law, municipal authorities also perform state administration. In such cases, it is the exercise of delegated competence. Municipalities are annually entitled to a contribution to fulfil tasks within delegated competence. The contribution is intended to partially cover the expenses associated with the performance of state

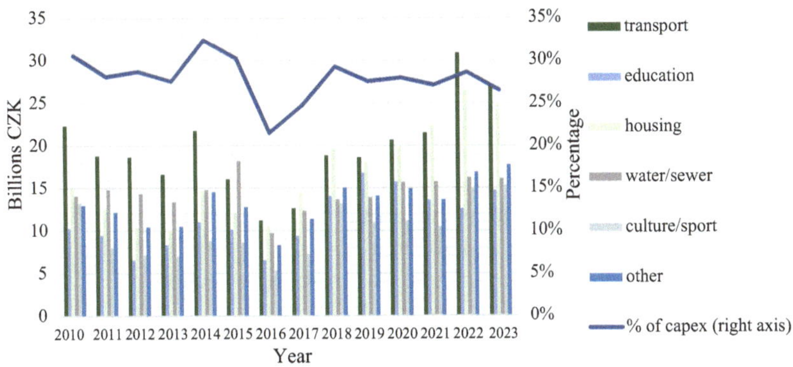

Fig. 3.3 Municipal capital expenditure (*Source* Authors, based on Monitor data [2024])

administration and has the character of a block grant (Ministry of Interior, 2022). The volume of the grant is determined in the law on the state budget for the particular year, and the Ministry of Interior publishes the volume for each municipality after the law on the state budget is approved.

The first part of this transfer is determined based on the population served in the given service. This applies to basic services, registry offices, building authorities, and the delegated and extended competences of the assigned municipalities.

The second part of the transfer is based on past performance, and the Ministry of Interior gradually expands its share in the total transfer for delegated services. The introduction of payments for actions stems from the long-term efforts of municipalities for a more targeted method of financing agendas in delegated competencies. This model increases offices' motivation for client-oriented behaviour. At the same time, it strengthens the competitive environment among various offices, leading to outreach to more citizens (clients), especially in areas with short distances between offices.

Performance financing includes the issue of identity cards and driver's licenses, the trade licensing agenda, public guardianship, urban planning, registry offices, and driver's exams (Ministry of Interior, 2022).

The remaining current transfers are targeted except for 2020 when a block grant compensated for lower tax collection due to COVID-19. Transfers from own funds are intra-municipal transfers from entrepreneurial funds (see Fig. 3.4).

There are many different grants to finance capital investment projects from different types of donors: national grant titles provided by the individual ministries, EU programs including the National Recovery Plan and the Modernization Fund, and the regions. These are target grants and require co-financing from municipal own resources (Union of Towns and Municipalities of the Czech Republic, 2022).

The current system of tax-sharing and local taxes provides minimum incentives or rewards for municipalities that pursue local policies conducive to local business development (Herrmann, 2022). Using a case study of the municipality of Kostelec (population 600, maximum property tax rate, new production hall with an area of 25,000 m^2 employing 140 workers for 30 years), KPMG (2024) estimates that the municipality's total revenue amounts only to approximately 0.75% of the plant's total contribution to public budgets (Table 3.1).

3.3 Case Study: Fiscal Autonomy Versus Uncontested Election

The aim of this case study is to analyse the relationship between fiscal autonomy (share of municipal expenditures financed from transfers) and local democracy using a very specific and unique approach—we compare the share of municipal expenditures financed from transfers in municipalities with and without electoral competition.

Elections are fundamental to the functioning of a democracy. They ensure that governments remain responsive and accountable to the people. Participation in elections is active when citizens cast their ballots and passive when they are eligible to be elected and when they run for office. Active participation is expressed by turnout, and passive participation is expressed by electoral completion, i.e. the number of parties or candidates.

Participation, whether at the voter turnout or competition level, is influenced by the degree of fiscal autonomy. An increase in fiscal autonomy promotes citizen engagement (Suzuki & Han, 2019), but weak fiscal autonomy can undermine voters' interests (Geys et al., 2010).

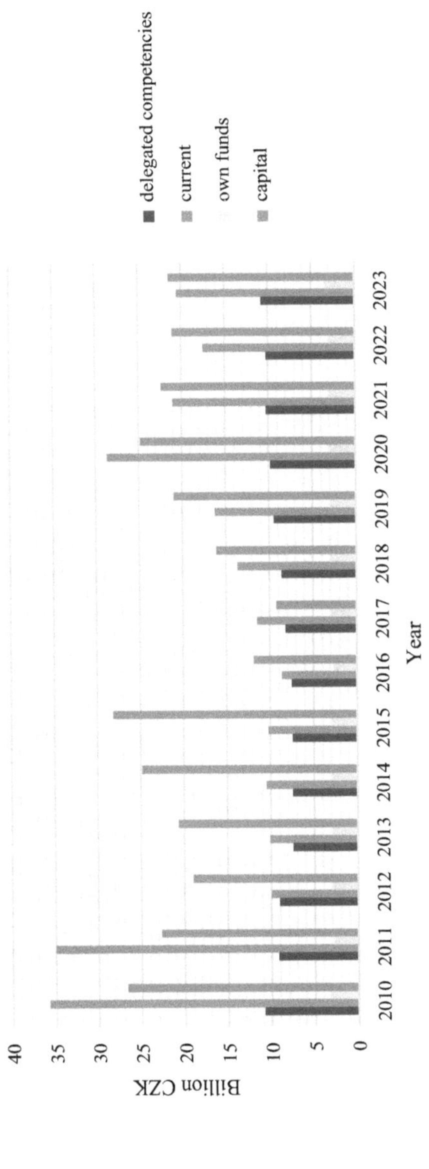

Fig. 3.4 Received transfers (Municipalities Excluding Prague) (*Source* Authors, based on Monitor data [2024])

Table 3.1 Tax revenues (30 Years of Operation of a Production Plan, Millions CZK)

Tax	*Total tax paid*	*All municipalities*	*Regions*	*State budget*	*Municipality Kostelec*
PIT	314	83	31	201	0.005
CIT	1,397	348	136	912	0.069
Social and health insurance	938	–	–	951	
Property tax	20	20	–	–	20.250
Total	2,763	532	167	2,064	20.324

Source Authors, based on KPMG data (2024)

This is related to the problem of the principal and agent and the exercise of responsibility. The citizens/voters (principal) hire politicians (agent) to administer public affairs. This relationship is burdened with the problem of information asymmetry (the agent has much more information than the principal and the principal can only control it with difficulty) and moral hazard (the agent fulfils goals other than those preferred by the principal). This problem is at least partially solved by the mechanism of political accountability (Bovens, 2007), where the agent has to account to the principal and the dissatisfied principal has the option to punish the agent, i.e. not to vote for them in the next election. If there is no electoral competition and the voter must vote for someone they are unsatisfied with, their interest in voting decreases, and voter turnout decreases.

Fiscal autonomy refers to the capacity of local governments to generate and use their own revenues independently from higher levels of government. While local taxes and non-tax revenue comply with generation and use, shared taxes comply with use only, and transfers with neither.

Politicians possess significant discretion in the case of high fiscal autonomy, which may have both positive and negative impacts. Positive impact is related to higher allocative efficiency when voter preferences are well met. Negative impact leads to rent extraction (Ashworth et al., 2014) through corruption or inefficiency. The environment of high fiscal autonomy attracts political candidates regardless of whether they have good or bad intentions and increases the voters' effort to hold the politicians accountable. Low fiscal autonomy has the opposite effect: lower or no electoral competition.

In the Czech Republic, we observe a stable turnout and an increasing trend of uncontested municipal council elections (Fig. 3.5). Uncontested elections are electoral races in which citizens are unable to choose among political alternatives. Their vote does not affect the outcome because there is only one list of candidates, or the number of candidates equals the number of council seats. Uncontested elections challenge democracy because the lack of competition skews representation, discourages citizen involvement in politics, and weakens the mechanism of accountability.

The share of uncontested elections has grown since 1998, reaching 28.3% in 2022. The share of uncontested elections in municipalities with less than 500 inhabitants exceeded 40% in 2022. There are many changes between the individual election years; however, more elections become uncompetitive from previously competitive scenarios rather than vice versa (Kouba & Lysek, 2023).

Uncontested elections have a strong negative effect on turnout (a 17-percentage point drop relative to competitive elections in 2022, controlling for many socio-economic features). This trend is more common in small municipalities but is not exclusive to them (Kouba & Lysek, 2023).

The difference of means test (t-test) was used to determine whether the share of expenditure financed from transfers over the period 2019 to 2022 is different for municipalities with and without electoral competition in the 2022 municipal election. The confidence level of the test was 95%.

Our results are shown in Fig. 3.6. Municipalities with uncontested elections in 2022 operated with a significantly higher share of expenditure financed from targeted transfers. This implies that they enjoyed less local autonomy than municipalities with competitive elections.

While the share of expenditure financed from transfer is significantly higher in municipalities with uncontested elections, the per capita volume of transfers is significantly higher only in all and small municipalities. The volume of capital expenditure per capita does not differ significantly between the two types of municipalities, and the volume of current expenditure per capita is significantly higher only in bigger municipalities (Table 3.2).

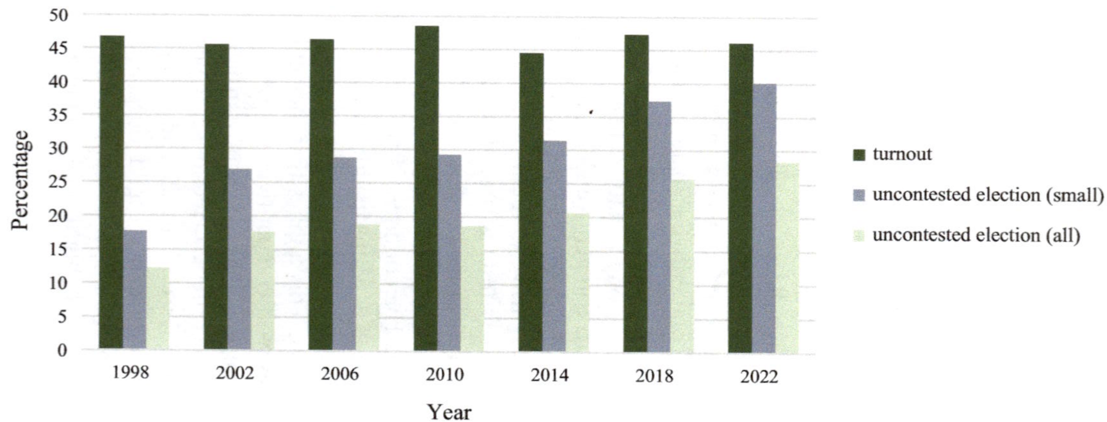

Fig. 3.5 Turnout and share of uncontested election in small and all municipalities (*Note* Small municipalities are municipalities with less than 500 inhabitants in 2022. *Source* Authors, based on the data by the Czech Statistical Office [2024], and of Kouba and Lysek [2023, p. 1535])

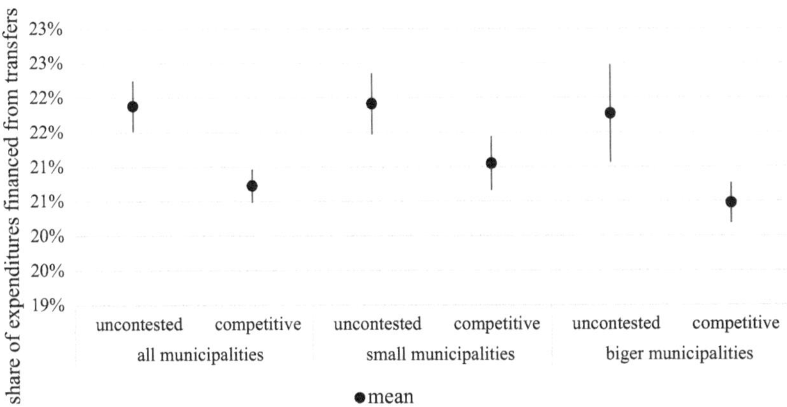

Fig. 3.6 Fiscal autonomy in municipalities with uncontested and competitive elections (2019–2022) (*Note* The differences between uncontested and competitive are statistically significant at 95% confidence level in all samples of municipalities. *Source* Authors, based on the data from Monitor and volby.cz [2024])

Table 3.2 Transfers and expenditure per capita in municipalities with uncontested and competitive elections (CZK, 2019–2022)

Municipal size	*Variable*	*Uncontested*	*Competitive*	*Significant at 95% confidence level*
All municipalities	curex	70,640.2	71,051.2	no
	transfers	28,437.8	25,384.9	yes
	capex	41,369.3	41,010.7	no
Large municipalities	curex	57,703.7	67,741.8	yes
	transfers	25,219.9	24,020.3	no
	capex	44,587.9	42,238.3	no
Small municipalities	curex	74,252.7	75,311.4	no
	transfers	29,336.4	27,141.4	yes
	capex	40,470.5	39,430.5	no

Note curex = current expenditure per capita, capex = capital expenditure per capita, transfers = received transfers per capita, all variables are a sum of the given budget line from 2019 to 2022
Source Authors, based on data from Monitor (2024)

3.4 Conclusions

The Czech Republic is a decentralised country where municipalities and regions have substantial autonomy regarding decision-making and budget. Revenue autonomy, however, is quite limited due to the construction of the tax-sharing mechanism, when municipalities do not have any possibility to influence their revenue and have a low volume of their local taxes and non-tax revenues. This revenue structure creates little to no incentives for local officials to foster economic growth (Weingast, 2009). At the same time, the availability and guarantee of intergovernmental revenues in the form of tax sharing and transfers keep more than six thousand municipalities in operation without any economic pressure to amalgamate.

Our case study shows that the negative impact of low fiscal autonomy on electoral competition suggested in the existing literature (Geys et al., 2010; Suzuki & Han, 2019) is observed in the Czech Republic. This topic is rarely analysed in the academic literature, and our findings provide important value added to the theory of fiscal decentralisation.

Acknowledgements This research was carried out with the institutional support of the Prague University of Economics and Business, No. IP 100040.

Annex: Country Profile: Czech Republic

See Tables 3.3.

Local self-government autonomy in the Czech Republic is not merely formal but substantial. Municipalities have the right to decide on their tasks (referred to as independent competence), except in areas where responsibilities have been explicitly assigned to other levels of government. This autonomy is guaranteed by Act No. 128/2000 Coll. on Municipalities (Municipal Establishment), which states that "the municipality manages its affairs independently." State and regional authorities can only intervene in this independent competence when necessary to protect the law and strictly follow legal provisions. Moreover, the scope of this independent competence can only be limited by law, ensuring that local governments retain significant control over their own affairs.

From the perspective of local self-government's freedom to decide on its political organisation and electoral system, it enjoys a certain degree of autonomy in the Czech Republic. Members of the council, known as

Table 3.3 Subnational political power structures

Criteria	*Results*
The level of autonomy of municipal governments over their functional mandates: the question of whether municipal governance institutions can only perform mandated tasks or can choose from a predefined scope of tasks Indicator: yes, partly, no	Yes
The level of freedom of municipal governments to decide their own political organisation and electoral system (can they, for example, determine their own electoral districts, number of seats, electoral system, etc.) Indicator: yes, partly, no	Partly
The constitutional or legal mechanisms to assert the autonomy of municipal governments. Examples of specific constitutional or legal mechanisms that allow municipal governments to assert their autonomy include (a) constitutional clauses or other statutory regulations protecting local self-government; (b) recourse to the judicial system through constitutional courts to settle disputes with higher authorities; or (c) other constitutional or legal protections of municipal autonomy exist (e.g. higher-level governments are prevented from forcing municipal governments to merge) Indicator: yes, partly, no	Yes
Municipal governments' right to use the legal system against higher-level government (de jure and de facto—do they use such right?) Indicator yes (both de jure and de facto), partly, no	Yes
The level to which decisions made by municipal governance institutions are subject to administrative supervision for their responsibilities and if higher-level approval is needed to act in their own matters Indicator yes, no	No
Does the higher-level have the right to remove local executives [or other local officials] without judicial intervention? Indicator yes, no	No

Source Authors, based on own research (2025)

executives, are elected by the municipal assembly. Municipalities have the authority to decide on some minor aspects of the political system, but they must adhere to the general rules established in the municipal and electoral laws. These regulations include the minimum and maximum number of elected representatives and council members and a proportional electoral system. However, municipalities can create electoral districts according to their needs.

In the Czech Republic, legal mechanisms enforce local autonomy. The autonomy of subnational governments in the Czech Republic is constitutionally guaranteed. According to Article 8 of the Constitution of the Czech Republic (Act No. 1/1993 Coll.), "self-government of territorial self-governing units is guaranteed." Furthermore, Article 87

(1)(c) provides that the Constitutional Court has the authority to adjudicate constitutional complaints by territorial self-governing bodies against unlawful interference by the state. Article 101 (4) further stipulates that "the state may interfere in the activities of territorial self-governing units only when required for the protection of the law, and only in the manner prescribed by law." These constitutional provisions ensure that local governments can assert their autonomy and seek protection from unlawful state interference, including through the judicial system. This legal framework, anchored in the Constitution, strengthens the independence of municipalities and regions and provides them with recourse to the Constitutional Court in cases of conflict with the central government.

In the Czech Republic, as regards the criterion of the right of lower territorial units to use the legal system against higher territorial units (both de jure and de facto), it is noteworthy that since the adoption of Act No. 128/2000 Coll. on Municipalities, local governments have enjoyed considerable autonomy with minimal direct supervision by state institutions or public administration. State supervision is limited to the control of legality, which is focused solely on ensuring compliance with legal regulations and not suspending municipal decisions. Only a court can annul or suspend a municipal decision if it is deemed unlawful, meaning that municipalities are protected from direct intervention by the state and have judicial recourse to maintain their autonomy.

In the Czech Republic, decisions made by subnational institutions are not subject to administrative oversight and do not require approval from a higher level. Local governments have full decision-making freedom. They can, for example, determine their organisational structure, number of employees, remuneration, task delegation, and subordination issues.

In the Czech Republic, higher authorities have no right to remove local officials or other officials. Officials (including the mayor) can only be dismissed by the municipal council. A supermajority must approve the recall of all council members. Neither the government, the courts, nor other higher administrative units have the authority to remove members of the officials.

Act No. 491/2001 Coll determines the election of subnational councillors. According to this law (§4), the right to vote in municipal council elections is granted to citizens who have permanent residence in the municipality, are citizens of the Czech Republic, are at least 18 years old on the day of the election, and have no legal impediment to the exercise of voting rights (these impediments are also listed in the law). Eligible candidates for municipal councils are citizens with permanent residence in the municipality who meet the conditions for voting and are not employees of the relevant offices performing state administration (§5). The elections to the council are general, equal, direct, and secret, based on the principle of proportional representation. The size of the municipality determines the number of council members, and Act No. 128/2000 Coll. sets a range within which the municipal council must determine the exact number of councillors for the upcoming term at least 85 days before the election day. The council then elects the municipal board, which consists of 5 to 11 members, depending on the size of the municipality. The board serves as the executive body of the municipality. From among its members, the council then elects the mayor (and deputy mayors). Thus, the mayor is elected indirectly (Table 3.4).

At the local and regional government level, the mandate of subnational councils is 4 years.

The level of citizen participation in subnational elections: The highest voter turnout in municipal elections was in 1990, with a participation rate of 73.24%. Since then, voter turnout has gradually declined; since 1998, it has fluctuated between 44 and 48%.

In the Czech Republic, various entities can participate in subnational elections. These include officially registered political parties and movements, coalitions formed by multiple political parties, and independent candidates. Groups of independent candidates may also run, and they

Table 3.4 Structure and quality of subnational electoral systems

Criteria	*Results*
How are municipal councillors elected? Indicator—election mode	Indirect election
For what term are municipal councils elected (years)? Indicator—years of mandate	4
What is the level of citizen participation in municipal elections? Indicator: Low—("Normal") voter turnout is below 35% of eligible (registered) voters Average—Voter turnout is between 35 and 60% of eligible (registered) voters High—Voter turnout is over 60% of eligible (registered) voters	Average

Source Authors, based on own research (2025)

are often a strong presence in municipal elections. Independent candidates need to gather a required number of voter signatures to qualify (Table 3.5).

Internal party mechanisms generally select candidates for subnational council elections in the Czech Republic. This can involve party primaries or decision-making processes by the party leadership. Independent candidates, however, go through a self-nomination process, where they independently decide to run for office and are required to gather signatures from voters to appear on the ballot.

Unlike parliamentary or presidential campaigns, municipal campaigns in the Czech Republic are not directly regulated by law. While Act No. 424/1991 Coll., on Association in Political Parties and Political Movements, and other legislation focus on financing political parties and campaigns for higher levels of elections, specific rules for financing campaigns for municipal elections are not laid down in Czech legislation.

While national parties in power at the central government level may exert some influence over subnational elections due to their resources and visibility, local issues and candidates often dominate subnational elections in the Czech Republic. Independent candidates and smaller regional parties frequently perform well in municipal elections. For instance, during the 2018 municipal elections, independent candidates won a

Table 3.5 P3 nature of subnational political party systems

Criteria	*Results*
Which subjects can run in municipal elections? Indicator—define who can participate	Political parties and movements, coalitions of political parties, independent candidates, groups of independent candidates
How are party candidates for municipal council elections selected? Indicator—selected by party, elected by party, self-nomination, other	Selected by party, self-nomination
Are there established rules for financing municipal political campaigns? Indicator—yes, no	No
Does the ruling national party have a dominant position in municipal elections? Indicator—yes, no	No

Source Authors, based on own research (2025)

significant number of mayoral and councillor positions, often outpacing national parties.

According to Act No. 128/2000 Coll. on Municipalities (Municipal Establishment), the municipal council meetings must be public (§93, paragraph 2). This law does not allow for any exceptions to this rule, meaning that the public must be informed about the meetings and must have the opportunity to attend them. Non-public meetings of the municipal council are not permitted. However, council members can hold informal working meetings, which are not public, but no binding decisions can be made at these meetings. Decisions can only be made at a properly convened and publicly held municipal council meeting (Table 3.6).

The right to access public records and documents at the subnational level is guaranteed by Act No. 106/1999 Coll. on Free Access to Information, commonly known as the Freedom of Information Act. This act obliges public authorities, including municipalities and regions, to make their records available to the public upon request unless such records are protected by other legislation (e.g. personal data protection, trade secrets).

Czech legislation does not explicitly require councils to engage in a participatory planning process where citizens can actively contribute. While public hearings and consultations are often part of the planning process, these are generally formalities rather than fully participatory platforms. Public involvement is encouraged but not mandated by law in a binding sense.

Table 3.6 Subnational political participation and accountability

Criteria	*Results*
Are all council meetings (required to be) open to the public? Indicator—yes, no	Yes
Are municipal records and documents (required to be) available to the public? Indicator—yes, no	Yes
Is the council (required to) engage in an open, participatory planning process? Indicator—yes, no	No
Are alternative participatory mechanisms, such as referendums or participatory budgeting, used? Indicator—yes, partly, no	Partly

Source Authors, based on own research (2025)

Alternative participatory mechanisms, such as local referendums and participatory budgeting, are possible but not widely institutionalised or mandatory. Act No. 22/2004 Coll. on Local Referenda allows citizens to initiate local referendums under specific conditions, and some municipalities voluntarily implement participatory budgeting, where citizens can vote on how a portion of the municipal budget is spent. However, these practices are not uniformly applied nationwide and depend on local government initiatives.

References

Act No. 250/2000 Coll. (2000). *On budgetary rules for territorial entities.*

Act No. 128/2000 Coll. (2000). *On municipal establishment.*

Act No. 243/2000 Coll. (2000). *On tax sharing assignment.*

Ashworth, J., Geys, B., Heyndels, B., & Wille, F. (2014). Competition in the political arena and local government performance. *Applied Economics, 46*(19), 2264–2276. https://doi.org/10.1080/00036846.2014.928800

Bečica, J. (2015). Property of self-governing regions in the Czech Republic. In: Vaňková, I. (ed.) Proceedings of the 11th International Scientific Conference Public Economics and Administration 2015. Ostrava: VŠB – Technical University of Ostrava, 2015. pp. 22–26.

Blöchliger, H., & Petzold, O. (2009). *Taxes or grants: What revenue source for sub-central governments?* (OECD economics department working papers, 706). OECD Publishing. https://doi.org/10.1787/223111363085

Bovens, M. (2007). Analysing and assessing accountability: A conceptual framework 1. *European Law Journal, 13*(4), 447–468. https://doi.org/10.1111/j.1468-0386.2007.00375.x

Geys, B., Heinemann, F., & Kalb, A. (2010). Voter involvement, fiscal autonomy and public sector efficiency: Evidence from German municipalities. *European Journal of Political Economy, 26*(2), 265–278. https://doi.org/10.1016/j.ejpoleco.2009.12.001

Herrmann, B. (2022). *Local taxes on economic activity in municipalities in EU member states* (No. JRC129095). Joint Research Centre (Seville site). https://publications.jrc.ec.europa.eu/repository/handle/JRC129095

Kouba, K., & Lysek, J. (2023). The return of silent elections: Democracy, uncontested elections, and citizen participation in Czechia. *Democratization, 30*(8), 1527–1551. https://doi.org/10.1080/13510347.2023.2146524

KPMG. (2024). *Rozpočtové určení daní: Srovnání přínosů průmyslu obcím v Česku, Německu a Rakousku.* https://assets.kpmg.com/content/dam/kpmg/cz/pdf/2024/Studie%20o%20zdan%C4%9Bn%C3%AD%20pr%C5%AFmyslu%20v%20%C4%8CR%20SRN%20a%20Rakousku.pdf

Local Public Sector Alliance. (2022). *The Local Governance Institutions Comparative Assessment (LoGICA) Framework*. Decentralization Net. https://decentralization.net/resources/logica-framework/

Lysek, J. (2021). *Local autonomy index 2.0 (2015–2019): Czech Republic (CZ)*. http://local-autonomy.andreasladner.ch/

Ministry of Interior. (2022). *Příspěvek na výkon státní správy na rok 2023: Příručka pro obce*. https://prispevekobce.cz/media/0/Pspvek_pruka_pro_obce_2023.pdf

Monitor. (2024). *Monitor—Complete overview of public finance*. Ministry of Finance. https://monitor.mfcr.cz

Sedmihradská, L. (2008). Tax sharing mechanism and municipal management in the Czech Republic. *Nispacee Journal of Public Administration and Policy, 1*(2), 119–133. https://doi.org/10.2478/v10269-009-0004-2

Suzuki, K., & Han, Y. (2019). Does citizen participation affect municipal performance? Electoral competition and fiscal performance in Japan. *Public Money & Management, 39*(4), 300–309. https://doi.org/10.1080/09540962.2019.1612763

Union of Towns and Municipalities of the Czech Republic. (2022). *Financování obcí*. https://www.smocr.cz/Shared/Clanky/11310/ins-10-2022.pdf

Weingast, B. R. (2009). Second generation fiscal federalism: The implications of fiscal incentives. *Journal of Urban Economics, 65*, 279–293. https://doi.org/10.1016/j.jue.2008.09.001

CHAPTER 4

India

Amitava Basu

4.1 Introduction

India, a socialist, secular republic in South Asia, extends from the snow-covered Himalayas in the north to the tropical rain forests in the south and tapers off into the Indian Ocean between the Bay of Bengal on the east and the Arabian Sea on the west. It spreads over 3.28 million square kilometres and is the 7th largest country in the world, consisting of 28 provinces or states and 8 union territories administered by the national government. The country houses over 1.45 billion people from diverse cultures, traditions, and religions. India has a federal framework with parliamentary democracy. It has a three-tier government—the national or the central government, the provincial or the state government, and the local government at the village and town level.

India witnessed rapid urbanisation following liberalisation in the 1990s and subsequent rapid economic growth. This trend is expected to continue. It is projected by the United Nations Department of Economic and Social Affairs (UNDESA), Population Division, that by 2025, about

A. Basu (✉)
Centre for Environmental Management and Participatory Development, Delhi, India
e-mail: amitava_basu18@rediffmail.com

J. Nemec et al. (eds.), *Local Government and Fiscal Transfers*, Governance and Public Management,
https://doi.org/10.1007/978-3-031-95674-4_4

46% of the population of India will be residing in towns and cities, which is a significant increase from 31% urban population as per the 2011 Census. However, till the 74th Constitutional Amendment Act in 1992, urban local governments, which are municipal bodies, had no constitutional status.

Municipal governance in India has a long and rich history, dating back to the early seventeenth century. The first municipality was established by the Dutch in Fort Kochi in 1664, followed by the creation of the Madras (now Chennai) Municipal Corporation in 1687, and later, the formation of the Calcutta (now Kolkata) and Bombay (now Mumbai) Municipal Corporations in 1726. By the early 1800s, most towns across India had some form of municipal governance in place. Following India's independence in 1947, the focus shifted to strengthening local self-governance. The Government of India set up various committees to improve urban governance. A key milestone was the 74th Constitutional Amendment Act of 1992, which, as mentioned earlier, granted constitutional recognition to municipalities and introduced a standardised framework for local governance across the country. The Amendment aimed to empower urban local bodies and foster greater democratic participation at the grassroots level, marking a pivotal moment in the evolution of municipal governance in India.

Municipal governance in India is vital for ensuring effective local self-governance. It is categorised into three primary types of urban local bodies, outlined in Table 4.1, each serving urban areas and populations within their respective geographical jurisdiction.

The municipal bodies (hereinafter collectively referred to as municipalities) are governed by the State Municipal Acts enacted by the state governments to establish and manage municipal governments within the cities. Each State typically has its own municipal legislation, and some States have multiple municipal legislations to govern different types of municipalities. These legislations cover various processes such as elections, recruitment of staff, and urban area demarcation. These legislations apply to most urban areas, except cantonment areas. In 2003, the central government introduced a model municipal law to streamline and update municipal governance laws across the States in alignment with the 74th Constitutional Amendment Act. The municipalities are under the administrative control of the state governments. The municipalities

Table 4.1 Types and structure of urban local bodies

Type of Urban Local Bodies	*Description of Jurisdiction*	*Administrative Structure*
Municipal Corporation	The largest urban local body, typically found in cities with a population exceeding 1 million	Councillors are elected on universal adult suffrage from each ward of the city and represent the citizens of the respective wards The councillors elect the mayor and the deputy mayor. The mayor is the head of the Corporation, and the deputy mayor is the second in command The state government appoints a municipal commissioner as the chief executive officer
Municipalities	Cities with a population between 100,000 and 1 million	Councillors are elected on universal adult suffrage from each ward of the city and represent the citizens of the respective wards The councillors elect the chairperson and the deputy chairperson. The chairperson is the head of the municipal council, and the deputy chairperson is the second in command The state government appoints an executive officer as the chief executive officer
Nagar Panchayats	Transitional areas with a population between 20,000 and 100,000	The similar structure to that of municipal councils

Source Author, based on own research (2025)

are responsible for urban planning, public health and sanitation, education, social welfare, and economic development within their respective geographical jurisdiction.

4.2 Fiscal Federalism

4.2.1 Local Government Revenues

The sources of revenue of the municipalities are broadly categorised as follows:

- Own revenues
  - Tax Revenue: Primarily property taxes but also includes other local taxes.
  - Non-Tax Revenue: Fees, licenses, user charges, and other income generated by municipal services.
- Transfers of funds from the central and state governments
- Other Sources
  - Borrowings
  - Miscellaneous income.

The 74th Constitutional Amendment Act has recognised the municipalities. Although they do not have independent taxing power under the Constitution, they derive their authority from the state governments. The States can assign taxes from the State List to the municipalities. Common taxes allocated to the municipalities include property tax, entertainment tax, vehicle tax, profession or trade/calling tax, and license fees. This Constitutional Amendment Act also introduced provisions related to measures that augment the Consolidated Fund of the State (one account in which all government revenues and expenditures are consolidated) to support the resources of the municipalities.

The municipalities face serious challenges in the management of finances. These challenges are especially limited funds, which restrict the ability to deliver services effectively; mismanagement of funds that leads to inefficiencies, misallocation of resources, and ultimately, a decline in service quality; misalignment between municipal fund requirements and the funding from the States, which creates gaps and significant obstacles in delivering consistent and effective services.

Further, the autonomy of the municipalities is often impaired by political interference, which hinders the ability of these bodies to make decisions that best suit their specific needs. Besides, state-level policies may not always align with local priorities, leading to further complications. As a cumulative effect, the financial status of most of the municipalities has been weak and dismal. In 2023–2024, the municipalities in India contributed only 0.6% to the nation's Gross Domestic Product (GDP), which, compared to the 9.2% generated by the Central Government and 14.6% by State Governments, reflects a significant gap. Tax revenues comprised 30% of the income for the municipalities, with grants, contributions, and subsidies contributing 24.9% and fees and user charges accounting for 20.2%.

4.2.2 *Local Government Expenditures*

The municipalities have two main categories of expenditure:

A. Capital expenditure involves spending on creating assets or city infrastructure such as water treatment plants, sewerage treatment plants, roads, parks, primary healthcare centres, etc.
B. Current expenditure include: (i) Establishment Costs that cover salaries, wages, bonuses, and post-retirement benefits for employees and usually form the most significant component of revenue expenditure; (ii) Administrative Expenses for office operation and management, such as utility bills, office supplies, transportation costs, and communication expenses, printing, and stationery, etc.; (iii) Operational and Maintenance Costs are incurred for maintenance of capital assets, such as buildings, roads, and water and sewerage treatment plants, and cover routine inspections, repairs, upgrades, and refurbishments of the capital assets, and these expenses are essential to provide civic services to the public; (iv) Program Expenses for specific events or public outreach activities, such as raising awareness about safety measures during the COVID-19 pandemic; (v) Financial Costs include interest on loans or borrowings; and (vi) Miscellaneous Expenses.

A recent study by the Reserve Bank of India (RBI) on the municipal finances in India revealed that the total expenditure of Municipal Corporations, which are the largest form of municipalities in the country, increased slightly from 1.2% of Gross Domestic Product (GDP) in 2019–2020 to 1.3% of GDP in 2023–2024. This is significantly lower compared to countries like Brazil, where it stands at 7.5%, and South Africa at 6%. Capital expenditure rose from 56.1% of total spending in 2019–2020 to 61.5% in 2023–2024. This shift indicates a growing emphasis on enhancing public infrastructure in urban India. However, a concerning trend is the increasing operational costs within revenue expenditures. Establishment expenses, including salaries, pensions, and administrative costs, account for over 50% of revenue spending. For the budgeted establishment expenditure of INR 697.45 billion in 2023–2024, salaries, wages, bonuses, and pensions alone amount to INR 564.50 billion (100 INR–1.1 EUR).

4.2.3 *Transfers to Local Governments*

The tax powers in India, between the central and the state governments, are specified in the Constitution. Though the state governments are empowered to collect significant taxes, the central government oversees higher revenue-yielding taxes such as income tax and customs duties. In contrast, the state governments manage relatively low revenue-yielding taxes such as land revenue. As a result, the central government collects a more considerable amount of revenue than the state governments and the local governments. Hence, fiscal transfers from the central government to the state governments and then to municipalities are necessitated.

Intergovernmental fiscal transfers in India date as far back as 1919. It has experienced many changes since the independence of the country in 1947. The economic rationale behind intergovernmental fiscal transfers is addressing vertical and horizontal fiscal imbalances. Vertical imbalance refers to the mismatch between the revenue-raising capacity of the central government and the expenditure responsibilities of the states and municipalities. Horizontal imbalance occurs when some states and municipalities are economically stronger than others, creating disparities in their ability to provide public services. Transfers help equalise these imbalances by redistributing resources from the wealthier to the poorer regions. As in other countries, India's fiscal transfer system today includes correcting vertical fiscal imbalances between the central government and the subnational governments by compensating for disparities between expenditures and revenues and correcting horizontal imbalances in the fiscal capacity among the subnational governments to facilitate equal access to public services across the country. These two aims are not always independent of each other, and both have been integrated into the system's operation.

In the process, intergovernmental fiscal transfers in India play a crucial role in the distribution of resources between the central government and the subnational governments to foster fiscal decentralisation, equitable development, and cooperative federalism.

Article 280 of the Constitution of India mandates the establishment of an independent Finance Commission, appointed by the President every five years, to recommend the distribution of central taxes and grants to the States. The Commission consists of a Chairman and four members. Its "Terms of Reference" (ToR), as specified in the Constitution, include: (i) determining the distribution of the net proceeds from central taxes between the central government and the state governments; (ii) advising on grants-in-aid to be allocated to the states; (iii) suggesting ways to enhance the Consolidated Funds of the States, to support the resources of rural and urban local governments; and (iv) addressing any other matter referred to it by the President to promote sound financial management. Under the latter provision, the Commission has been tasked with various responsibilities in the past, such as setting fiscal rules and targets for the central government and the state governments, recommending sustainable development strategies and environmental protections, restructuring or waiving States' loans, evaluating public expenditure management systems, reviewing disaster management frameworks, formulating strategies for public enterprise reforms, and encouraging States to implement tax reforms. The Finance Commission is a non-permanent body established for a specific period. Its mandate concludes with submitting its report on the devolution of central taxes. Fifteen Finance Commissions have been constituted since 1952.

The role of the Finance Commission as envisaged in the Constitution was curtailed when the Planning Commission was appointed through a Cabinet Resolution in 1950. Historically, fiscal transfers in India were of two types: those allocated by the Finance Commission (fiscal transfers) and those allocated through the Planning Commission (discretionary transfers). The latter were often criticised for being politically motivated and lacking objectivity in distribution. After the dissolution of the Planning Commission in 2015, the role of the Finance Commission was strengthened. Since then, two main routes for transferring resources from the central government to the state governments have been established: (i) statutory transfers through awards of the Finance Commission, which include (a) formula-based tax devolution and (b) grants-in-aid, and (ii) discretionary transfers from various ministries of the central government.

Following the 74th Constitutional Amendment, steps have been taken to strengthen the municipalities' financial bases and improve the fiscal relationship between the central, state, and local governments. The intergovernmental fund transfer mechanism has also been redesigned.

As stated earlier, municipal revenue comes from two primary sources: own revenue generated by the municipalities and intergovernmental fiscal transfers from the central and state governments. Fiscal transfers, particularly when consistent, predictable, and recurring, are robust funding sources because they do not require repayment and incur no financing costs. Municipalities often prefer fiscal transfers. Furthermore, their predictable nature strengthens their creditworthiness by ensuring a stable revenue stream.

Since the implementation of Goods and Services Tax (GST) from 2017 to 2018, the proportion of own tax revenue to total revenue for the municipalities decreased. In contrast, the share of transfers in total revenue has grown, reflecting an increased reliance on higher levels of government. This trend, however, does not undermine the significant benefits that GST has brought to the economy. The introduction of GST on 1 July 2017, marked a transformative shift in the country's indirect tax system by simplifying the tax structure and establishing a unified market. GST consolidated several local taxes, including entry tax, entertainment tax, and advertisement tax, which were key sources of revenue for the municipalities. One of the significant taxes subsumed under GST was octroi, an entry tax. While the GST Constitutional Amendment Act of 2016 ensures compensation for the state governments, it does not extend this obligation to local governments, leaving it up to the state governments to decide whether to compensate the municipalities. In the post-GST era, different States implemented varying policies to address the loss of octroi revenues for the municipalities. For example, Maharashtra compensated for octroi losses, while Kerala did so for entertainment tax revenue. Conversely, some States allowed the municipalities to impose additional taxes, such as a tax on movie tickets in Bhopal, Madhya Pradesh. Despite implementing GST, municipal tax revenues remained relatively stable compared to 2015 levels. However, the municipalities saw increased revenue through grants, contributions, and subsidies in compensation for the lost tax sources.

In 2022–2023, grants from both the central and state governments to the Municipal Corporations, the largest types of municipal bodies, increased by 24.9% and 20.4%, respectively. Transfers from the State

Governments, including assigned revenues, compensation, State Finance Commission (SFC) grants, and other State grants, constituted around 30% of the Municipal Corporations' revenue receipts from 2019–2020 to 2022–2023 and were projected to be 28.7% in 2023–2024. Meanwhile, transfers from the Central Government accounted for 2.5% of the Municipal Corporations' total revenue receipts in recent years. Intergovernmental transfers from the central and state governments to the Municipal Corporations, the country's largest municipal bodies, are summarised in Table 4.2 for the years 2019–2020 to 2022–2023.

Table 4.2 Grants to the municipal corporations from the central and the state governments in billions of INR

	2019–2020	*2020–2021*	*2021–2022*	*2022–2023*
Total Grants from the Central Government to the Municipal Corporations	138.81	143.15	117.95	147.31
Finance Commission Grants as reported by the Municipal Corporations	53.86	70.99	60.76	70.67
Grants from the Central Government other than Finance Commission Grants	84.95	72.16	57.19	76.64
Total Grants from the State Governments to the Municipal Corporations	321.48	335.48	347.72	418.72
State Finance Commission Grants as reported by the Municipal Corporations	68.61	71.68	65.92	86.05
Grants from the State Governments other than State Finance Commission Grants	252.87	263.80	281.80	332.67
Memo Item				
Finance Commission Grants as reported in the Budget of the Central Government	250.98	267.10	161.47	177.79

Source Author, based on the RBI Report on Municipal Finance (2025)

Table 4.3 Grants recommended versus actual releases in millions of INR

Grants	*Recommended*	*Released*	*% Released*
Finance Commission (FC) X	10,000	8,340	83.4
FC XI	20,000	17,520	87.6
FC XII	50,000	44,700	89.4
FC XIII	231,110	189,800	82.1
FC XIV	871,440	742,590	85.2

Source Author, based on the Fifteenth Finance Commission Report (2025)

4.3 Major Challenges Related to Transfers to Municipalities

This part documents three critical aspects connected with the impacts of fiscal transfers to municipalities on local democracy: transfers are frequently delayed, states do not manage the fiscal transfer system well, and transfers decrease municipalities' incentives to generate their own revenues.

4.3.1 Delay of Transfers

Though transferring funds from the central and state governments to the municipalities is vital for providing essential services and infrastructure, this process faces several significant challenges that hinder the efficient and equitable allocation of resources.

The actual disbursements have been lower than the amounts suggested by the Central Finance Commissions, with shortfalls ranging from 10 to 18% for urban local bodies. As shown in Table 4.3, these shortfalls were mainly due to the municipalities not meeting the conditions required to receive the performance grants recommended by the Central Finance Commissions.

4.3.2 Ineffectiveness of State Finance Commissions

As stated earlier, the Constitution mandates that the state government establish State Finance Commissions (SFCs) every five years. Similar to the Central Finance Commission, SFCs play a crucial role in allocating state resources to local governments, including municipalities. However,

Table 4.4 Status of constitution of SFC

State	*Last SFC constituted*
Assam, Bihar, Punjab, Rajasthan	VI
Haryana, Himachal Pradesh, Kerala, Madhya Pradesh, Maharashtra, Odisha, Sikkim, Tamil Nadu, Tripura, Uttarakhand, and Uttar Pradesh	V
Andhra Pradesh, Karnataka, and West Bengal	IV
Chhattisgarh, Goa, Gujarat, Jharkhand, and Manipur	III
Arunachal Pradesh, Mizoram	II
Erstwhile Jammu and Kashmir, Telangana	I

Source Author, based on the Fifteenth Finance Commission Report (2024)

the timely constitution and effective functioning of SFCs have been a significant challenge in many States. Table 4.4 shows the status of the formation of SFCs in various states.

Many states have not constituted SFCs within the mandated time-frame, leading to delays in their recommendations. For example, the State of Telangana was created in 2014 and its first SFC was constituted in 2017. Besides, SFCs in several States often have inadequate administrative support and insufficient resources, which impact their effectiveness. The average delay in SFCs submitting their reports has been around sixteen months, hindering the timely flow of resources to local governments. It has also been noticed that there are a few instances where, even when the SFC submits recommendations, implementation by the state government is often delayed or inadequate. All of these issues have disrupted the smooth flow of resources to the municipalities, impacting their ability to efficiently and effectively deliver services to the citizens.

4.3.3 Low Generation of Own Revenues

The municipalities depend heavily on property tax as a source of revenue. Nearly 50% of the municipalities generate less than 23% of their total revenue, heavily relying on tax revenue. Alarmingly, a few municipalities derive over 80% of their total revenue from taxes alone. Dependence on one source of revenue restricts their ability to generate diverse revenue streams and limits their capacity to address increasing infrastructure demands. Hence, dependence on the transfer of funds from higher levels of government becomes predominant. The absence of an enhanced range of revenue sources and lack of efficiency in revenue collection led to the municipalities' ineffective funds management. This phenomenon is reflected in low spending by the municipalities to provide basic urban services and support growth, productivity, and quality of life. The spending must be significantly increased to meet the rising demands of the city's infrastructure, amenities, and facilities.

With heavy reliance on transfers, the municipalities also do not manage their borrowing policies well. A World Bank Report of 2022 on "Financing India's Urban Infrastructure Needs" estimates India will need to invest about $840 billion in urban infrastructure over the next 15 years. Currently, over 75% of funding comes from the central and state governments, with the municipalities contributing only 15% of their revenues. Grant-in-Aid remains the main source of funds.

Municipal bonds could be a key tool to enable funding of city infrastructure projects like roads, bridges, and water supply systems. In 1997, Bengaluru Municipal Corporation was the first to issue a municipal bond, followed by Ahmedabad Municipal Corporation in 1998 and subsequently by Pune Municipal Corporation and Hyderabad Municipal Corporation. However, the municipal bond market is underdeveloped, with most bonds privately placed, limiting investor participation. According to a recent report by the RBI, the total municipal bonds outstanding as of the end of March 2024 is INR 42.04 billion, which is only 0.09% of the total corporate bonds. Further, the Green Bond market is still nascent, and issuing Green Bonds involves additional costs for green audits and monitoring key performance indicators. The central government and the Securities and Exchange Board of India (SEBI) have taken several initiatives to promote municipal bonds, introduced guidelines to improve transparency and accountability, and required issuers to disclose project details and associated risks. With support from regulatory bodies such as SEBI and the involvement of credit rating agencies, the municipal bond market is set for substantial growth. By utilising municipal bonds, the municipalities can diversify their funding options, draw long-term investments, and foster the development of modern, resilient urban infrastructure.

4.4 Conclusions

India's economic growth is mainly dependent on effective urbanisation. Cities need to drive the nation's growth and development. Municipalities play a crucial role in addressing the challenges and seizing the opportunities for this urban growth. Additionally, efforts to mitigate climate change and ensure equitable resource distribution must be driven through active engagement at the municipal level. States with a higher share of urban economic activity have witnessed greater per capita income growth and reduced poverty, suggesting a strong link between urbanisation, economic growth, and poverty reduction. It is, therefore, crucial to strengthen municipal finances to transform urban governance in India and enhance urban facilities and services. The path forward involves improving the financial transfers from higher levels of government and empowering the municipalities to generate their revenue. By adopting innovative financial tools and reforming existing systems, the municipalities in India can enhance their fiscal stability and independence, allowing them to meet the growing demands of urbanisation and drive sustainable development in cities across the country.

In this perspective, the Fifteenth Finance Commission made five major recommendations that could contribute to better management and governance of cities in India. These recommendations are: (i) substantive increase in provision of funds to the municipalities, (ii) tied-financing with performance indicators on air quality, water supply, and sanitation service, (iii) publication of audited annual accounts and notification of floor rate of property tax by the municipalities to be eligible for accessing grant, (iv) setting of time deadline for the States to strengthen SFC and present action taken report in the State legislature, and (v) publication of all service level benchmarks and annual accounts on national level platform by the municipalities to be entitled to avail funds.

Effective functioning of cooperative federalism and state-municipal fiscal relationships assume paramount significance concerning how the recommendations of the Fifteenth Finance Commission are implemented. Besides, SFCs play a crucial role in resource allocation to the municipalities. However, as stated hereinbefore, the timely constitution and effective functioning of SFCs have been a significant challenge in many States. To address these deficiencies, it is paramount for the States to constitute SFCs within the mandated timeframe, provide adequate administrative support and resources to SFCs, and ensure timely implementation of SFC recommendations. The Fifteenth Finance Commission advised that all States must constitute SFCs, act upon their recommendations, and lay the explanatory memorandum as to the action taken before the State legislature on or before March 2024. After March 2024, no grants should be released to a State that has not complied with the Constitutional provisions in respect of the SFC and these conditions.

Further, to promote responsible borrowing by the municipalities, the municipal laws should incorporate a Comprehensive Debt Limitation Policy (CDLP) or a similar guideline, which will help steer borrowing decisions and maintain fiscal responsibility. The state governments may consider creating or engaging suitable expert institutions to support the municipalities, provide guidance, and build the capacity of the municipalities to access and manage capital effectively.

The municipalities also have a role to optimise their own revenue streams. Property tax is a predominant source of own revenue for the municipalities. The revenue from this source needs to be augmented to strengthen the finances of these organisations and requires reform of the property tax system. The reform should include regular property surveys with the State, making GIS facilities accessible to all the municipalities. Unit Area Valuation (UAV) and self-assessment methods should be gradually adopted. Property Tax Boards are needed for independent guidance, and tax exemptions must be transparently justified. The property tax register should be made public online with key property details while ensuring privacy. An integrated property tax system is crucial for billing, reminders, online payments, and digital records. Penalties for late payments and publication of defaulter lists are essential. Normative staffing standards and cost-benefit analyses of outsourcing should be developed, and the experiences of Ranchi Municipal Corporation in Jharkhand can serve as valuable guidance in this regard. Concerning fees and user charges, it is essential to implement functional costing, which involves comparing the cost of service delivery with the corresponding fees and user charges, identifying any revenue gap, and suitably bridging the gap. Besides, the Ministry of Housing and Urban Affairs (MoHUA) of the central government can conduct a comprehensive study of all revenue streams, apart from property tax, and provide the state governments and municipalities guidance on optimising these revenue streams.

Additionally, the municipalities must improve transparency and accountability, making financial data easily accessible to the public, strengthening service delivery through defining the service standards, establishing grievance redressal mechanisms, and implementing the same. Also, a Fiscal Responsibility and Budget Management (FRBM) framework for the municipalities must incorporate medium-term fiscal planning, realistic budget projections, standardised accounting practices, timely audited annual accounts presentation, performance tracking, and public involvement in budgeting and financial decision-making. This will require significant revision in the municipal laws and regulations. The laws and rules relating to budget preparation and management need to be structured around the FRBM framework. It may be mentioned in this connection that the Karnataka Local Fund Authorities Fiscal Responsibility Act 2002, along with the Karnataka Municipal Accounting and Budgeting Rules 2006, provides a model that the other States could adopt. In addition, it is incumbent to strengthen the revenue and accounting capabilities of the municipalities. This requires updating recruitment rules, especially for revenue and finance positions, defining clear roles, skills, competencies, and performance standards, regularly reviewing workforce needs based on city growth, upskilling the staff, introducing standardised software for revenue and finance functions, and facilitating adoption of this software by the staff. In essence, these initiatives enhance the professional capacity of the staff, improve their efficiency, and ultimately strengthen the financial health of the municipalities.

In sum, to increase and more efficiently fund municipal services in India, it is critical to build robust municipal own-source revenue, facilitate effective transfers from higher levels of government to the municipalities, and ensure consistent guidelines from SFCs to support sustainable urban development.

Annex: Country Profile: India

See Table 4.5.

Municipal governance in India has evolved over time, beginning in colonial times and continuing through a series of reforms. The system has been shaped by significant changes, particularly with the introduction of various urban local bodies such as Municipal Corporations, Municipal Councils, and Nagar Panchayats (as stated earlier, collectively referred to

Table 4.5 Municipal political power structures

Criteria	*Results*
The level of autonomy of municipal governments over their functional mandates: the question of whether municipal governance institutions can only perform mandated tasks or can choose from a predefined scope of tasks Indicator: yes, partly, no	Yes
The level of freedom of municipal governments to decide their own political organisation and electoral system (can they, for example, determine their own electoral districts, number of seats, electoral system, etc.) Indicator: yes, partly, no	Partly
The constitutional or legal mechanisms to assert the autonomy of municipal governments. Examples of specific constitutional or legal mechanisms that allow municipal governments to assert their autonomy include (a) constitutional clauses or other statutory regulations protecting local self-government; (b) recourse to the judicial system through constitutional courts to settle disputes with higher authorities; or (c) other constitutional or legal protections of municipal autonomy exist (e.g., higher-level governments are prevented from forcing municipal governments to merge) Indicator: yes, partly, no	Yes
Municipal governments' right to use the legal system against higher-level government (de jure and de facto—do they use such right?) Indicator yes (both de jure and de facto), partly, no	The rights are enshrined in law but not generally used
The level to which decisions made by municipal governance institutions are subject to administrative supervision for their responsibilities and if higher-level approval is needed to act in their own matters Indicator yes, no	Yes
Does the higher-level have the right to remove local executives [or other local officials] without judicial intervention? Indicator yes, no	Yes

Source Author, based on own research

as municipalities). A pivotal moment in the history of municipal governance came with the enactment of the Seventy-Fourth Amendment to the Indian Constitution in 1992. This amendment created a constitutional framework for the municipalities, delineating their structure, powers, and responsibilities. It aimed to decentralise governance and give municipalities more authority in urban planning and development. The main focus of the municipalities includes public health, urban planning, and social welfare, all aimed at improving the community's living standards. In managing these areas, the municipalities handle a wide range of tasks, from sanitation and healthcare to infrastructure development. Financial management is a key aspect of municipal governance, with the municipalities relying on diverse revenue sources while grappling with budgetary constraints.

The structural framework of the municipalities is provided in Table 4.6.

The purpose of the Seventy-Fourth Constitutional Amendment has been to establish democratically run Municipalities with independent powers and finances, addressing key local issues like water supply and sanitation. While the State legislatures enacted laws to fulfil the spirit of the Constitutional Amendment, the transfer of responsibilities often remained ambiguous. In Kerala, for instance, while the law aimed to transfer powers to the municipalities, implementation was hindered by a lack of action of the State Government for over two decades, keeping control over staff, equipment, and administration. In contrast, Gujarat had a history of local autonomy predating the Seventy-Fourth Constitutional Amendment, with the municipalities holding powers from as early as the 1940s. However, recent trends have eroded this legacy. The main issue across the States is the reluctance of bureaucracies to decentralise power, which led to slow progress.

The State Governments were given authority to make rules and were led by political executives. However, in reality, the actual rulemaking is done by the state bureaucracy. The bureaucracy's motivation and interests did not necessarily align with the democratic intentions of decentralisation outlined in the Seventy-Fourth Constitutional Amendment. Established practices influence the process of rulemaking and have often shaped the outcome. There are inconsistencies among the States concerning the devolution of authority and responsibilities to the municipalities.

Table 4.7 contains the critical factors that indicate that despite the Constitutional Amendment, legislative reform, and policy initiatives, the

Table 4.6 Structural framework of municipalities

Parameter	*Status*
Constitutional Recognition	The Seventy-Fourth Constitutional Amendment granted constitutional recognition to the municipal bodies in India. came into effect on 1 June 1993
Governance Guidelines and Regulations	Each State has municipal laws that provide the rules and regulations for the governance structure, process, financial management procedures, powers, and functions of the municipalities. The powers, duties, and responsibilities of the key municipal functionaries are also laid down in the municipal legislation States have separate Acts for Municipal Corporations and Municipalities. Some States have separate Acts for large Municipal Corporations, especially in metropolitan cities, such as the Kolkata Municipal Corporation Act for Kolkata Metropolis in West Bengal and the Mumbai Municipal Corporation Act for Greater Mumbai Metropolis in Maharashtra
Governing Body	According to municipal legislation, the municipality's governance vests with an elected council headed by the Municipal Corporation's Mayor or the Chairperson of the Municipality and Nagar Panchayat The municipalities are governed by three key authorities: the Council, the Standing Committee, and the Municipal Commissioner or the Chief Executive Officer. The council, comprising the elected Councillors, is the deliberative and legislative wing of the municipalities. The standing committees are formed to facilitate the work of the council, and their members are selected from among the council members. The Municipal Commissioner or the Chief Executive Officer is the executive wing of the municipalities and is responsible for implementing the decisions of the council and the standing committees

Source Author, based on own research

dominance of the state government largely continues, and the autonomy of the Municipalities is constrained (Table 4.8).

Therefore, it is evident that the municipalities are not autonomous in the real sense.

Municipal elections in India are held according to the municipal laws of each State. However, the overall framework of the municipal elections, presented in Table 4.9, is, by and large, uniform across the country and is in line with the provisions of the Constitution of the country.

Despite the rules and regulations that have been laid down, municipal elections in the country face several challenges. These challenges are as follows:

1. Untimely Holding of Election: Many states failed to hold timely elections. As a result, there were over 1500 municipalities which did not have elected councils between 2015 and 2021.

Table 4.7 Relationship between state government and municipalities

Parameter	*Status*
Transfer of authority to the municipalities for revision of tax rates and introduction of new taxes and charges	Despite the provision in Article 243X of the Constitution, some States have not yet granted municipalities independent authority to revise the existing tax rates. Similarly, Municipalities face challenges in introducing new taxes or charges
Compliance by the state governments with respect to SFCs	Only nine States have established their Sixth SFC, despite it being due by 2019–2020, and many States stagnated at earlier stages. Besides, some State Governments resist fully devolving powers and resources to Municipalities as per the 74th Constitutional Amendment
Interference or intervention by the state government	The municipalities are administratively under the state government's supervision, direction, and control. They also depend heavily on the state government for financial resources. Given their administrative subordinate status and overdependence on finance, several state governments often intervene in decision-making and impose decisions on the municipalities

Source Author, based on own research

Table 4.8 Structure and Quality of Subnational Electoral Systems

Criteria	*Results*
How are municipal councillors elected? Indicator—election mode	Local elections
For what term are municipal councils elected (years)? Indicator—years of mandate	5
What is the level of citizen participation in municipal elections? Indicator: Low—("Normal") voter turnout is below 35% of eligible (registered) voters Average—Voter turnout is between 35 and 60% of eligible (registered) voters High—Voter turnout is over 60% of eligible (registered) voters	High

Source Author, based on own research

Table 4.9 Framework of municipal election

Parameter	*Status*
Electorate	The geographical area of each municipality is divided into territorial constituencies known as wards. The adult residents of each ward elect their representatives who constitute the council of the Municipal Corporations, Municipalities, and Nagar Panchayats (i.e. collectively referred to as municipalities)
Election Authority	The electoral roll is prepared under the supervision, direction, and control of the Election Commission of each State, and the election process is managed and conducted by the respective State Election Commissions
Periodicity of Election	Municipal Elections are held every five years
Reservation of Electoral Wards	Certain numbers of electoral wards or election seats are reserved for weaker sections, women, and marginalised groups
Election of Mayor or Chairperson	In some States, the mayor or chairperson of the municipal body is elected by the councillors. In some other States, the mayor or chairperson of the municipal body is directly elected by the people of the municipal area

Source Author, based on own research

2. Inadequate Power of SECs: SECs depend on the State Governments for important processes like delimitation and reservations.
3. Delays in Determination of Electoral Ward Boundaries and Reservation of Electoral Seats: At times, State Governments delay the process of ward delimitation and seat reservations, affecting election schedules. In several states, the power of delimitation of wards and reservation of electoral seats is vested with the State Government.
4. Delay in Formation of Municipal Council: Even after elections, municipal councils, the governing body of municipalities, and key positions such as the mayor are often not in place on time. For example, in Karnataka, there was a delay of 12 to 24 months in the formation of elected municipal councils after the declaration of election results in most of the cities.

All these factors lead to the creation of voter apathy that results in low voter turnout for municipal elections. It is observed that voter turnout in the municipal elections has been consistently lower than in the parliamentary and state assembly elections. For example, in the December 2022 municipal elections in Delhi, it was about 50.74% as against the voter turnout of 62.59% for the Delhi State Assembly elections in 2021 and 60.6% voter turnout in the parliamentary elections in 2019 (Table 4.10).

India has a multi-party system. There are national parties, as well as regional or state-level parties. The political parties have played a critical role in India, shaping democracy, equality, social justice, and empowerment of marginalised communities. Over time, they have facilitated political engagement and representation for a broad range of societal interests, and their electoral success has been central to governance. During the past four decades, regional parties have grown in number and influence and contributed to the federalisation of India's party system. The regional parties have played a critical role in evolving coalition politics and reinforced the cooperative aspects of India's federal structure.

The political parties in India operate as institutions that channel the ambitions of their members while relying on the grassroots level to sustain their influence. To meet the challenges of marginalised groups seeking political representation, grassroots-level activities are significant for the working of the political parties. The parties adapt to voters' demands, employing emotional and material appeals to attract support. However,

Table 4.10 Nature of subnational political party systems

Criteria	*Results*
Which subjects can run in municipal elections? Indicator—define who can participate	Any person whose name exists in the relevant part of the existing electoral rolls of the State Legislative Assembly constituency or a part thereof till the last date of filing of nomination of the municipality All persons who are enrolled as electors in the electoral rolls of the concerned ward of the municipality
How are party candidates for municipal council elections selected? Indicator—selected by party, elected by party, self-nomination, other	Selected by the party
Are there established rules for financing municipal political campaigns? Indicator—yes, no	No
Does the ruling national party have a dominant position in municipal elections? Indicator—yes, no	Generally, not. Usually, the ruling party in the State dominates the municipal elections due to its proximity to the local level

Source Author, based on own research (2025)

despite claims of inclusivity, social inequalities and the influence of privileged, established, upper-caste male leaders continue. At the municipal level, the selection process of party candidates for election is largely opaque and heavily influenced by informal lobbying and elite preferences. Women and lower-caste candidates face additional hurdles due to the entrenched biases of the parties. Although the signs of elite preferences to shape continue, of late, the importance of local-level engagement is clearly emerging. The status of the political system at the municipal level is summarised in Tables 4.11 and 4.12.

Table 4.11 Status of municipal political system

Parameter	*Status*
Participation of Political Parties	Political parties, both national and regional or state-level parties, contest the municipal elections. Depending on political exigencies, the parties enter into alliances or make coalition arrangements to contest the election
Nomination of Candidates	Candidates are selected by the respective political parties or political alliances, as the case may be. In the case of an alliance, there is a mutually agreed-upon seat-sharing arrangement The candidates for the reserved constituencies are either women or from the marginalised community, in accordance with the requirements prescribed by the SEC for the reserved seats. However, in selecting the candidates, the influence of the privileged established echelon of the political parties and informal lobbying continue
Domination	Usually, the ruling party in the State dominates the municipal elections due to its proximity to the local level
Accountability of the Elected Municipal Council	There are rules and regulations for different municipal activities and functions that must be followed. However, these rules, including the financial regulations, are often not strictly adhered to

Source Author, based on own research

Public participation plays an essential role in ensuring transparency and accountability in governance. Engaging citizens and civic societies in decision-making processes fosters a democratic environment and strengthens the relationship between the municipalities and the communities. In this connection, the Seventy-Fourth Constitutional Amendment established a framework for decentralising urban governance, connecting citizens to municipalities. Ward Committees, consisting of the ward Councillor and diverse local representatives, such as citizens, municipal experts, representatives of civic groups, and women, are created to promote citizen participation in municipal affairs. These committees

Table 4.12 Subnational political participation and accountability

Criteria	*Results*
Are all council meetings (required to be) open to the public? Indicator—yes, no	No
Are municipal records and documents (required to be) available to the public? Indicator—yes, no	Yes, on request
Is the council (required to) engage in an open, participatory planning process? Indicator—yes, no	No
Are alternative participatory mechanisms, such as referendums or participatory budgeting, used? Indicator—yes, partly, no	No

Source Author, based on own research (2025)

address local issues and are involved in planning, financial, and administrative functions affecting their wards. However, a few States have formed Ward Committees. Even in the States where these Committees are formed, most of them are dormant or inactive.

References

Athar, S., White, R., & Goyal, H. (2022). *Report on financing India's urban infrastructure needs*. The World Bank. https://documents1.worldbank.org/curated/en/099615110042225105/pdf/P17130200d91fc0da0ac610a1e3e1a664d4.pdf

Fifteenth Finance Commission. (2021). *The fifteenth finance commission report*. https://fincomindia.nic.in/commission-reports-fifteenth

Government of India. (1950). *The constitution of India*. https://www.india.gov.in/my-government/constitution-india

Government of India. (1992). *The constitution (seventy-fourth amendment) act, 1992*. https://www.india.gov.in/my-government/constitution-india/amendments/constitution-india-seventy-fourth-amendment-act-1992

Government of India. (2016). *Goods and Services Tax (GST) constitutional amendment act*. https://www.gstcouncil.gov.in/gst-council-0#:~:text=The%20Constitution%20Amendment%20Bill%20was%20passed%20by%20more%20than%2015,governing%20goods%20and%20services%20tax

Janaagraha Centre for Citizenship and Democracy. (2022). *A municipal finance blueprint for India*. https://www.janaagraha.org/files/Municipal-Finance-Blueprint-for-India-Janaagraha.pdf

Reserve Bank of India. (2024). *Report on municipal finances*. Reserve Bank of India.

CHAPTER 5

Indonesia

Irwanda Wisnu Wardhana and Amrie Firmansyah

5.1 Introduction

As of 2025, Indonesia is the world's largest archipelagic nation, with 17,000 islands, comprising 38 provinces led by governors, 416 regencies led by regents, and 98 cities led by mayors (Statistics Indonesia, 2025). Both regents and mayors have equal status as the second local government level after governors. Additionally, there are over 84,000 villages called *desa* in rural areas and *kelurahan* in urban areas. The country's territory stretches over 5,120 kilometres from east to west, making it comparable in width to the European continent. Indonesia is home to over 273 million people, making it the fourth most populous country in the world. It is a highly diverse nation with more than 1,300 ethnic groups. This diversity is reflected in its linguistic richness, where over 700 local languages and dialects are spoken.

I. W. Wardhana (✉)
Indonesia National Research and Innovation Agency, Jakarta, Indonesia
e-mail: irwandawisnu@gmail.com

A. Firmansyah
Universitas Pembangunan Nasional Veteran, Jakarta, Indonesia
e-mail: amriefirmansyah@upnvj.ac.id

J. Nemec et al. (eds.), *Local Government and Fiscal Transfers*,
Governance and Public Management,
https://doi.org/10.1007/978-3-031-95674-4_5

Indonesia's current governance system is rooted in its decentralisation reforms, which were introduced after the fall of the New Order regime in 1999. As a result, local governments now play a critical role in public service delivery and regional development. Local governments manage approximately 25% of the national spending (*APBN*), demonstrating substantial fiscal transfers from the central government.

5.2 Fiscal Federalism

Indonesia's journey towards fiscal federalism has undergone significant transformation, particularly with the revolutionary decentralisation measures in 1999. Since then, fiscal decentralisation policy has developed into an evolutionary process.

Before 1999, Indonesia's governance was characterised by highly centralised control under the New Order regime (1966–1998) as stated in Law No. 32 of 1956 on Financial Balance Between Central and Regional and Law No. 5 of 1974 on Regional Government. Fiscal and political authority was concentrated in the central government, with provinces and regencies/cities serving as administrative extensions. Local governance was weak, as heads of subnational governments were appointed by the central government. Furthermore, regional resources were limited, as revenue-sharing mechanisms, mainly from natural resources, were minimal, leading to growing dissatisfaction in resource-rich regions such as Sumatra, Kalimantan, and Papua. This centralised system resulted in regional disparities, inefficiencies in public service delivery, and mounting demands for greater autonomy, which became critical drivers of reform following the political and economic crisis of 1998 (*Reformasi* era).

In 1999, the *Reformasi* era (1998–now) brought revolutionary changes to Indonesia's governance and fiscal systems. The decentralisation reforms, enacted through Law No. 22 of 1999 on Regional Government and Law No. 25 of 1999 on Fiscal Balance Between Central and Local Governments, fundamentally reshaped intergovernmental relations. Political decentralisation shifted authority from the central government directly to regencies (*kabupaten*) and cities (*kota*), bypassing provinces, which were assigned coordinating roles. Subnational government heads were elected by subnational councils (*DPRD*), paving the way for direct elections in later reforms (2005). They have independently developed local policies (*Perda*) and managed their budgets (*APBD*) with fiscal transfers governed by transparent formulas.

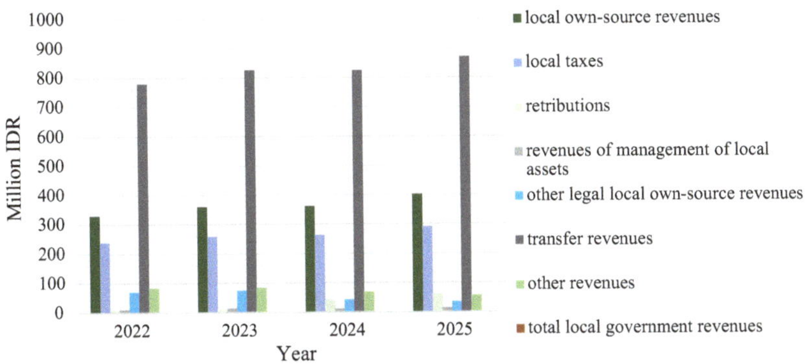

Fig. 5.1 Local government revenues (*Note* The 2025 data is projection meanwhile 2023 and 2024 are realisation. *Source* Authors, based on Ministry of Finance data [2025])

5.2.1 Local Government Revenues and Expenditures

Figure 5.1 shows the structure of local government revenues. This Figure highlights that the primary sources are central transfers and local taxes (100,000 IDR–5.5 EUR).

The structure of local government expenditure based on the expenditure classification is shown in Fig. 5.2.

5.2.2 Transfers to Local Governments

Fiscal decentralisation grants local administrations control over their budgets, which are supported by financial transfers from the central government, primarily through the General Allocation Fund (DAU), Special Allocation Fund (DAK), Revenue Sharing Fund (DBH), and Village Fund for villages as shown in Table 5.1.

The General Allocation Fund serves for fiscal equalisation, the Specific Allocation Fund supports sector-specific needs like health and education, and the Revenue Sharing Fund allocates a portion of revenues from natural resources.

The decentralisation reforms in 1999 established the framework for a decentralised Indonesia but also revealed significant challenges, particularly disparities in the capacity of local governments and an overreliance on fiscal transfers. To address those problems, a series of refinements have

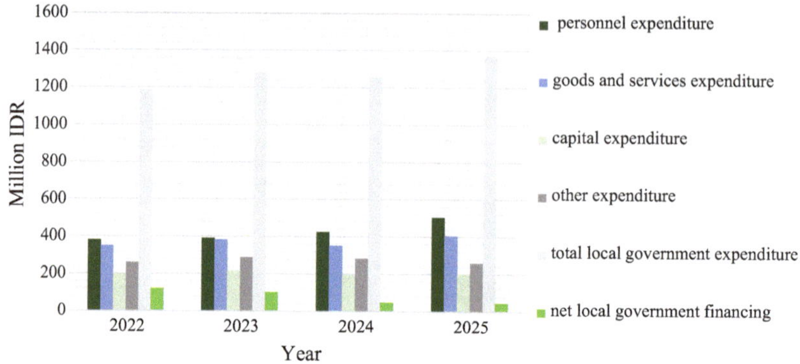

Fig. 5.2 Local government expenditure (*Note* The 2025 data is projection meanwhile 2023 and 2024 are realisation. *Source* Authors, based on Ministry of Finance data [2025])

Table 5.1 Break-down of fiscal transfers in Indonesia in trillions of IDR

Description	*2023*	*2024*	*2025*
1. Revenue Sharing Fund	136.3	143.1	192.28
2. General Allocation Fund	396.0	427.7	446.63
3. Specific Allocation Fund	185.8	188.1	185.24
4. Special Autonomy Fund	17.2	18.3	17.52
5. Privilege Fund for DI Yogyakarta	1.4	1.4	1.20
6. Village Fund	70.0	71.0	71.00
7. Fiscal Incentive Fund	8.0	8.0	6.00
Total Transfers	814.7	857.6	919.87
Total National Spending	3061.2	3325.1	3621.3
Proportion of fiscal transfers over the national spending	26.6%	25.8%	25.4%

Note 2023, 2024, 2025 data are projection, 2025 before efficiency measures
Source Authors, based on Ministry of Finance (2025)

been conducted. The first revised regulation is Law No. 32 of 2004 on Regional Government and Law No. 33 of 2004 on Fiscal Balance, which aimed to strengthen governance and fiscal systems. Further evolutionary changes occurred with the passage of Law No. 1 of 2022 on Financial Relations Between Central and Local Governments, which modernised Indonesia's fiscal decentralisation framework. The policy evolution on fiscal decentralisation since 1999 is exhibited in Table 5.2.

Table 5.2 Evolutionary changes in fiscal transfers policy in Indonesia

Instrument	*Law No. 25/1999*	*Law No. 33/2004*	*Law No. 1/2022*
General Allocation Fund (*DAU*)	Equalise fiscal capacities among regions by redistributing resources based on population, area, and basic needs	It is the same as in 1999, but with a refined formula incorporating fiscal gaps (needs vs. capacity)	Equalisation remains the primary goal but introduces a performance component
Specific Allocation Fund (*DAK*)	Targeted funding for specific projects like education, health, and infrastructure	Broadened to include more sectors like environment and disaster management	Expanded to align with national priorities, with stricter conditions and reporting
Revenue Sharing Fund (*DBH*)	Share revenue from natural resources and taxes with producing regions	Continued revenue-sharing but refined formulas to balance producing and non-producing areas	Broadened revenue sources to include digital economy (e-commerce) and carbon trading

Source Authors, based on own research (2025)

5.3 Transfers and Local Democracy

Before the fiscal decentralisation system in Indonesia was implemented, the Indonesian government's fiscal policy system was implemented centrally. This provision resulted in local governments having limited authority to prepare their budgets and spending. This condition hampered the local government's ability to address these regions' needs and increased development inequality between regions (Ayu et al., 2024). In addition, this condition resulted in local governments only acting as implementers of policies designed centrally, without much room to adjust policies to the needs or priorities of their regions (Akita et al., 2021; Lewis, 2023). This fiscal centralisation approach hampered the development of local democratic governance by limiting community participation and public accountability. The decision-making process was top-down, where local communities had little opportunity to determine development priorities or resource allocation (Gracio et al., 2023; Saptono & Mahmud, 2023). Less developed regions such as East Nusa Tenggara (*NTT*) have historically faced significant challenges in meeting basic infrastructure needs, including access to clean water, electrification, and health facilities. These difficulties were compounded by limited fiscal authority and reliance on central government allocations, often inadequate to address the region's unique geographic and development constraints. Ineffective infrastructure spending in NTT further exacerbated the situation, with limited road networks and inadequate water infrastructure hampering public service delivery and economic growth (Asyahra et al., 2022; Kause et al., 2013; Luter et al., 2019).

In resource-rich regions such as Kalimantan and Papua, the centralised fiscal system benefited the central government more than the regions, contributing significantly to national income. With its extensive coal mining industry, Kalimantan and Papua's large gold and copper reserves contributed to government revenues every year (Hidayat, 2022; Kusumawati et al., 2024). However, both regions only received low returns for local development in their regions. For example, Papua still faces low literacy rates, minimal health facilities, and poor transportation infrastructure. This condition shows a significant imbalance between Papua's economic contribution to the country and the benefits received by the region. The same thing happens in Kalimantan, which still faces poor road conditions and severe environmental degradation due to uncontrolled mining activities, so these unfavourable conditions hinder the socioeconomic development of this region (Rakhman et al., 2021).

In addition to creating economic inequality, a centralised fiscal system also undermined democratic accountability by excluding local communities from the decision-making process. The central government often made key decisions regarding resource allocation without considering the local specific needs, creating a gap between the governance structure and the reality in the regions (Rakhman et al., 2021). This low inclusiveness in local community decision-making reduced public trust in the governance system. In addition, this centralised system failed to address the social and environmental impacts of natural resource exploitation. In Kalimantan and Papua, uncontrolled resource extraction has led to deforestation, major flooding, and the displacement of local communities, further exacerbating the socioeconomic and environmental challenges in these regions (Kusumawati et al., 2024). These weaknesses in centralised fiscal control point to an urgent need to build a more equitable and participatory governance model. Awareness of the negative impacts of this centralised fiscal system has ultimately led to reforms to decentralise fiscal authority so that local governments can more effectively address challenges specific to their regions.

The enactment of Law No. 22 of 1999 on Regional Government and Law No. 25 of 1999 on Fiscal Balance Between Central and Local Governments, followed by Law No. 32 of 2004 on Regional Government and Law Number 33 of 2004 on Fiscal Balance, was a turning point in fiscal decentralisation efforts in Indonesia. These laws introduced greater fiscal autonomy for local governments and implemented participatory budgeting mechanisms. Furthermore, the fiscal decentralisation policy was combined with direct election to choose subnational heads of government and subnational councils. With this framework, local communities can be directly involved in decision-making regarding resource allocation and their leaders, thereby creating inclusiveness and empowering regions to set development priorities that align with their needs (Musviyanti et al., 2022).

One of the main advantages of this fiscal decentralisation policy reform is the potential to improve resource utilisation and encourage transparency. Through the new regulations, local governments are incentivised to optimise budget allocations for more appropriate results by linking fiscal transfers to the performance that needs to be achieved by the region. For example, regions with a stronger institutional framework, such as Kalimantan, have shown their ability to leverage resources and governance systems to secure larger fiscal allocations. These regions are better positioned to meet the desired performance criteria, so fiscal incentives can be realised by improving basic services to the community (Mitra & Pal, 2022).

Subnational governments with relatively strong institutional capacity, such as Java and Bali, have successfully implemented participatory budgeting to channel fiscal resources to community-based projects that have real impact (Rangkuti et al., 2024). These regions' infrastructure, education, and health investments have been tailored to community needs. This condition shows that fiscal autonomy supported by strong institutions can significantly improve the provision of public services (Gracio et al., 2023). Despite its success, the implementation of Law Number 33 of 2004 also revealed gaps in institutional capacity between regions. Many local governments, especially in less developed areas, have difficulty managing their newly acquired fiscal autonomy. Limited administrative expertise and technical resources hinder effective budget planning and implementation, resulting in inefficiencies and errors in budget allocation (Syarif, 2023). These challenges further emphasise the importance of regional capacity-building initiatives. Training programs that focus on financial management, governance, and anti-corruption are essential to strengthen the ability of local governments to manage decentralised resources responsibly (Hamzah et al., 2024). Strengthening institutional capacity, especially in less developed regions, remains an important factor in reducing regional disparities in Indonesia so that the objectives of fiscal decentralisation can be achieved.

Weak accountability mechanisms further exacerbate this problem. Up to 40% of the General Allocation Fund allocation in some regions is used for non-productive expenditures, contrary to fiscal decentralisation objectives, namely poverty alleviation and improving public services (Hamzah et al., 2024). Similarly, the lack of planning on the Specific Allocation Fund has reduced the potential to improve essential services to the community through education, health, and infrastructure (Alpi & Sirait, 2022; Gulo et al., 2023).

The enactment of Law Number 1 of 2022 marks a significant shift in fiscal decentralisation in Indonesia by emphasising a performance-based transfer scheme linked to achieving measurable development outcomes. This policy change in fiscal decentralisation aims to address systemic challenges in resource utilisation by aligning fiscal allocations based on indicators such as poverty reduction, access to education, and improving health services.

Concerning this regulation, regions with high natural resource capacity, such as Kalimantan and Papua, show more significant potential to adjust to performance criteria due to the significant contribution of resources from both regions to the central government. However, challenges remain in converting this economic contribution into equitable local development. In Papua, revenues from natural resources have not been followed by comparable improvements in public infrastructure or essential services (Kusumawati et al., 2024). A similar situation also occurred in Kalimantan, where infrastructure weaknesses and environmental degradation were due to uncontrolled mining activities (Rakhman et al., 2021). Conversely, due to limited fiscal capacity and institutional readiness, this performance-based approach challenges regions highly dependent on fiscal transfers from the central government. This disparity suggests the importance of more targeted central government support for less developed regions so that these regions can compete on an equal footing in the new fiscal framework (Ayu et al., 2024).

In addition, the focus on performance indicators may also raise concerns about its impact on regional autonomy. Subnational governments may feel compelled to prioritise nationally set goals over their regional needs, which risks sidelining local priorities in favour of meeting national indicators (Lewis, 2023). Therefore, a careful balance between maintaining accountability and promoting optimal regional autonomy and the challenges faced by each region needs to be considered. Performance-based systems pose significant challenges for less developed regions, such as the eastern of the country. This region faces structural constraints, including limited administrative capacity and weak institutional frameworks, that hinder its ability to meet the complex criteria required to receive performance-based funds.

Focusing on planned performance indicators also raises concerns about regional and local autonomy. Local governments often feel compelled to prioritise initiatives that align with national targets, potentially sidelining specific regional needs. For example, prioritising education improvements to meet central performance criteria can divert resources from addressing other pressing local issues, such as access to clean water, basic education, or disaster mitigation efforts (Hamzah et al., 2024). This condition suggests that there are still obstacles in adjusting the achievement of national accountability goals and maintaining the flexibility needed for local governance (Saptono & Mahmud, 2023).

Since the implementation has just started, it is very soon to judge the policy outcome. However, the general notion is that the successful implementation of this law depends on strong governance reforms and capacity-building initiatives in the regions. Strengthening the institutional framework, especially in disadvantaged regions, needs to be done to ensure that all regions in Indonesia can feel the benefits of performance-based fiscal decentralisation. Investment in digital integration and real-time monitoring systems can further increase transparency and public trust (Musviyanti et al., 2022; Syarif, 2023).

5.4 Conclusions

The transition from a centralised government system to fiscal decentralisation has allowed local governments to manage their areas but with some challenges and risks. This shift allows local governments to manage budgets and prioritise development based on local needs. However, implementing fiscal decentralisation still shows significant gaps in institutional capacity, especially in less developed regions in Indonesia. These regions still show limited human resource expertise in administrative management, weak institutional frameworks, and inadequate financial management systems.

Capacity-building programs designed explicitly for underperforming regions must be instituted to mitigate these risks. Training programs in fiscal management, project evaluation, and development planning seek to equip local officials with the competencies required to navigate the intricacies of performance-based systems. In addition, mechanisms such as bailout funds or technical support for disadvantaged regions are recommended to level the playing field and ensure equitable access to fiscal resources (Musviyanti et al., 2022).

Providing flexibility in implementing performance-based systems and better integration into regional development plans is essential to balance accountability with regional autonomy. The integration of digital technology, alongside training, can be revolutionary. Real-time monitoring systems must be implemented to oversee the movement and utilisation of transfer funds, guaranteeing that all transactions are documented clearly.

Reforms in the administration of fiscal transfers are necessary, particularly concerning the Revenue Sharing Fund and the General Allocation Fund, which are pertinent to addressing issues of regional imbalances. This reform should utilise these two sources for strategic development initiatives, including infrastructure enhancement, broadening access to quality education, and advancing health care. Establishing explicit objectives for development expenditure on *DBH* and *DAU* allocations might assist local governments in prioritising initiatives that directly affect local populations.

The implementation of fiscal decentralisation reforms, exemplified by Law No. 1 of 2022, underscores the essential function of regulatory transformation in promoting fiscal decentralisation. These policies enhance transparency, accountability, and equitable development throughout Indonesia by correlating resource allocation with metrics such as poverty alleviation, educational access, and enhanced healthcare services.

These reforms acknowledge the necessity of closing the disparity between resource-abundant and underdeveloped regions. These reforms concentrate on equitable allocation procedures to rectify historical disparities that have resulted in the underdevelopment and marginalisation of numerous regions. Incorporating performance indicators enables local governments to efficiently utilise central government fiscal resources and deliver tangible advantages to people. Consequently, regulatory modifications are crucial in establishing an effective and equitable governance framework harmonising local growth with national objectives.

Annex: Country Profile: Indonesia

See Table 5.3.

Table 5.3 Subnational political power structures

Criteria	*Results*
The level of autonomy of municipal governments over their functional mandates: the question of whether municipal governance institutions can only perform mandated tasks or can choose from a predefined scope of tasks Indicator: yes, partly, no	Partly
The level of freedom of municipal governments to decide their own political organisation and electoral system (can they, for example, determine their own electoral districts, number of seats, electoral system, etc.) Indicator: yes, partly, no	No
The constitutional or legal mechanisms to assert the autonomy of municipal governments. Examples of specific constitutional or legal mechanisms that allow municipal governments to assert their autonomy include (a) constitutional clauses or other statutory regulations protecting local self-government; (b) recourse to the judicial system through constitutional courts to settle disputes with higher authorities; or (c) other constitutional or legal protections of municipal autonomy exist (e.g., higher-level governments are prevented from forcing municipal governments to merge) Indicator: yes, partly, no	Yes
Municipal governments' right to use the legal system against higher-level government (de jure and de facto—do they use such right?) Indicator yes (both de jure and de facto), partly, no	Partly
The level to which decisions made by municipal governance institutions are subject to administrative supervision for their responsibilities and if higher-level approval is needed to act in their own matters Indicator yes, no	Yes
Does the higher-level have the right to remove local executives [or other local officials] without judicial intervention? Indicator yes, no	Yes

Source Authors, based on own research (2025)

Law No. 23 of 2014 on Local Government defines the division of authority among the three tiers of government: central, provincial, and regencies (rural areas) or cities (urban areas). Given autonomy under a unitary state system, subnational governments can choose tasks from a predefined scope determined by the central government to align with national priorities. Local governments' authority is subject to legal constraints and oversight by the central or provincial government to ensure compliance with national laws and standards.

The central government determines the electoral system under Law No. 10 of 2016 on the Election of Governor, Regent, and Mayor. The subnational governments do not have the authority to alter electoral procedures, such as the number of seats or the mode of elections. Similarly, Law No. 23 of 2014 on Local Government prescribes the organisational structure of subnational governments, including the composition of subnational councils or legislative bodies (*DPRD*), the roles of executives, and decision-making processes.

The 1945 Constitution (*UUD* 1945) explicitly guarantees regional autonomy in Article 18 by granting administrative, fiscal, and political authority to subnational governments. Law No. 23 of 2014 on Local Government provides a detailed framework for dividing authority between central, provincial, and local governments. Specifically, Law No. 6 of 2014 on Villages strengthens village-level governance. Subnational governments have judicial recourse to resolve disputes with the central government through the Constitutional Court (*MA*) or Supreme Court (*MK*). Additionally, higher-level governments cannot force mergers of subnational entities without fulfilling specific conditions, such as population thresholds and local agreements.

Subnational governments have the legal right (*de jure*) to challenge decisions or actions by higher-level governments through the judicial system as regulated by Law No. 23 of 2014 on Local Government. However, in practice (de facto), using judicial mechanisms is uncommon and typically limited to specific administrative or legal disputes. Most conflicts are resolved through political or administrative means.

Decisions made by subnational governance institutions are subject to administrative supervision by higher-level governments. Law No. 23 of 2014 on Local Government mandates oversight to ensure compliance with national laws and higher-level regulations. Aside from the central government, provincial governments also play a supervisory role in ensuring that regencies and cities adhere to national policies. As an illustration, local regulations (*Perda*) are reviewed for alignment with national laws, with higher authorities having the power to annul conflicting regulations.

Law No. 23 of 2014 on Local Government grants the central government authority to suspend or remove governors, regents, or mayors if suspected of criminal acts (e.g., corruption, treason, or terrorism) or disrupting public order. The Minister of Home Affairs plays a key role in this process, with recommendations for removal forwarded to the President for governors and in consultation with provincial governors for regents and mayors. On the other hand, local executives can appeal removal decisions to the Administrative Court (*PTUN*) if they believe the decision was unlawful. Several local executives have been removed or suspended for corruption or legal violations.

Members of the subnational councils or legislative bodies (*DPRD*) at the provincial, regency, and city levels are elected directly by citizens, as regulated by Law No. 7 of 2017 on General Elections. The members of DPRD are elected by employing a proportional representation system with an open-list mechanism under a multiparty system (Table 5.4).

The term of subnational councils (*DPRD*) is 5 years, as established under Law No. 23 of 2014 on Local Government and Law No. 7 of 2017 on General Elections. The term is aligned with the duration of the national council or legislative body (*DPR*), the senators (*DPD*), and the President under a simultaneous general election nationwide.

Table 5.4 Structure and quality of subnational electoral systems

Criteria	*Results*
How are municipal councillors elected? Indicator—election mode	Direct election
For what term are municipal councils elected (years)? Indicator—years of mandate	5
What is the level of citizen participation in municipal elections? Indicator: Low—("Normal") voter turnout is below 35% of eligible (registered) voters Average—Voter turnout is between 35 and 60% of eligible (registered) voters High—Voter turnout is over 60% of eligible (registered) voters	High

Source Authors, based on the own research (2025)

This standardised 5-year cycle supports continuity and alignment within Indonesia's legislative framework.

There are two different elections for subnational government. The first is to elect a subnational legislative body (DPRD) that has the same time as the national general election, consisting of a legislative election (Pileg) and a presidential election (Pilpres). The second is to elect the subnational head of government (Pilkada), i.e., governor, regent, and mayor. Based on the National Election Commission (KPU), the highest voter turnout in elections is the general election, in which the subnational legislative election's turnout voter rate is tied up. In this case, the voter turnout rate is above 80% since 2004. However, the subnational head of government election's turnout voter rate has consistently been lower than the national election, around 70%.

Under Law No. 2 of 2011 on Political Parties and Law No. 7 of 2017 on General Elections, the subjects eligible to run in subnational elections as head of subnational government are candidates nominated by political parties and coalitions of political parties. Additionally, Law No. 10 of 2016 on Regional Elections permits individuals to run as independent candidates without party affiliation. To be eligible as a candidate, an independent must collect specific endorsements from registered voters in their electoral district. However, to run as a subnational council member, a candidate must be a political party member and represent a single party only.

Candidates for subnational council elections (*DPRD*) are selected by their political parties through internal mechanisms as regulated by Law No. 2 of 2011 on Political Parties and Law No. 7 of 2017 on General Elections. These centralised or hierarchical processes ensure that party leadership has significant control over candidate selection.

Campaign financing is governed by Law No. 7 of 2017 on General Elections, Law No. 10 of 2016 on Regional Elections, and specific guidelines issued by the General Election Commission (*KPU*). These rules include legally defined limits, sources of funds, and spending limits. Candidates and parties must submit detailed financial reports to the KPU for auditing and publication. Violations of these regulations can result in penalties, including fines or disqualification of the candidates (Table 5.5).

Indonesia's multiparty and proportional representation systems ensure a low probability for a single party to consistently dominate subnational elections across all regions. Local dynamics heavily influence subnational

Table 5.5 Nature of subnational political party systems

Criteria	*Results*
Which subjects can run in municipal elections? Indicator—define who can participate	Political parties, coalitions of political parties, and independent candidates
How are party candidates for municipal council elections selected? Indicator—selected by party, elected by party, self-nomination, other	Selected by party
Are there established rules for financing municipal political campaigns? Indicator—yes, no	Yes
Does the ruling national party have a dominant position in municipal elections? Indicator—yes, no	No

Source Authors, based on the own research (2025)

elections, such as the candidates' popularity, issues, and coalitions. Empirical evidence since the introduction of direct elections in 2004 has demonstrated that no single party in Indonesia can dominate national and subnational elections. Furthermore, either opposition parties or independent candidates have secured victories in subnational elections. Even in Jakarta, notable governors were elected when they were opposition figures of the national ruling party (Table 5.6).

Table 5.6 Subnational political participation and accountability

Criteria	*Results*
Are all council meetings (required to be) open to the public? Indicator—yes, no	Yes
Are municipal records and documents (required to be) available to the public? Indicator—yes, no	Yes
Is the council (required to) engage in an open, participatory planning process? Indicator—yes, no	Yes
Are alternative participatory mechanisms, such as referendums or participatory budgeting, used? Indicator—yes, partly, no	Partly

Source Authors, based on the own research (2025)

Under Law No. 14 of 2008 on Public Information Transparency and Law No. 23 of 2014 on Local Government, subnational council meetings (*DPRD*) must uphold transparency and public access. All meetings related to public decision-making, such as local budgets (*APBD*) or local regulations (*Perda*), are mandated to be open to the public. Subnational councils must also notify the public in advance about meeting schedules and grant citizens the right to attend, observe, and participate in public hearings. Non-compliance with these requirements can lead to public complaints or sanctions under the Public Information Transparency law.

Law No. 14 of 2008 on Public Information Transparency mandates that public institutions, including subnational governments, provide citizens with access to public records and documents. Subnational governments must publish public information, namely the local budget (APBD), local regulations (Perda), and local development plans (RPJMD), which are accessible except for records classified as confidential under specific laws. Citizens can request that subnational governments fulfil records. The Information Commission (*Komisi Informasi*) oversees compliance and mediates disputes.

Law No. 25 of 2004 on the National Development Planning System and Law No. 23 of 2014 on Local Government mandate participatory planning at the subnational level. The laws require structured mechanisms such as the Development Planning Conference (*Musrenbang*) to enable citizens, local organisations, and community leaders to provide input on local development plans. Additionally, public hearings allow the subnational council (*DPRD*) to consult with citizens on regional regulations (*Perda*) and budget plans (*APBD*). Proposals and feedback from these participatory processes are integrated into planning documents such as the Regional Medium-Term Development Plan (*RPJMD*) and Annual Work Plan (*RKPD*).

No specific law in Indonesia regulates referendums as a mechanism for national issues, such as passing laws or other strategic decisions. The only exception is Law No. 6 of 2014 on Villages, which permits village-level referendums for decision-making. Similarly, there is no specific national legal framework to regulate and require participatory budgeting. Therefore, its implementation is highly dependent on the initiative of the heads of subnational governments.

References

Akita, T., Riadi, A. A., & Rizal, A. (2021). Fiscal disparities in Indonesia in the decentralization era: Does general allocation fund equalize fiscal revenues? *Regional Science Policy and Practice, 13*(6), 1842–1865. https://doi.org/10.1111/rsp3.12326

Alpi, M. F., & Sirait, R. F. (2022). Pengaruh pertumbuhan ekonomi, pendapatan asli daerah (PAD), dana alokasi umum (DAU) dan dana alokasi khusus (DAK) terhadap belanja modal pada kabupaten/kota di provinsi Sumatera Utara. *Jurnal Akuntansi Dan Pajak, 23*(1), 1–20. https://doi.org/10.29040/jap.v23i1.5557

Asyahra, M. L., Beliab, N., Anggaryadi, O. M. P., Rangkuti, R. A., & Syahfitri, V. N. (2022). Krisis penyediaan air bersih di Provinsi Nusa Tenggara Timur. *Konferensi Nasional Ilmu Administrasi, 6*(1), 150–155. https://knia.stialanbandung.ac.id/index.php/knia/article/view/710

Ayu, D., Daulay, M., & Gowasa, R. K. (2024). Dinamika perekonomian Indonesia: sebuah tinjauan historis dari sentralisasi ke desentralisasi. *Polyscopia, 1*(2), 36–42. https://doi.org/10.57251/polyscopia.v1i2.1299

Gracio, F. E., Kartono, D. T., & Suharto, D. G. (2023). The challenges of economic decentralization: A systematic literature review against research trends for 2013–2023. *Review of Economics and Finance, 21*, 1288–1294. https://doi.org/10.55365/1923.x2023.21.141

Gulo, H., Fitrawaty, F., & Arwansyah, A. (2023). Analisis pengaruh dana alokasi khusus, dana alokasi umum dan pendapatan asli daerah terhadap indeks pembangunan manusia di Sumatera Utara. *SOSIOHUMANIORA: Jurnal Ilmiah Ilmu Sosial Dan Humaniora, 9*(1), 59–73. https://doi.org/10.30738/sosio.v9i1.13725

Hamzah, M. Z., Sofilda, E., & Kusairi, S. (2024). How do socioeconomic indicators and fiscal decentralization affect stunting? Evidence from Indonesia. *International Journal of Development Issues*. https://doi.org/10.1108/IJDI-05-2024-0150

Hidayat, K. F. (2022). Kinerja keuangan daerah Pemerintah Provinsi Papua dalam kerangka otonomi khusus tahun 2014–2020. *Dialogue: Jurnal Ilmu Administrasi Publik, 4*(2), 394–414. https://doi.org/10.14710/dialogue.v4i2.14585

Kause, W. L., Helfiarne, M. R., Komba, Y. T., Salim, A., & Djesse, S. T. (2013). Kajian status provinsi Nusa Tenggara Timur sebagai provinsi kepulauan ditinjau dari perspektif hukum. *Jurnal Borneo Administrator, 9*(2), 137–161. https://doi.org/10.24258/jba.v9i2.102

Kusumawati, A., Badriah, L. S., & Arifin, A. (2024). Pengaruh desentralisasi fiskal, IPM, panjang jalan terhadap kemiskinan di Papua. *Jurnal Ekonomika45, 12*(1), 1–13. https://doi.org/10.30640/ekonomika45.v12i1.3506

Lewis, B. D. (2023). Indonesia's new fiscal decentralisation law: A critical assessment. *Bulletin of Indonesian Economic Studies, 59*(1), 1–28. https://doi.org/10.1080/00074918.2023.2180838

Luter, M., Indrocahyo, I., & Resti, I. L. V. (2019). Pengaruh belanja infrastruktur terhadap pertumbuhan ekonomi Provinsi Nusa Tenggara Timur. *Jurnal Ekonomi Pembangunan, 17*(2), 38–48. https://doi.org/10.29259/jep.v17i2.9533

Ministry of Finance—Indonesia. (2025). *National budget information 2025.*

Mitra, A., & Pal, S. (2022). Ethnic diversity, social norms and elite capture: Theory and evidence from Indonesia. *Economica, 89*(356), 947–996. https://doi.org/10.1111/ecca.12423

Musviyanti, K., Bone, H., Syakura, M. A., & Yudaruddin, R. (2022). Structure of local government budgets and local fiscal autonomy: Evidence from Indonesia. *Public and Municipal Finance, 11*(1), 79–89. https://doi.org/10.21511/pmf.11(1).2022.07

Rakhman, O., Ma'rufah, U., Ardi, A., Kausan, B. Y., & Sembiring, B. J. E. (2021). Analisis pengaruh rencana pembangunan proyek prioritas jalan trans Papua (MP-31) terhadap aspek sosial-ekologis Papua. *Eksekutif Nasional WALHI (Wahana Lingkungan Hidup Indonesia).* https://www.walhi.or.id/analisis-pengaruh-rencana-pembangunan-proyek-prioritas-jalan-trans-papua-mp-31-terhadap-aspek-sosial-ekologis-papua

Rangkuti, M. R., Sihombing, M., Kusmanto, H., & Ridho, H. (2024). Fiscal decentralization and community participation in education services in Deli Serdang regency, Indonesia. *International Journal of Sustainable Development and Planning, 19*(5), 1639–1653. https://doi.org/10.18280/ijsdp.190502

Saptono, P. B., & Mahmud, G. (2023). Stimulus or enforcement? How intergovernmental transfers crowd-in local taxes in Indonesia. *Public Finance Review, 51*(6), 782–837. https://doi.org/10.1177/10911421231191961

Statistics Indonesia. (2025). *National statistics report 2025.* https://www.bps.go.id/id

Syarif, A. (2023). Fiscal decentralization and corruption: The facts of regional autonomy policies in Indonesia. *Jurnal Ilmu Sosial dan Ilmu Politik, 27*(1), 60–73. https://doi.org/10.22146/jsp.69007

CHAPTER 6

Japan

Tatsuro Niikawa

6.1 Introduction

Japan is an archipelagic state with an area of 370,000 sq km and a population of 124 million in 2023 (Statistics Bureau of Japan, 2024). Japan is a constitutional monarchy, and a centralised (unitary) state restored to a democratic political system in 1947 following the defeat in the Pacific War in 1945. The House of Councillors and the House of Representatives, which are directly elected by the public, make up the Diet. The Prime Minister, whom the Diet appoints, appoints his ministers and heads the central government. The parliamentary cabinet system is like that of the United Kingdom.

The local government system in Japan is governed by the 1947 Constitution of Japan and the Local Autonomy Act, which provides for a two-tier subnational government system consisting of 47 prefectures (regional governments) and 1,741 municipalities (local governments) (Japan Local Government Centre, 2024). The Constitution of Japan guarantees a local self-government system based on the rights of resident autonomy and collective self-government (National Diet of Japan, 1947a). It stipulates

T. Niikawa (✉)
Doshisha University, Kyoto, Japan
e-mail: tniikawa@mail.doshisha.ac.jp

J. Nemec et al. (eds.), *Local Government and Fiscal Transfers*,
Governance and Public Management,
https://doi.org/10.1007/978-3-031-95674-4_6

that local governments shall have councils and heads. The public shall directly elect the heads and members of the councils. It also guarantees local governments the right to enact bylaws, administrative execution and self-financing administration. The Local Autonomy Law (National Diet of Japan, 1947b) details the organisation and functioning of local government per the Constitution.

6.2 Fiscal Federalism

Local government finances in Japan refer to the general situation and rules governing the money coming in and going out of local governments. The basis of the institutional framework of local government finance in Japan is first stipulated in Chapter 9, "Finance" of the Local Autonomy Law. Section 1 of the Bill stipulates the "Fiscal Year and Classification of Accounts", which states that the fiscal year of a local government shall be from 1 April of each year to 31 March of the following year and that the revenue of the year must be used for the expenditure of each fiscal year. It is statutory that the finances of local governments are based on the income and expenditure of a single fiscal year. Although there are criticisms of the single-year accounting principle, this is the principle from the viewpoint of democratic control, which is voted on by the local council of local government every year. Regarding local governments' accounting, in addition to the general account, a special account can be established by ordinance. However, of course, it is based on the principle of single-year accounting (National Diet of Japan, 1947b).

Another important feature of local government fiscal management is the budgetary principle. By the beginning of each fiscal year, all revenues and expenditures for the fiscal year must be included in the revenue and expenditure budget. This principle is considered the total budget since all revenues and expenditures are included. It is said that a budget must be prepared in advance and approved by the local council before the execution of revenue and expenditures. It is a fiscal democracy.

Regarding budgeting, the matters to be stipulated in the budget are defined in detail by law. Although there are exceptions, like long-term borrowing, revenues and expenditures are to be balanced in the budget in accordance with accounting principles. The budget system aims to achieve democratic fiscal control, implement rational and systematic fiscal management from a comprehensive perspective, and aim to effectively and efficiently manage each revenue and expenditure item.

6.2.1 Local Government Revenues

Local government revenues consist mainly of local taxes, subsidies from the central government, and municipal bonds (debt). On the revenue side, local tax revenues total 40 trillion yen (1000 yen–6 EUR), local allocation taxes total 17 trillion yen and local government bonds total 9 trillion yen (Fig. 6.1). The most well-known taxes are the inhabitant tax and the fixed asset tax. In addition, dues, user fees, commissions and subscriptions may be collected. In addition, local allocation tax subsidies based on the Local Allocation Tax Law and national expenditure framework, which are subsidies and contributions from the national government, also account for a large percentage of revenues. Local governments also borrow money by issuing municipal bonds. The revenue budget is divided into "sections" and "subsections" according to its nature.

The tax system of local governments is basically based on the tax items specified in the Local Tax Law. The Local Tax Law establishes general procedures for levying, collecting and paying local taxes, special provisions for prefectural ordinary taxes, municipal ordinary taxes and special purpose taxes, which consist of special provisions for metropolitan areas and special districts and special provisions for large-scale fixed assets. It also provides a system of non-statutory general tax and non-statutory special purpose tax, which allows local governments to establish their own

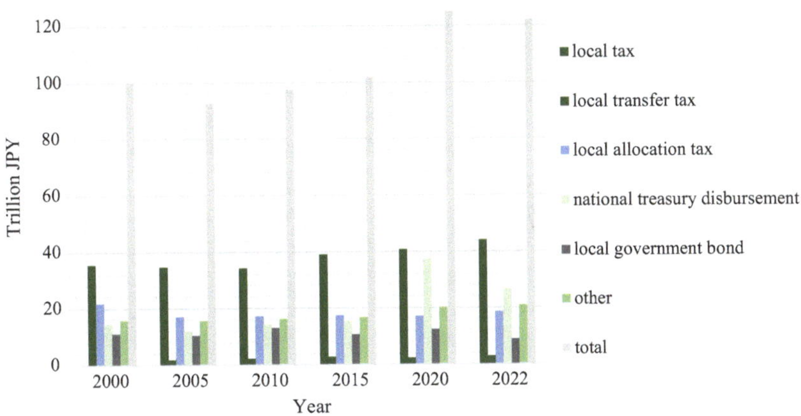

Fig. 6.1 Trends of local government revenue (*Source* Author, based on the data of the Ministry of Internal Affairs and Communication [2025])

tax systems by ordinance within the scope of the law. In addition, the local tax law sets standard tax rates for residents, property, and other taxes and a limited tax rate that allows for excess taxation with an upper limit. Some of them do not have a tax rate limit, but in any case, the tax rate is set by ordinance and collected as a tax. The tax rate is set, levied and collected by ordinance (National Diet of Japan, 1950a).

Municipal ordinary taxes include municipal resident tax, fixed asset tax, light oil excise tax, municipal tobacco tax, mineral tax, special land use tax and non-statutory municipal ordinary tax. Prefectural and municipal taxes of special purposes include hunting tax, water use and benefits tax, municipal bathing tax, business tax, urban planning tax, common facilities tax, residential land development tax, national health insurance tax and non-statutory purpose taxes (Mochida, 2001).

According to the Local Tax Law, local government taxes are broadly divided into prefectural and municipal tax systems. In addition, the Tokyo Metropolitan Government and special wards are treated somewhat differently, corresponding to the metropolitan county system. The basic tax categories of prefectures include prefectural resident tax (for individuals and corporations), business tax and local consumption tax. The basic tax categories of municipalities include municipal resident tax (for individuals and corporations) and fixed asset (real estate) tax. According to the Local Tax Law, local taxes are broadly divided into ordinary taxes and special purpose taxes. General taxes are generally positioned as a source of revenue that can be used to pay for any administrative expenses.

On the other hand, the special purpose tax must use that revenue for its purpose. For example, in the case of bathing tax, Article 701 of the Local Tax Law provides that "municipalities with mineral bathing facilities shall establish environmental sanitation facilities, facilities for the protection and management of mineral springs, firefighting facilities and other facilities necessary for firefighting to protect guests and tourists, and tourism promotion" (including the development of tourism facilities). The municipality where a mineral spring bathhouse is located shall collect a bathing tax from bathhouse visitors to cover the abovementioned costs. The tax shall be used to cover the costs of improving facilities and firefighting equipment, and so on.

As a major source of revenue for local governments, local taxes accounted for 40.2% of total revenue in fiscal year 2018, making it the first significant revenue component. In recent years, local tax revenue has amounted to approximately 40 trillion yen for the total local government finances. The main source of local tax revenue is the inhabitant tax, which is levied on individuals and corporations. The inhabitant tax consists of a flat-rate portion and an income-based portion. For example, in fiscal year 2018, about 36% of local tax revenue came from the inhabitant tax. Furthermore, about 80% of the inhabitant tax is levied on individuals, while 20% is levied on corporations as an inhabitant. In addition, local consumption tax revenues totalled 4.8 trillion yen. The consumption tax of 8% for foods and 10% for others is levied on consumption, and a certain percentage (2.2% of the standard tax rate of 10% and 1.76% of the reduced tax rate of 8%) falls under the local consumption tax.

There are cases in which a local government needs to make a one-time payment for significant expenses for land acquisition or construction costs, such as rebuilding government buildings or constructing facilities for residents' use. If funds need to be secured for a project that is politically necessary but cannot be raised through normal revenues and expenditures, a loan can be taken out to be repaid over several years in future. If the funds are used this way, local governments can issue municipal bonds to simultaneously raise all the necessary amounts, even for large projects. Consider, for example, the purchase of land or buildings or the construction of roads and bridges.

Of course, this issuance of municipal bonds means borrowing money simultaneously, so the repayment of these bonds is usually made over several subsequent fiscal years as a sequential reimbursement of bond expenses. Just as a household's finances will go bankrupt if it does not systematically borrow money, local governments must be prudent in their financial management when it comes to borrowing. For this reason, the Local Autonomy Law and the Local Finance Law impose certain conditions on the purpose, method and amount of issuance of municipal bonds. For example, the Local Finance Law limits the types of expenditures for which local government bonds may be used, emphasising public facility construction projects.

The Local Government Law regulates the issuance of local government bonds and their legal conditions in Article 230. In the case of the preceding paragraph, the purpose, maximum amount, method of issuance, interest rate and method of redemption of municipal bonds shall be specified in the budget.

Although the budget determines the purpose, amount, method of issuance, interest rate and method of redemption of local government bonds, they are regulated by the Local Finance Law. Article 5 of the

Local Finance Law (National Diet of Japan, 1956) stipulates that local government expenditures must be financed by sources other than local government bonds. However, it also specifies when local government bonds may be used for the following: (1) public enterprises such as waterworks, (2) capital contributions and loans, (3) refinancing of municipal bonds, (4) disaster-related project expenses and (5) project expenses for public facilities such as schools and roads and the purchase of their land. Article 5-2 of the Local Finance Law stipulates that the repayment period of local government bonds for construction project expenses may not exceed the facility's useful life. The same applies to refinancing.

Local governments may raise funds by issuing municipal bonds. The same applies to changes in the method of issuing bonds, interest rates and repayment methods. Article 5-3 of the Local Finance Law requires local governments to consult with the Minister of Internal Affairs and Communications or prefectural governors when issuing bonds. By Cabinet Order, the Minister of Internal Affairs and Communications must be consulted in the case of prefectures and designated cities, and the prefectural governor in the case of municipalities. Consultation with prefectural governors is a statutory duty of the governor. Paragraph 2 of the same article stipulates that the consultations shall include clarification of the purpose, maximum amount, method of issuing bonds, funds, interest rates and method of redemption of bonds.

Article 5-3, Paragraph 3 of the Local Finance Law stipulates that consultation with the national government or prefectural governor is not required if funds other than public funds specified by governmental regulation are used (specified public funds are considered to be fiscal loan funds and funds of the Local Public Finance Organization) and if the real debt cost ratio, real deficit, consolidated real deficit ratio and future burden ratio meet the conditions specified by governmental regulation. If the real debt cost ratio, real deficit ratio, consolidated real deficit ratio and future burden ratio meet the conditions specified by government regulation, consultation is not required. This provision specifies whether or not consultation is required for issuing bonds per the standards outlined in the Law on the Financial Soundness of Local Public Entities. Even in cases where consultation is not required (i.e. organisations that are not subject to consultation), Article 6, Paragraph 6 of the same article requires that the purpose, maximum amount and method of redemption of the bonds must be notified in advance when consultation is not required.

In general, borrowers of municipal bonds can be divided into domestic and foreign funds, with foreign funds being divided into foreign currency-denominated funds and yen-denominated funds. As for domestic funds, as mentioned above, public funds include the Fiscal Loan Fund and the Local Public Finance Organization funds, while private funds are the main source of funds. Private funds include publicly offered funds and funds underwritten by banks and other financial institutions. Municipal bonds underwritten by banks and other financial institutions were formerly known as "hypothecated bonds" because they are financed by designated financial institutions that have close relationships with local governments and handle the disbursement of their funds. As the term "banks and the like" implies, banks, insurance companies, mutual aid associations, and local businesses with close ties to the local government have historically underwritten crony bonds. Of course, now that the policy has shifted to a public offering type and competition from the private sector has become the basic policy, banks and other financial institutions are underwriting smaller amounts of bonds that the municipalities issue.

While there are various ways to issue municipal bonds, public funds have accounted for about 40% in recent years. 60% of public funds are national fiscal loan funds, and 40% are Local Public Finance Organization funds, which account for the bulk of the public funds. Of course, public funds account for a large proportion of municipal bond issues, but in contrast, the proportion of public funds in prefectures is small. Private-sector funds account for 60% of municipal bonds issued by prefectures, with nationwide publicly offered municipal bonds accounting for half of the private-sector funds. Similarly, private-sector funds are the main source of municipal bonds in large cities. In addition, about 30% of municipal bonds are underwritten by banks and other financial institutions (Ministry of Finance, 2024; Ministry of Internal Affairs & Communications, 2022, 2023, 2025).

6.2.2 *Local Government Expenditures*

Expenditures are carried out per the budget. By law, the budget's appropriations begin with "articles", which are large items for each purpose, such as council expenses and general affairs expenses, and are subdivided into "sections", which are approved by the council as part of the budget.

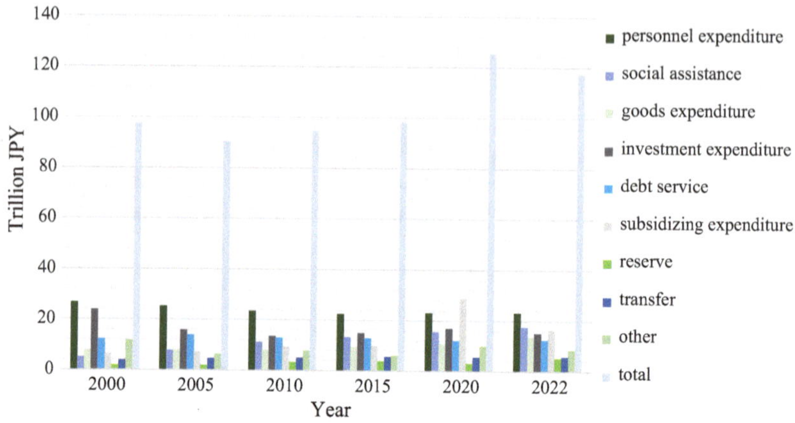

Fig. 6.2 Trends of local government expenditure (*Source* Author, based on the data of the Ministry of Internal Affairs and Communication [2025])

The most important expenditure areas are personnel and capital expenditures. Figure 6.2 provides data about the trends of local government expenditures.

6.2.3 *Intergovernmental Fiscal Transfers*

In order to maintain the role of local government finances, there is a local fiscal adjustment system. As mentioned earlier, the finances of Japanese local governments are closely related to those of the national government, as clearly shown by the fiscal transfers from the national government to local governments, such as the local allocation tax and national expenditures (subsidies and contributions) described below and is also reflected in the fact that the fiscal management of local governments is regulated by national law. On the other hand, as stipulated in the Local Finance Law, it is important to ensure the autonomy and soundness of local finances, and the extent of national government intervention in local finances has been limited. The scope of state intervention in local public finances is strictly regulated by each related law, as seen in the areas of welfare and health services. The principle is that both national and local finances should be mutually autonomous and not cause inconvenience to others.

From the point of view of providing administrative services to citizens and residents, it is impossible to separate the work of the central government from that of local governments, and even in such cases, they cannot be equal. In many cases, one or the other is forced to carry a heavy burden. In some cases, the roles of the central and local governments are divided into a single task, which takes the form of a percentage share of the expenses required for the service. In fact, there are some areas where only local governments can provide administration tailored to the lives of individual citizens. For example, public assistance spending is legally delegated to local governments, and the law stipulates that local governments should carry out the work of the central government. The central government bears three-fourths of the cost of public assistance, and prefectures and municipalities with welfare offices that administer public assistance bear one-fourth of the cost. Local governments have questioned why local governments have to bear one-fourth of the cost and the basis for the one-fourth share. They have repeatedly pointed out that the central government is shirking its responsibility and shifting the burden to local governments.

On the other hand, it should be noted that local finances have very different characteristics depending on each local government's social and economic circumstances. Simply put, a place like Tokyo, with a population of more than 10 million and a high concentration of business and other economic activities, has substantial tax revenues and is financially rich. In contrast, a town with a population of only 1,000 or a rural village with a population of a few hundred is said to be fiscally poor because its local tax revenues are small. However, the system of local self-government basically assigns equal authority and responsibility to all prefectures and municipalities. It requires them to perform the same tasks under the same system, regardless of size. For example, establishing a publicly elected head and council is common to all local governments. Of course, economies of scale come into play when the number of residents and the target population are large. In terms of absolute costs themselves, larger local governments obviously have higher costs. However, they also have higher revenues relative to their population, which increases the likelihood that they can take advantage of economies of scale to run their affairs more efficiently. On the other hand, smaller local governments are less efficient when performing administrative tasks, whether required by law or autonomous.

Under these circumstances, it seems that small municipalities with weak economies and little tax revenue potential would soon go bankrupt. But, in fact, this is not the case. The local fiscal adjustment system compensates for the disparity in fiscal strength among local governments. Specifically, the local allocation tax system corrects the imbalance in fiscal strength among local governments: since the early 2000s, local tax revenue has accounted for 50–80% of municipal fiscal revenue in cities but only about 30% in towns and villages. However, some towns and villages have secured 80% of the general revenue, which is a source of revenue that is not restricted for use. The local allocation tax compensates for the revenue gap among local governments, and it can be said that the local fiscal adjustment system is working well.

The local fiscal adjustment system is based on the Local Allocation Tax Law (National Diet of Japan, 1950b), under which the national government collects a portion of taxes (an indirect form of levy) considered a source of local revenue and redistributes them according to certain standards to correct disparities. The standard for this is the measurement of standard fiscal demand and standard fiscal revenue, which is the formula for calculating the local allocation tax, and the local allocation tax is used to compensate for the shortfall in revenue and expenditure based on this measurement. Under this system, the difference between Tokyo, which has the highest per capita local tax revenue at the prefectural level, and Okinawa, which has the lowest per capita local tax revenue, would be corrected by spending the local allocation tax. This local fiscal adjustment system allows both prefectures and municipalities to provide a certain level of welfare to residents based on the idea of guaranteeing a national minimum for a healthy and cultured life for the people.

The basic nature of the local allocation tax is financial equalisation among local governments. The local allocation tax is a source of revenue temporarily collected by the central government as a national tax and distributed to local governments based on specific criteria. The Local Allocation Tax Law specifies the source and method of distribution. Although the central government levies and collects the tax (indirect levy), it is considered an inherent financial resource of local governments (local tax). Since it is an inherent financial resource equivalent to a local tax, it is a general financial resource whose purpose is not specified, and local governments can decide how to use it at their own discretion. The law stipulates that the central government may not restrict the local government's use of such funds.

The reason for the development of the distribution concept to each local government is that each local government has a large difference in population size and economic strength, resulting in a large difference in the amount of revenue from each local financial resource. Despite the differences in financial strength, local governments must operate at a certain level per the principles of resident autonomy and organisational autonomy secured by the Constitution and the law. In the local government system, matters other than those prescribed by law are defined as self-government matters. While there is a principle that the central government should bear the burden of the legally entrusted affairs to local governments, there are many other affairs that local governments must carry out, such as those mandated by law. In reality, there are cases where it is difficult for local governments to cover their administrative expenses, or in other words, to provide the financial resources needed for administrative services, with only their own financial resources, mainly local taxes collected from local residents. When the local taxes collected directly cannot cover the necessary administrative expenses of the local government, it may be possible to ask the local residents to bear the burden. However, in some cases, it may not be possible to ask more from the standpoint of the residents' ability to bear the burden and have a fair and equitable burden. Moreover, these circumstances are complex and vary from locality to locality, and the shortfall amount differs from one local government to another. The role of the local allocation tax distribution is to compensate for this imbalance in financial resources by calculating it for each local government based on certain objective and rational criteria. Conversely, some local governments with abundant financial resources, such as directly collected local taxes, may not be in a state of financial resource deficiency according to a particular formula and thus may not receive any local allocation tax as "non-allocating organisations".

6.2.3.1 Local Allocation Tax

Based on this concept, the local allocation tax system is also called the local fiscal adjustment system. This system aims to adjust the uneven distribution of financial resources or the imbalanced financial strength among prefectures and municipalities. If a region of specific local government is economically active, it can expect to receive local tax revenue and provide sufficient administrative services. However, if other local governments have to cut back on administrative services due to low revenue, this is not a guarantee of local autonomy based on resident autonomy and organisational autonomy secured by the Constitution. The purpose of the local allocation tax is to compensate for the lack of financial resources and to coordinate finances among local governments so that all local governments can provide at least a certain level of services (Mochida, 2001).

There are two types of local allocation tax: general allocation tax and special allocation tax. According to the Local Allocation Tax Law, the general allocation tax accounts for 94% of the total allocation tax, and the special allocation tax accounts for 6%. The local allocation tax is financed by the sum of 33.1% of corporate income tax and personal income tax revenue, 50% of liquor tax revenue, 20.8% of excise tax revenue and local business tax revenue.

The general allocation tax, which accounts for the bulk of the local allocation tax, is a general allocation of financial resources to realise the goals of the local fiscal adjustment system. In fiscal 2019, 15.21 trillion yen was allocated as a general local allocation tax, a slight increase from the previous year. Of this amount, 8,179.6 billion yen was allocated to prefectures and 7,030.4 billion yen to municipalities. The Tokyo Metropolitan Government is the only prefectural government not receiving this distribution, while 85 municipalities did not. Among prefectures, Hokkaido received the most significant amount of grants at 601.7 billion yen, while Aichi Prefecture received the smallest amount at 71.5 billion yen. Of course, the Tokyo Metropolitan Government is a non-allocating organisation, so it received 0 yen. Some municipalities are also not allocated because they have considerable revenue resources from nuclear power plants, large public facilities, large business and factory clusters, active economies or wealthy urban residents (Ministry of Finance, 2024; Ministry of Internal Affairs & Communications, 2022, 2023, 2025).

The special allocation tax system is designed to compensate for fiscal balance problems that cannot be adequately adjusted under the regular allocation tax system. Prefectures and municipalities may be required to incur unexpected expenses or to cope with sudden shortfalls in revenue. For example, in recent years, natural disasters such as earthquakes, storms and floods have occurred throughout Japan, but not to the same extent in all prefectures and municipalities. Local governments that experience disasters are entitled to a special tax revenue allocation. Specifically, in fiscal 2019, the redistribution of special allocation tax was 1,065.8 billion yen. Of this amount, 147.1 billion yen is for disaster-related expenses, followed by 95.5 billion yen for ensuring regional medical care at public hospitals and 72.2 billion yen for regional transportation, including support for buses, shipping routes and railways. Disasters in fiscal 2019 include the heavy rains in August, the Boso Peninsula typhoon and the East Japan typhoon, for which the special allocation tax covers disaster-related expenses. In addition, 1.5 billion yen has been allocated for measures against new coronavirus infections (COVID-19).

The general local allocation tax calculation must be based on objective criteria to ensure fair distribution. At the same time, however, the calculation cannot be said to be fair unless it reflects the geographical characteristics, population structure, socioeconomic environment, and administrative conditions of each local government. For this reason, a method is used in which the revenues and expenditures of each local government are calculated based on a common unit per specific standards, and the difference between revenue and expenditure is used as the amount of local allocation tax as a shortage in financial resources. Specifically, it is as follows:

If there is a revenue shortfall, the difference between the standard fiscal demand, which corresponds to the standard amount of expenditure required by a certain local government, and the standard fiscal revenue, which is the standard tax revenue forecast multiplied by a certain percentage, is distributed as the amount of general allocation tax. If there is no shortfall, i.e. if the revenue is larger than the expenditure, the local allocation tax amount is 0 yen, and the local government is a non-allocating organisation.

6.2.3.2 *National Treasury Funds Expenditures*

National Treasury Funds expenditures accounted for 15,785.4 billion yen, or 15.3% of the central government's total revenue, in the fiscal year that ended 31 March 2019. It is about the same size as the local allocation tax and is a valuable source of revenue for local governments. Because the use of national expenditures is limited and strongly reflects the will of the central government, there has been much debate on the reform of national expenditures from the perspective of securing the autonomy and independence of local governments. Decentralisation reforms and trinity reforms (composed of reforms in Local Tax, Local Allocation Tax and National Treasury Funds Expenditure) called for the reduction or elimination of national expenditures, and these reforms have had a certain effect, reducing the share of national expenditures to about 11% of local government revenues. However, the economic measures taken after the Lehman Shock and reconstruction measures after the Great East Japan Earthquake led to a large increase in government expenditures, and in

2009 and 2011, the ratio rose to the 16–17% range. The ratio has been gradually reduced since then, but as mentioned above, it has remained around 15%.

The general definition of "National Treasury Funds Expenditures" is a generic term for the central government's expenditures to local governments that specifies the use of the funds. The central government makes partial or total disbursements to local governments to pay for administrative projects that the local governments perform. They are in three types: (1) primarily like central government affairs, (2) projects in which the central government has an interest and projects that are necessary to promote central government policies and (3) special necessity in terms of the finances of the local governments. The central government pays a part or all of the cost of these projects. The central government grants these funds for specific administrative projects undertaken by local governments, collectively called National Treasury Funds Expenditures.

The term "national treasury fund expenditure" covers various activities. They are classified according to their nature and other factors, but the main categories are national treasury contributions, subsidies and consignment payments. National treasury contributions are defined as the mandatory burden borne by the central government per a particular burden classification for the affairs the central government performs jointly with local governments. For example, the national treasury's share of public assistance expenses is well known.

National treasury subsidies are conditional (categorical) grants from the central government to local governments. Typical examples are subsidies for public works projects such as the establishment of parks by local governments.

National treasury consignment payments (Commissions) are government-commissioned affairs for which the central government bears the entire cost, including national elections and the issuance of passports implemented by local governments.

Among the nearly 15 trillion yen in National Treasury Funds Expenditures in the fiscal year ending 31 March 2018, the most significant amount, at about 20%, is for the cost of public assistance, followed by about 10% for expenditures on general construction projects, another 10% for comprehensive grants for social infrastructure development and the remaining grants are for child allowances, for the cost of services and supports for persons with disabilities, and the like.

In municipalities, nearly 30% of the total national treasury funds expenditures are for public assistance expenses, followed by subsidies for child allowance and subsidies for services and support for persons with disabilities, and the like, which account for more than 10% of the total amount of national treasury funds expenditures.

6.3 Fiscal Relations Between the State and Local Governments from the Perspective of Local Democracy

The Local Finance Law establishes principles regarding the management of local government finances, as well as basic principles regarding the relationship with central government finances, to ensure the soundness of local government finances and contribute to the development of local self-governance. The Local Finance Law mandates sound management of local government finances and prohibits measures that would affect the finances of the central government or other local governments. In addition, when preparing budgets, local governments must calculate expenses based on reasonable standards, accurately capture financial resources and calculate revenues in line with economic reality. At the same time, it is required that expenditures be limited to the minimum necessary to achieve objectives and that revenues be appropriately and strictly secured. These are the basic principles of local government financial management based on local democracy (National Diet of Japan, 1956).

Since local government finances are closely related to those of the central government, the law prohibits local governments from taking measures contrary to central policies or negatively impacting central finances. It also requires the central government to promote the independent and sound management of local government finances. It prohibits any actions that impair local government independence or shift burdens to local governments.

The Local Finance Law stipulates how local governments should be fiscally disciplined, how inter-year finances should be adjusted through reserves, the conditions for issuing local government bonds, the conditions and purposes of borrowing, and how property should be managed and operated. It also clarifies the principle that local governments shall bear all administrative costs. In contrast, the national government shall bear all or part of the costs of administrative tasks based on laws and regulations, such as construction projects and welfare programmes (Ministry of Finance, 2024).

6.3.1 Centralised Control Tendency Through Fiscal Transfers

Figures 6.1 and 6.2 clearly show that the transfers of financial resources from the central government to local governments represent an important part of local revenues. Within this framework, local governments are expected to promote effective and efficient fiscal management with autonomy based on the primary purpose of local autonomy (Cabinet Office, 2024; Council for Decentralization Reform, 2023).

Clearly, local government finances in Japan are heavily influenced by the national fiscal system and its management, and both the central and local governments are subject to a common fiscal discipline and framework. At first glance, this is one of the reasons local government finances are seen as belonging to an accounting speciality and as the exclusive domain of an administration almost entirely integrated through the central and local governments. However, it is clear from the perspective of local democracy that this is not the case at all. Financial management as a local government policy decision must result from local democracy through the council's deliberation.

In reality, local government finances are restricted to the overall framework of regulation of local government finances per related laws and national financial policy. However, within that framework, there is a degree of freedom, which means local governments can operate policy-oriented, aligning with local autonomy's primary purpose. Local governments are supposed to manage their finances on their own initiative through financial policy decisions based on the budget. On the other hand, the central government's finances are closely related to local finances, and the central government's finances and national policies are affected by the financial policies of local governments, so there is an interdependent relationship in terms of both money and policy (Muldoon-Smith et al., 2024).

Local governments are established as democratic political institutions as provided by the constitution. Following this democratic principle, local government finances are also subject to institutional control. Specifically, local government finances are controlled by the council and the head, which is an indirect democratic system. In addition, the local residents are guaranteed the right to request an audit of their local government finances and the right to file a lawsuit against the financial operation of the local government.

Japan has a presidential-type representative democracy. Its council is comprised of directly elected members, and mayors and prefectural governors are also directly elected by the public. Fiscal policy-making by local governments is based on the budgetary principle, which requires the mayor or governor to prepare a budget proposal and the council to deliberate and resolve it. The budget sets the annual fiscal policy in advance, and the decision-making process is based on democracy.

The municipality's mayor and governor of prefectures have the authority to execute the budget, allowing room for discretion within the budget framework. The system allows for changes in the amount of money at the budget execution stage and transfers within a specific range. However, the council must prepare and approve a supplementary budget proposal for projects requiring new revenues or expenditures. Supplementary budgets are also subject to democratic control.

After a year's budget process, the accounts are settled. After an audit by the audit committee members, the council reviews the settlement of accounts. The council must deliberate on the appropriateness of the budget execution. The council may vote to approve or disapprove the settlement of accounts. In case of disapproval, the municipality's mayor or the governor will review the matter again, take necessary measures, report to the council and announce the results to the public.

Audit committee members are an important appointment proposed by the mayor or governor of a municipality or a prefecture and appointed by the council. Up to half of the audit committee members may also serve as council members. Audit committee members are also constituted from a democratic perspective. The primary roles of the committee members are to inspect monthly cash receipts and disbursements and to audit financial statements.

Residents have the right as local government taxpayers to request a resident audit and file a resident lawsuit. When residents are dissatisfied with the handling of local government financial accounts, they may request the audit committee conduct an audit. In addition, if they are dissatisfied with the auditor's audit results, they may file a resident lawsuit with the court. Residents have the right to file a taxpayer lawsuit.

The above means that local governments' finances are basically subject to the decisions of local democracies. However, as also mentioned above, local government finances are simultaneously subject to state control, in terms of both revenues and expenditures, through financial transfers from the central government.

The Constitution of Japan recognises the right of local governments to manage their own finances (National Diet of Japan, 1947a), but the specific systems and powers of local governments are to be determined by law. As a result, local governments are subject to various restrictions by law. Concerning local government finances, there are many laws, including the Local Autonomy Law, the Local Finance Law, and the Local Tax Law. In addition, national fiscal laws also have provisions that affect local government finances. For example, there is the Law for Appropriation of Subsidies. The problem is not limited to fiscal laws but also includes a large body of laws that define the responsibilities of local governments. Local governments must fulfil their duties in such profound areas as welfare, health and sanitation, education, environmental conservation and infrastructure development, constraining local budget and finance.

The impact of fiscal transfers from the central government on local autonomy and local democracy is significant. One problem is the local allocation tax system as a general revenue source. The local allocation tax is a mechanism to compensate for the shortfall between standard local government revenues and expenses. The calculation is based on the total amount of various local government projects, and the difference between tax revenues and expenditures is compensated for. As a result, local governments choose standard fiscal management in line with the framework of the local allocation tax system. The local allocation tax is a general source of revenue initially collected by the national government on behalf of local governments and distributed to local governments. It is also a source of revenue at the disposal of local governments.

In other words, the local fiscal adjustment system under the Local Allocation Tax Law tends to keep local governments at a standardised level. For example, in the calculation of the local allocation tax, if a local government increases its tax revenue, the local allocation tax is reduced by a corresponding percentage. Even if local governments strive to increase their revenues through voluntary efforts, there will be pressure to level the playing field. Local governments can set local tax rates on their initiative. However, not only the opposition of residents to higher taxes but also the local allocation tax system could curb such efforts.

As so-called subsidised projects, central government subsidies (categorical grants) significantly influence local governments' project choices. It is customary for local governments to be able to commercialise a project only after it has been selected for a central government subsidy project. The intent of central government subsidy projects may be to contribute to national policy goals, support local governments' autonomous activities or play both roles. One criticism is that they distort the democratic policy-making of local governments. However, they are meant to provide financial support to enable the national government to implement projects reflecting residents' will. One of the problems is that the subsidy projects take the form of individual subsidies (categorical grants), leaving little room for local governments to exercise discretion in selecting projects. It is the job of local governments to select projects that meet the conditions proposed by the central government. The second problem is that it deprives the local governments of autonomy and opportunities for creativity and ingenuity. Since the framework of central government-subsidised projects will be uniformly provided to all local governments, it will be difficult for local democracies to exercise their policy-making functions, which the local government can only do whether they adopt or not.

6.4 Conclusions

In Japan, the entire country is highly centralised and welfare state-oriented, and local governments are expected to play a role within this system. As public interpersonal services and public facility provision are largely the responsibility of local governments, the local government implements much for the public. Japan's central government budget and the overall budget of local governments are roughly equal. However, after transferring payments from the central government to local governments, the central government to local government ratio of finances is one to two. On the other hand, local governments seem to have great fiscal authority and are caught in the middle of a separate and detailed local fiscal management statute frame. At first glance, the local autonomy system based on local democracy appears functioning. However, fiscal management is heavily distorted by fiscal management rules through the central government, specifically by fiscal transfers from the national government to the local governments (Muldoon-Smith et al., 2024).

In order to revitalise local democracy and achieve democratic management of local governments, some points need to be considered in future through the local fiscal system. In particular, we would like to indicate policy issues that require future fiscal transfer reform. One is to simplify the local fiscal adjustment system by making fiscal transfers a mechanism for guaranteeing local financial resources. As long as there are economic disparities among regions, a certain amount of financial resources should be secured for the maintenance and survival of local governments. The financial resources should be collected through local taxes and distributed based on an objective proposal. Second, the state regulation of central government-led fiscal management of local governments should be abolished, as is the case with the policy guidance represented by central government subsidies. This is the liberalisation of local government finances, where local governments are responsible for managing their own finances on their own initiative and autonomy.

Finally, it is important to point out that liberalisation of local government finances may become unregulated freedom if the enhancement of local democracy does not accompany it. In order to realise democratic fiscal management, local democracy and local autonomy will become a mere formality unless a mechanism for broad-based public participation in fiscal management is realised, for example, through the introduction of a participatory budget system. In addition, in order to revitalise local government financial democracy, it is necessary to revise the current situation where the authority of the head is bigger than the council in the decision of the budgetary process and to expand the authority of the council to be involved in financial matters. It is also necessary to strengthen the democratic nature of the audit committee system with the introduction of the direct election system for committee members and citizen participation in the audit system.

Annex: Country Profile: Japan

See Table 6.1.

Local self-government autonomy in Japan is not merely formal but substantial. Municipalities and Prefectures have the right to decide on their tasks, except in areas where responsibilities have been explicitly assigned to other levels of government. This autonomy is guaranteed by the Constitution (1947), Chapter 8 Local Autonomy, Articles 92, 93, 94, and 95 (National Diet of Japan, 1947a). The Local Autonomy Act

Table 6.1 Subnational political power structures

Criteria	*Results*
The level of autonomy of municipal governments over their functional mandates: the question of whether municipal governance institutions can only perform mandated tasks or can choose from a predefined scope of tasks Indicator: yes, partly, no	Yes
The level of freedom of municipal governments to decide their own political organisation and electoral system (can they, for example, determine their own electoral districts, number of seats, electoral system, etc.) Indicator: yes, partly, no	Yes
The constitutional or legal mechanisms to assert the autonomy of municipal governments. Examples of specific constitutional or legal mechanisms that allow municipal governments to assert their autonomy include (a) constitutional clauses or other statutory regulations protecting local self-government; (b) recourse to the judicial system through constitutional courts to settle disputes with higher authorities; or (c) other constitutional or legal protections of municipal autonomy exist (e.g. higher-level governments are prevented from forcing municipal governments to merge) Indicator: yes, partly, no	Yes
Municipal governments' right to use the legal system against higher-level government (de jure and de facto—do they use such right?) Indicator yes (both de jure and de facto), partly, no	Yes
The level to which decisions made by municipal governance institutions are subject to administrative supervision for their responsibilities and if higher-level approval is needed to act in their own matters Indicator yes, no	No
Does the higher level have the right to remove local executives [or other local officials] without judicial intervention? Indicator yes, no	No

Source Author, based on own research (2025)

(1947), Articles 12, 13, and 14 also guarantees the discretion power of local governments except in the case of explicit exclusion of local engagement by laws. State and prefectural authorities can only intervene in this municipal competence when necessary to protect the law and strictly per legal provisions or judicial decisions.

Local governments are subject to the political system established by Local Autonomy Law and Public Officials Election Law. These regulations include the direct general election of governors, mayors and council members by residents, positive lists of election campaigns, and an electoral system. However, the councils of prefectures and municipalities have the right to decide the number of council members and modify electoral districts according to their needs for fairness and equality.

In Japan, there are legal mechanisms that enforce local autonomy. The autonomy of subnational governments in Japan is constitutionally guaranteed. According to Chapter 8 of the Constitution of Japan (1947), self-government of the local public body is guaranteed along with the local autonomy principle (Article 92). Furthermore, the institutions and functions of local government are stipulated only by law establishment. Article 93 of the Constitution provides that the local council must be established, and the council members and chief executives of a local public body must be elected by direct general election of residents. Article 94 of the Constitution provides the authority of local governments to manage local affairs and local finance and to make local ordinances by themselves. Article 95 further stipulates that the Diet of Japan cannot make a law for one designated local government without the approval of a residents' majority vote for that local government. These constitutional provisions ensure that local governments can assert their autonomy and seek protection from unlawful state interference. The legal framework, including Local Autonomy Law and related laws anchored in the Constitution, strengthens the independence of municipalities and prefectures (Council for Decentralization Reform, 2023).

In Japan, the local governments have the right to use the legal system against higher territorial units (prefecture and central government). The above is the dispute resolution procedure in the Local Autonomy Law. If a dispute arises between the national government and a local government or between a prefecture and a municipality, an impartial, neutral third-party organisation will resolve the dispute, and a judgement of the High Court will resolve any illegal acts. In addition, in the case of disputes between the national government and local governments, the National and Local Dispute Resolution Commission will work to resolve the dispute as a third-party organisation. Regarding disputes between prefectures and municipalities, the Local Dispute Resolution Commissioners will work to resolve the dispute as a third-party organisation.

In Japan, decisions made by subnational institutions are not subject to administrative oversight and do not require approval from a higher level except in case of a law provision which orders local governments to have permission for their decision from the central government or prefecture. Although there may be extraordinary cases of intervention from higher levels of government, local governments usually have full decision-making freedom. The local governments have the power to establish ordinances that can mandate forceful articles with sanctions. They can determine their budget, organisational structure, number of employees, remuneration, delegation of tasks, and subordination issues.

In Japan, higher authorities cannot remove local officials or other officials. Elected officials (including the mayor and governor) can only be dismissed by the municipal council or its residents. A supermajority of all council members or residents' recall votes must approve the recall. Neither the central government, the courts, nor other higher administrative units have the authority to remove members of the officials (Table 6.2).

The Japanese political system of local government is the presidential system, with a local council and executive (mayor and governor). The election of subnational councillors, mayors and governors is determined by Public Office Election Law (1947). According to this law, the right to vote in municipal council elections is granted to citizens who have permanent residence in the municipality, are citizens of Japan, are at least 18 years old on the day of the election and have no legal impediment to the exercise of voting rights (these impediments are also listed in the law such as criminals serving time in prison, election law violators, incompetent persons and the like). Eligible candidates for municipal councils are citizens with permanent residence who meet the conditions for voting and are not employees or other officials of the central and local governments. Candidates of municipal public officials must be over 25 years old. The elections to the council are general, equal, direct, and secret, based on the principle of a single-member or multi-member constituency system. The local council itself determines the number of council members. The mayor

Table 6.2 Structure and quality of subnational electoral systems

Criteria	*Results*
How are municipal councillors elected? Indicator—election mode	Direct election
For what term are municipal councils elected (years)? Indicator—years of mandate	4
What is the level of citizen participation in municipal elections? Indicator: Low—("Normal") voter turnout is below 35% of eligible (registered) voters Average—Voter turnout is between 35 and 60% of eligible (registered) voters High—Voter turnout is over 60% of eligible (registered) voters	High

Source Author, based on own research (2025)

and governor are elected directly by its citizens and must be Japanese nationals over 25 years old in the case of mayors and over 30 years in the case of governors.

At the local and regional government level, the mandate of subnational councils is 4 years. The terms of mayor and governor office are also 4 years (National Diet of Japan, 1947c).

The level of citizen participation in subnational elections: The highest voter turnout in municipal council elections was in 1951, with a participation rate of 91.02%. In 1951, the voter turnout of other local elections was also highest: mayor election turnout was over 90%, governor over 80% and prefectural council member over 80%. Since then, voter turnout has gradually declined, and in 2023, it marked the lowest turnout, which was between 41 and 47% of the mayor, governor and prefectural council elections (Table 6.3).

In Japan, various entities can participate in subnational elections. These include officially registered political parties and movements, coalitions formed by multiple political parties, and independent candidates and their movements. Usually, many candidates compose the campaign organisation for the election campaign movement. Independent candidates are the majority in small municipalities and often have a strong presence in town and village council elections. Independent candidates are used to getting support from conservative factions.

Table 6.3 P3 Nature of subnational political party systems

Criteria	*Results*
Which subjects can run in municipal elections? Indicator—define who can participate	Political parties and movements, independent candidates, groups of independent candidates
How are party candidates for municipal council elections selected? Indicator—selected by party, elected by party, self-nomination, other	Selected by party, self-nomination and recognised by party
Are there established rules for financing municipal political campaigns? Indicator—yes, no	Yes
Does the ruling national party have a dominant position in municipal elections? Indicator—yes, no	No

Source Author, based on own research (2025)

Candidates for subnational council elections in Japan are generally selected by local leaders or notables in their community. Majority of municipal council members are independent. Independent candidates, in some cases, go through a self-nomination process, while they have their supporters in the local community.

Public Office Election Law regulates prefectural and municipal election campaigns in Japan, same as national elections (National Diet of Japan, 1947c). The law strictly stipulates the activities and financing of election campaigns. The terms of election campaigns, campaign offices and personnel, using communication tools like letters, leaflets, brochures, meetings, SNS and home pages are restricted by law. In comparison, Japanese election campaigns do not have sufficient freedom like other democratic countries because Japan has been seeking excessively fair and cheap election campaigns in its history.

Approximately 80% of Japanese prefecture and large city council members are affiliated with political parties. However, middle-sized city council members who are political party affiliated are only 30%. Mayors and governors are usually independent and supported by multiple political parties because candidates for mayor or governor often want to have a wide range of voters across political wings. While national parties in power at the central government level may exert some influence over subnational elections due to their resources and visibility, local issues and candidates often dominate subnational elections (Table 6.4).

According to the Local Autonomy Law on municipalities and prefectures, council meetings must be public. This law allows for an exception

Table 6.4 Subnational political participation and accountability

Criteria	*Results*
Are all council meetings (required to be) open to the public? Indicator—yes, no	Yes
Are municipal records and documents (required to be) available to the public? Indicator—yes, no	Yes
Is the council (required to) engage in an open, participatory planning process? Indicator—yes, no	Yes
Are alternative participatory mechanisms, such as referendums or participatory budgeting, used? Indicator—yes, partly, no	Partly

Source Author, based on own research (2025)

to this rule if the council decides to close the meetings because of privacy protection, public interest and so on. However, the council must make the proceedings open to the public. This disclosure erases the documents, phrases or words that must be closed.

Each local ordinance guarantees access to public records and documents at the subnational level—Free Access to Information, commonly known as the Freedom of Information Act. In Japan, the central government has the Law on Disclosure of Information, which is held by Administrative Organs and is known as the Information Disclosure Law of 1999. The local governments also stipulated the ordinance of information disclosure, like the central government's. These ordinances oblige municipalities and prefectures to make their records available to the public upon request unless such records are protected by other legislation (e.g. personal data protection and trade secrets).

In Japan, the legislation does not explicitly require councils to engage in a participatory planning process where citizens can actively contribute. Usually, the Japanese local council does not allow the citizen participation procedure. Recently, some local councils have tried to start a dialogue with citizens. On the other hand, in some legal cases and with some local governments which provide citizen participation ordinances, legislation, or ordinances demand that mayors or governors implement the participation procedures in the planning process of urban planning, the infrastructure construction plan, welfare planning for older adults and the like. While public hearings and consultations are often part of planning and drafting proposed ordinances, these are generally formalities rather than fully participatory platforms.

Alternative participatory mechanisms, such as local referendums and participatory budgeting, are possible but not widely institutionalised or mandatory. Local Referendums in Local Autonomy Law allow citizens to elect and dismiss public officials, and some municipalities voluntarily implement other system referendums and participatory budgeting systems. In a participatory budget, citizens can vote on how much of the municipal budget is spent. The participatory mechanisms differ depending on whether the local government has chosen them or not. These practices are not uniformly applied nationwide and depend on local government initiatives.

References

Cabinet Office. (2024). *Annual report on the Japanese economy and public finance (White Paper).*

Council for Decentralization Reform. (2023). *Annual report on decentralization progress in Japan.* Government of Japan.

Japan Local Government Centre (JLGC). (2024). *Local government in Japan: Structure, finance, and challenges.* JLGC.

Ministry of Finance. (2024). *Japanese public finance fact sheet 2024.*

Ministry of Internal Affairs and Communications. (2022). *FY2019 settlement white paper on local public finance.*

Ministry of Internal Affairs and Communications. (2023). *FY2020 settlement white paper on local public finance.*

Ministry of Internal Affairs and Communications. (2025). *Local government revenue and expenditure trends.*

Mochida, N. (2001). *Taxes and transfers in Japan's local public finances.* World Bank Institute.

Muldoon-Smith, K., Forbes, C., Pearson, J., & Sandford, M. (2024). *A systematic analysis of local government finance in Japan.* LGIU's Local Democracy Research Centre.

National Diet of Japan. (1947a). *The Constitution of Japan.*

National Diet of Japan. (1947b). *Local Autonomy Law.*

National Diet of Japan. (1947c). *Public Offices Election Law.*

National Diet of Japan. (1950a). *Local Tax Law.*

National Diet of Japan. (1950b). *Local Allocation Tax Law.*

National Diet of Japan. (1956). *Local Finance Law.*

Statistics Bureau of Japan. (2024). *Statistical handbook of Japan 2024.*

CHAPTER 7

Lithuania

Andrius Puksas

7.1 Introduction

After the administrative reform, which took place nearly a quarter of a century ago, Lithuania comprises 60 municipalities, as defined in the Law on the Territorial Administrative Units and Their Boundaries of the Republic of Lithuania (1994). The population of the country is approximately 2.9 million. The average Lithuanian municipality has an area of approximately 1,200 square kilometers (total area is approximately 65,300 square kilometers). However, individual municipality sizes vary significantly, with larger rural municipalities often covering more area than urban ones. Four cities have more than 100,000 inhabitants (approximately 605,000 in Vilnius, 404,000 in Kaunas, 160,000 in Klaipėda, and 113,000 in Šiauliai) (data from the Official Statistics Portal of the Republic of Lithuania, 2025).

According to recent data, public sector expenditures are distributed as follows: the state budget accounts for 55%, while municipal budgets account for 16% (Ministry of Finance of the Republic of Lithuania, 2024).

A. Puksas (✉)
Vytautas Magnus University, Kaunas, Lithuania
e-mail: andrius.puksas@gmail.com; andrius.puksas@vdu.lt

J. Nemec et al. (eds.), *Local Government and Fiscal Transfers*, Governance and Public Management,
https://doi.org/10.1007/978-3-031-95674-4_7

In Lithuania, as in any other country, significant differences are observed between municipalities in terms of financial, quality of life, and other indicators. The Vilnius City Municipality stands out the most from the others.

As of October 2024, 52 out of 60 municipalities had implemented participatory budgets, and another three plan to do so soon. According to data from the Lithuanian chapter of Transparency International, residents have been deciding on the use of €14.4 million since 2018 (Transparency International, 2024).

7.2 Fiscal Federalism

The Law on the Budget Structure of the Republic of Lithuania (2024) establishes the composition of the state and municipal budgets, the rules for generating revenue for these budgets, the use of appropriations, and other regulations relevant to the budget structure.

Article 130 of the Constitution (1992) stipulates that the State Budget draft is prepared by the government and submitted to the National Parliament (Seimas) no later than 75 days before the end of the fiscal year. The Ministry of Finance of the Republic of Lithuania prepares the budget draft. The regulations of this ministry stipulate that it prepares and submits to the government the draft law for the approval of the financial indicators of the state budget and municipal budgets for the respective year, as well as the allocation of funds provided in the State Investment Program according to appropriation managers and investment projects. The ministry also ensures the proper alignment of the national budget with European Union fiscal policy requirements. It also manages the distribution of approved state budget appropriations through programs and drafts decisions on allocating funds from the government's reserve.

State budget revenue consists of taxes, mandatory payments, fees, income from budgetary institutions, income from state property, contributions from the European Union and other international financial assistance, and other receipts. In addition, EU membership has significantly influenced Lithuania's budgetary structure, as European Union funds contribute substantially to national and municipal budgets.

Since joining the eurozone in 2015, Lithuania has been submitting its national budget draft to the European Commission by October 15 each year. The above is part of the broader EU oversight of member states' budgetary policies under the Stability and Growth Pact.

According to Article 127 of the Constitution, Lithuania's budgetary system consists of the independent state budget of the Republic of Lithuania, as well as the independent budgets of local municipalities. Article 121 of the Constitution states as follows: "Municipalities shall draft and approve their budgets. Municipal councils shall have the right, within the limits and according to the procedure provided for by law, to establish local levies; municipal councils may provide for tax and levy concessions at the expense of their own budgets."

Article 5 of the Law on Local Self-Government of the Republic of Lithuania (2023) distinguishes between independent and state (state-delegated) municipal functions. The latter are delegated based on the interests of residents and grant municipalities the freedom to make decisions. The legislation also provides that functions may be delegated on a contractual basis. Article 6 of the aforementioned law lists the independent functions, while Article 7 provides a comprehensive list of delegated functions.

A municipality also has the right to delegate the implementation of some of its functions to another municipality or to authorize a regional development council on a contractual basis. The municipality transferring its functions remains responsible for implementing the delegated functions. The municipal council cannot delegate the powers assigned to its exclusive competence to any other municipal institution or entity.

Following the procedures established by its regulations, the municipal council oversees the municipal mayor and other entities directly implementing state (delegated to municipalities) functions.

Funds for state functions (delegated to municipalities) are allocated from the state budget or monetary funds and transferred to municipalities as a special targeted grant. Accordingly, the municipality has the right to demand the allocated funds from the central government to implement these functions.

7.2.1 Local Government Revenues

Each municipality has its own separate budget. Municipal budget revenue consists of taxes, mandatory payments, fees paid to municipal budgets as prescribed by law, state budget grants and other transferred funds, income from budgetary institutions, income from municipal property, contributions from the European Union and other international financial assistance, and other receipts. Municipalities increasingly rely on state budget grants and EU funds, as local tax revenue often falls short of essential services and investments. The structure of local government revenue for Lithuania (2015–2024) is shown in Fig. 7.1.

The main portion of revenues consists of income, profit taxes, and revenues from goods and services. The tax category includes income and profit taxes, property taxes, and taxes on goods and services. Other revenues comprise property income, goods and services, fines, confiscated property, and other unspecified income. Actual revenues are shown for 2015–2022, while planned data is presented for 2023 and 2024. According to Article 2 of the Law on Methodology of Determination of Municipal Budget Revenue of the Republic of Lithuania (2021), municipal budget revenues consist of tax, non-tax, and state budget grants.

7.2.2 *Local Government Expenditures*

The largest share of municipal allocations by functions is directed to the education sector, followed by allocations for the economy and general government services (Fig. 7.2).

It is important to note that the allocation forecast is assessed alongside potential borrowed funds. One of the fundamental principles of local self-government is the participation of municipal residents in managing municipal affairs. Municipalities inform residents about their activities, draft decisions and resolutions adopted, and create opportunities for residents to participate directly in planning and implementing municipal decisions. Essentially, this is one of the primary ways for residents to influence important municipal and state decisions. Accordingly, municipalities must be provided with adequate financial conditions to effectively implement a wide range of functions.

The National Audit Office assessed how municipalities executed their 2023 budgets and whether the approval of the 2024 budgets complied with the requirements set by legal regulations. The results indicated that municipal budgets adhered to fiscal discipline rules overall. However, certain comments regarding financial accountability remained. Overall, more comments requiring amendments were directed at five municipalities (compared to 14 in the previous year) (National Audit Office, 2024).

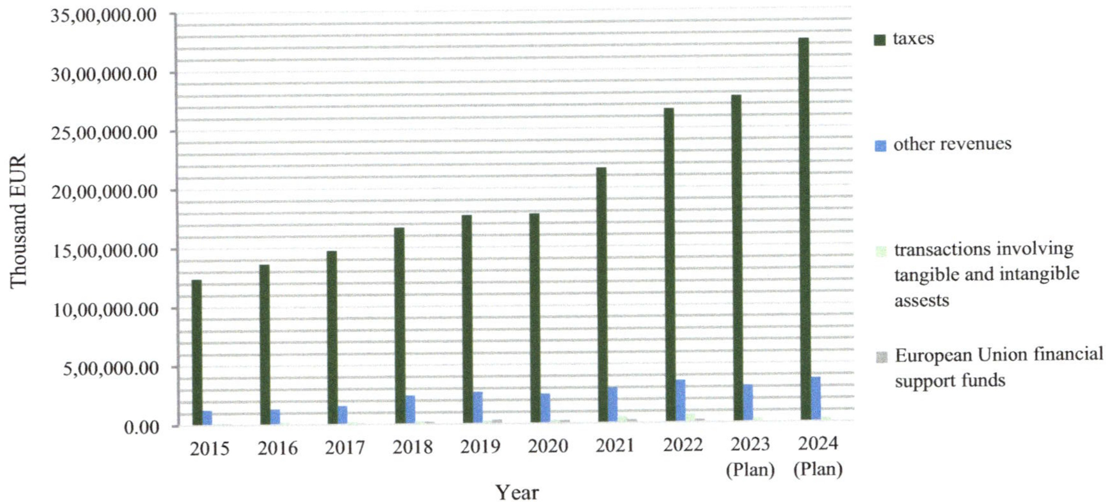

Fig. 7.1 Local government revenues (*Source* Author, based on Ministry of Finance of the Republic of Lithuania [2024])

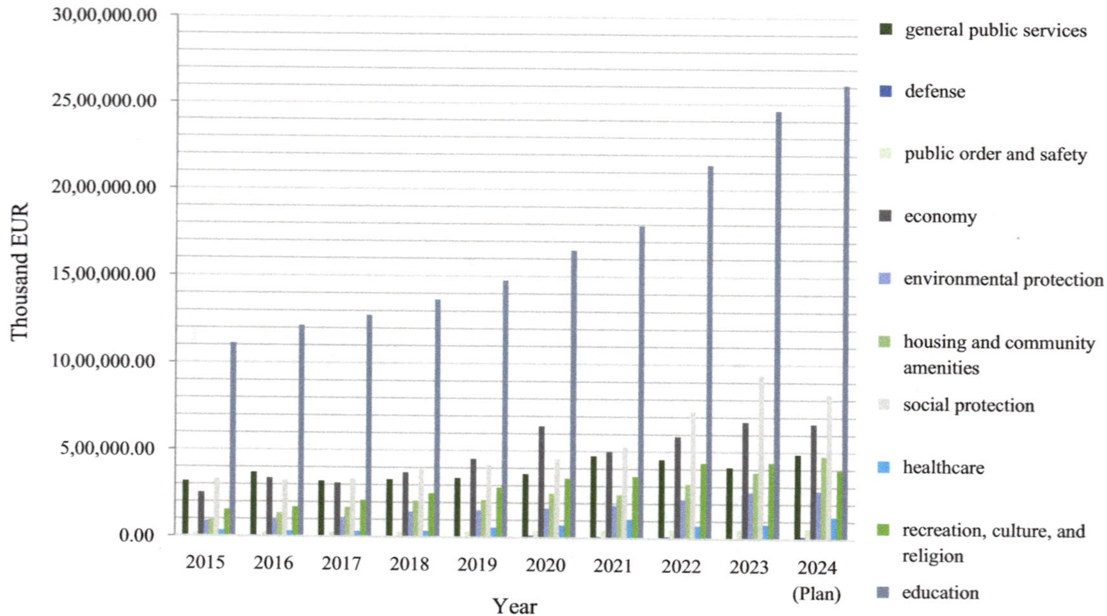

Fig. 7.2 Local government expenditures (*Source* Author, based on Ministry of Finance of the Republic of Lithuania [2024])

7.2.3 *Transfers to Local Governments*

Article 7 of the Law on Local Self-Government of the Republic of Lithuania (2023) specifies 35 state (state-delegated to municipalities) functions. It is noted that the list of functions is not exhaustive. Successful implementation of functions requires adequate funding.

Clause 1 of Paragraph 2 of Article 5 of the Law on Methodology of Determination of Municipal Budget Revenue of the Republic of Lithuania (2021) stipulates that special targeted grants from the state budget to municipal budgets are allocated for performing state (state-delegated to municipalities) functions, based on the established methodology for calculating the funds required for these functions. Other clauses also define targeted grants for financing educational needs, implementing programs or decisions approved by the National Parliament (Seimas) or government, and improving conditions for business development.

The approved methodology is relatively detailed and includes provisions for the risk that municipalities may not collect sufficient funds from taxes during the fiscal year. In such cases, at the end of the budget year, these uncollected personal income tax revenues are compensated by the appropriations approved in the state budget.

Municipalities return the unused amounts of state budget grants to the appropriation managers from whom they were received, except for the unused portion of European Union and other international financial aid and co-financing funds.

For example, the Law on the Approval of Financial Indicators of the State Budget and Municipal Budgets of the Republic of Lithuania for 2024 (2023) stipulates that the Ministry of Education, Science, and Sport of the Republic of Lithuania has the authority to allocate funds to municipalities for optimizing and renewing the pedagogical staff (teachers working under preschool, pre-primary, general education, and vocational training programs) of municipal schools. The Ministry is also authorized to allocate funds for career guidance, non-formal education, and ensuring preschool education for children at social risk.

Interestingly, in November 2024, an order by the Minister of the Interior of the Republic of Lithuania approved the description of the procedure for evaluating the assignment of municipal functions to either independent or state (state-delegated to municipalities) functions (2024). The legal act aims to determine whether the characteristics of already established or planned functions assigned to municipalities correspond to independent or state-delegated functions. An even more important goal is to identify the most efficient methods of performing these functions that best address the needs of the residents.

One of the five identified characteristics of a state (state-delegated to municipalities) function is that its execution is financed through a special targeted grant from the state budget (or other state budget appropriations essentially classified as special targeted grants) allocated for performing state (state-delegated to municipalities) functions.

7.3 Case Study—Own Versus Delegated Responsibilities

In the spring of 2019, the State Audit Office presented a report titled "Does the System of Functions Performed by Municipalities Create Conditions for Them to Operate Efficiently?" (2019). It was determined that municipalities carry out 44 independent functions and 36 state functions (delegated by the state to municipalities). In 2017, 1.1 billion EUR was allocated from the state budget to implement delegated functions, with target objectives defined for only 1 out of the 36 functions, which means that the effectiveness of funding for the remaining 35 functions was not assessed. Additionally, it was found that the procedure for utilizing funds for 11 out of the 36 state functions was not regulated.

Two core dysfunctionalities relate to the State Audit Office's findings. First, the main audit conclusion was that the funding system for functions does not motivate municipalities to achieve better performance results. Therefore, it was recommended that the government review the system of functions performed by municipalities, which directly includes the issue of funding. The overlap of functions undoubtedly creates tension between the entities sharing them. Although more serious disputes have been avoided, this still affects the efficiency of function execution.

Second, municipalities' main complaints relate to the fact that the funding allocated by the state only partially covers the delegated functions. One such example is the insufficient funding for the needs of social support recipients. Although the number of such individuals has recently increased, this has not been considered when allocating state funds. As a result, municipalities have to use their budget funds, reducing financing for other activities accordingly. To some extent, the situation is alleviated by the flexibility to use other available funds.

The effort to review the functions performed by municipalities highlights that it is not always clear which are independent and which are state functions (delegated to municipalities by the state) (Order by the Minister of the Interior of the Republic of Lithuania approving the description of the procedure for evaluating the assignment of municipal functions to either independent or state (state-delegated to municipalities) functions, 2024). One of the proposed criteria is to assess whether, based on actual cases of function execution and the allocated and utilized funding over the past three years, the function is permanent or performed on an ad hoc basis.

It is planned to assess situations where multiple municipalities are jointly responsible for implementing a specific function. Such situations may potentially pose challenges related to the use of financial resources and could lead to disputes over the share of financial contributions.

The process of reviewing functions has proven to be quite complex. The aforementioned Order includes a recommendation for ministries to conduct a function assessment by 2030. Essentially, this would involve reviewing the functions delegated to municipalities, which would, in turn, impact the allocated funding.

Although more municipalities are providing opportunities for residents to engage through participatory budgeting and other mechanisms, not all residents take advantage of these opportunities. One reason is the relatively complex involvement process.

Essentially, municipalities employ the mechanisms provided for understanding residents' positions and strive to consider their interests. However, practice shows that decisions do not always reflect the positions expressed by residents.

7.4 Conclusions

All 60 municipalities in Lithuania are granted fairly extensive rights and freedoms of self-government. Municipalities have their budgets, which they use as allocated. Each municipality performs both independent functions and state (state-delegated) functions. Funding is provided for the latter. Although the distinction between these functions is specified in national regulations by listing specific functions, a review is planned to assign them to a specific category (independent or state-delegated). The planned review of the categorization of functions is expected to enhance clarity and efficiency, potentially improving how municipalities manage resources and responsibilities.

Municipalities exercise financial autonomy, with their budgets primarily funded through local taxes, fees, and state transfers. This financial independence enables them to address local priorities within the framework of available resources. However, balancing independent functions with state-delegated responsibilities and proper financing of delegated responsibilities remain significant aspects of their governance.

Currently, the state-delegated functions to municipalities are being reviewed to identify an efficient mechanism for function implementation and funding. Until now, funding has been allocated without considering the effectiveness of function execution and without proper regulations regarding financing specific functions. Additional tensions arise due to insufficient state funding for specific functions delegated to municipalities by the government (e.g., the social security sector).

Annex: Country Profile: The Republic of Lithuania

See Table 7.1.

The autonomy of local self-government in Lithuania is ensured by law. According to Article 120 of the Constitution, "municipalities shall act freely and independently within their competence defined by the Constitution and laws." Article 5 of the Law on Local Self-Government stipulates that municipal functions are divided into independent and state (state-delegated to municipalities) functions based on the level of decision-making freedom.

Local self-government's involvement in the electoral process is primarily technical. Municipal mayors and council members are elected directly, with the number of council members defined by legislation and based on the municipality's population. Municipalities closely cooperate with the Central Electoral Commission and lower-level electoral commissions during elections.

Municipalities provide facilities and technical support for municipal and district electoral commissions. They also participate in the formation of polling stations by proposing district locations, adapting buildings for voters with disabilities, and performing other related tasks.

However, municipalities are strictly prohibited from interfering in the electoral process itself. Their primary role is to ensure that municipal and

Table 7.1 Subnational political power structures

Criteria	*Results*
The level of autonomy of municipal governments over their functional mandates: the question of whether municipal governance institutions can only perform mandated tasks or can choose from a predefined scope of tasks Indicator: yes, partly, no	Yes
The level of freedom of municipal governments to decide their own political organization and electoral system (can they, for example, determine their own electoral districts, number of seats, electoral system, etc.) Indicator: yes, partly, no	Party
The constitutional or legal mechanisms to assert the autonomy of municipal governments. Examples of specific constitutional or legal mechanisms that allow municipal governments to assert their autonomy include (a) constitutional clauses or other statutory regulations protecting local self-government; (b) recourse to the judicial system through constitutional courts to settle disputes with higher authorities; or (c) other constitutional or legal protections of municipal autonomy exist (e.g., higher-level governments are prevented from forcing municipal governments to merge) Indicator: yes, partly, no	Yes
Municipal governments' right to use the legal system against higher-level government (de jure and de facto—do they use such right?) Indicator yes (both de jure and de facto), partly, no	Yes
The level to which decisions made by municipal governance institutions are subject to administrative supervision for their responsibilities and if higher-level approval is needed to act in their own matters Indicator yes, no	Partly
Does the higher-level have the right to remove local executives [or other local officials] without judicial intervention? Indicator yes, no	No (exemption resolution to impose direct rule in the municipality's territory)

Source Author, based on own research (2025)

district electoral commissions have suitable working conditions and that voters have no obstacles to casting their ballots.

Lithuanian legislation and courts protect local self-government. Article 120 of the Constitution of the Republic of Lithuania states: "The State shall support municipalities. Municipalities shall act freely and independently within their competence defined by the Constitution and laws." Article 122 of the supreme legal act also stipulates: "Municipal councils and municipal mayors shall have the right to apply to a court regarding the violation of their rights."

Paragraph 1 of Article 69 of the Law on Local Self-Government of the Republic of Lithuania stipulates that municipalities may, depending on the nature of the violation, apply to the court for violations of their rights.

Any intervention by central authorities into municipal activities must be justified solely by law. The National Parliament (Seimas) can impose temporary direct rule in a municipality's territory only in cases and procedures specified by law.

Article 65, Part 5 of the Law on Local Self-Government of the Republic of Lithuania also stipulates that if changes occur in municipal budget revenues or expenditures and a dispute arises between the central government and municipalities, the dispute may be resolved in court.

The Association of Local Authorities in Lithuania, whose members are the country's municipalities, also ensures municipal representation and the protection of legitimate interests.

Municipalities have the right and proper tools to defend their rights and legitimate interests in court, including disputes with central state institutions. The above is ensured through the aforementioned rights of municipal council members and municipal mayors and the principle of judicial independence. Disputes between municipalities and central government institutions are resolved in administrative courts. Article 20, Part 2, Clause 2 of the Law on Administrative Proceedings of the Republic of Lithuania (2016) stipulates that the Regional Administrative Court hears cases based on municipal councils' requests regarding violations of their rights when the defendants are state administrative entities. Disputes may also arise concerning compliance with legal acts when making decisions. However, in certain cases, such disputes may be resolved by the Constitutional Court. Judicial protection in Lithuania is guaranteed to every entity.

Essentially, municipalities are free to make decisions related to their operations, including structural and personnel matters. However, it is natural that every municipal decision must comply with the law. Therefore, a certain oversight mechanism is in place. Article 123 of the Constitution of the Republic of Lithuania states: "The observance of the Constitution and laws and the execution of the decisions of the Government by municipalities shall be supervised by the representatives appointed by the Government."

The above does not mean that municipal decisions require approval, but the representatives appointed by the Government monitor whether the municipality complies with the applicable national regulations.

Government representatives can appeal to the court if they believe a municipality's decisions contradict the Constitution or the law.

In Lithuania, municipal council members and mayors can only lose their positions per the law. The list of grounds for losing authority is not short. Paragraph 4 of Article 176 of the Electoral Code of the Republic of Lithuania (2022) provides the list of such cases. These cases include resignation (for various reasons), the entry into force of a conviction, assuming duties incompatible with their position, death, being declared legally incapacitated by a court, and others. Municipal mayors can also lose their powers if they lose their citizenship.

If the Central Electoral Commission determines that a serious (called "harsh") violation led to the individual's election, they lose their mandate. There are also specific cases, such as if a council member permanently relocates to another municipality, they lose their powers. Similarly, a municipal council member may be removed if they, without a valid reason, miss three consecutive council meetings.

If there is reason to believe that a municipal council member or the municipal mayor has violated their oath, the municipal council itself may apply to the Supreme Administrative Court of Lithuania requesting an opinion. If it is confirmed that the oath was violated, their mandate is revoked.

An indirect way for the National Parliament (Seimas) to remove a municipal mayor or council members exists if the Parliament adopts a resolution to impose direct rule in the municipality's territory. However, this requires a grave reason as specified in legal acts. Even in the case of war, the Constitution allows extending the mandates of municipal council members and municipal mayors if regular elections are due at that time. Therefore, municipal council members and mayors can feel secure in their positions, provided they do not violate the imperative requirements established by legal acts.

In Lithuania, municipal council members and mayors are elected directly. The number of council members depends on the population of the municipality and is as follows:

51 council members in municipalities with over 500,000 residents;
41 council members in municipalities with 250,000 to 500,000 residents;
31 council members in municipalities with 100,000 to 250,000 residents;
27 council members in municipalities with 50,000 to 100,000 residents;
25 council members in municipalities with 20,000 to 50,000 residents;
21 council members in municipalities with 10,000 to 20,000 residents;
17 council members in municipalities with 5,000 to 10,000 residents;
15 council members in municipalities with fewer than 5,000 residents.

Article 10 of the Electoral Code of the Republic of Lithuania stipulates that municipal council members can be elected if they are permanent residents of that municipality and are at least 18 years old on election day. Similarly, municipal mayors can be elected if they are citizens of the Republic of Lithuania, permanent residents of the municipality, and at least 18 years old on election day. Legal acts define what constitutes a permanent presidentship of a municipality.

The Central Electoral Commission of the Republic of Lithuania organizes elections and forms municipal electoral commissions. Elections are organized in close cooperation with municipalities, which provide voting facilities, although municipalities primarily play a technical role in the process.

A proportional representation system is used for electing municipal council members, while a majoritarian system is applied for electing municipal mayors. Candidates are considered elected municipal mayor in the first round if they receive more than half of the votes cast in the election, provided that at least 40% of the voters on the electoral roll for that constituency participated. If less than 40% of voters participated, the candidates were elected if they received the most votes but not less than 1/5 of all voters on the electoral roll for that constituency.

Otherwise, a second round is held between the two candidates who received the most votes in the first round. If both candidates receive an equal number of votes in the second round, the candidate who received more votes in the first round is considered elected (Table 7.2).

Municipal councils and municipal mayors are elected for a four-year term. A person who has served as municipal mayor for three consecutive terms cannot be elected as municipal mayor for a fourth consecutive term. This term limit was introduced with the Electoral Code, which came into force in 2022. The first direct municipal mayoral elections were held in 2015. Since 2024, municipal mayors are no longer considered municipal council members, and their powers have been amended. This change aims to clarify the separation of executive and legislative functions at the local level.

The Electoral Code of the Republic of Lithuania assigns the Central Electoral Commission of Lithuania to encourage voters to participate in elections, essentially making it responsible for increasing voter turnout.

Table 7.2 Structure and quality of subnational electoral systems

Criteria	*Results*
How are municipal councilors elected? Indicator—election mode	Direct election, Proportional Representation System; for municipal mayors—Majority System
For what term are municipal councils elected (years)? Indicator—years of mandate	4
What is the level of citizen participation in municipal elections? Indicator: Low—("Normal") voter turnout is below 35% of eligible (registered) voters Average—Voter turnout is between 35 and 60% of eligible (registered) voters High—Voter turnout is over 60% of eligible (registered) voters	Average

Source Author, based on own research (2025)

During the first round of the 2023 municipal council and municipal mayoral elections, voter turnout reached 48.97% and 45.85% in the runoff, which is the highest turnout in recent decades: 41.30% in 2007, 44.08% in 2011, 47.17% in 2015, and 47.90% in 2019. It is important to note that since 2015, municipal mayors in Lithuania have been elected directly, introducing the need for runoff elections if a municipal mayor is not elected in the first round.

Article 65 of the Electoral Code of the Republic of Lithuania defines who can participate in election campaigns for different elections. In municipal council elections, the following can participate as election campaign actors:

Political parties and committees (both called political organizations) must be registered no later than 180 days before the election day. They can nominate candidate lists or individual candidates.

Independent candidates. Candidates not affiliated with any political party or committee can also participate in municipal council elections. However, they must collect the legally required signatures to validate their candidacy (Table 7.3).

Political parties and political committees decide which individuals will be candidates in the elections and determine the order of candidates on

Table 7.3 Nature of subnational political party systems

Criteria	*Results*
Which subjects can run in municipal elections? Indicator—define who can participate	Political parties and political committees, independent candidates
How are party candidates for municipal council elections selected? Indicator—selected by party, elected by party, self-nomination, other	Selected by party, committee, self-nomination
Are there established rules for financing municipal political campaigns? Indicator—yes, no	Yes
Does the ruling national party have a dominant position in municipal elections? Indicator—yes, no	No

Source Author, based on own research (2025)

the list. Practices among different political organizations can vary significantly—some organizations use democratic voting processes, while others may rely on decisions made by their leaders.

Independent candidates nominate themselves but are subject to additional requirements, such as collecting a certain number of voter signatures to validate their candidacy. These requirements ensure the candidate has sufficient public support to participate in the elections.

Until September 1, 2022, the financing and control of political campaigns in Lithuania were regulated by a separate Law on Funding of Political Campaigns and Control of Funding thereof of the Republic of Lithuania (2004). The key features of political campaign financing were incorporated into the Electoral Code of the Republic of Lithuania, which came into force in 2022. The entire Chapter XI of the Code is dedicated to financing election political campaigns, while Chapter XII addresses financial control. A serious (called "harsh") violation of the Code is considered to occur if an election campaign participant decides to use donations from individuals who are not eligible to finance election campaigns or from prohibited sources of campaign financing (Article 193, Paragraph 1, Clause 2).

The results of the municipal council and municipal mayoral elections can differ significantly from those of national parliamentary elections. Voters decide to whom they entrust their votes in each specific election. However, the results of both elections can sometimes be favorable for the same party. Notably, the most recent municipal and national parliamentary elections demonstrated increased voter confidence in the Social Democratic Party of Lithuania. In the 2023 municipal elections, they secured 358 council seats and 17 municipal mayoral positions, totaling 375 mandates. The ruling Homeland Union—Lithuanian Christian Democrats came in second, with 244 mandates. In the 2024 National Parliament (Seimas) elections, the Social Democratic Party of Lithuania won 52 of the 141 seats. By comparison, the Homeland Union—Lithuanian Christian Democrats secured 28 seats.

Currently, the results show that the Social Democratic Party of Lithuania performed successfully in the last municipal elections (2023) and the national parliamentary elections (Seimas) (2024). However, practice demonstrates that such outcomes cannot be considered a rule, as the same party does not consistently win both local and national elections.

Article 17 of the Law on Local Self-Government stipulates that municipal council meetings are open to the public. However, there is

Table 7.4 Subnational political participation and accountability

Criteria	*Results*
Are all council meetings (required to be) open to the public? Indicator—yes, no	Yes
Are municipal records and documents (required to be) available to the public? Indicator—yes, no	Yes
Is the council (required to) engage in an open, participatory planning process? Indicator—yes, no	Yes
Are alternative participatory mechanisms, such as referendums or participatory budgeting, used? Indicator—yes, partly, no	Yes

Source Author, based on own research (2025)

an exception to the principle of openness: when a meeting involves matters containing state, service, or commercial secrets or issues related to personal data and/or private life, the municipal council deliberates on these in a closed session (Table 7.4).

The legislation ensures that audio and video recordings of council meetings are publicly accessible to promote transparency and openness. Public access also includes documents discussed and adopted, as well as the voting records of council members. Audio and video recordings of municipal council meetings are not made public when their disclosure could reveal state, service, or commercial secrets or violate individuals' rights to privacy and personal data protection.

Legislation provides tools and mechanisms for citizens' involvement in addressing issues relevant to state and municipalities (for example, the Constitutional Law on Referendums of the Republic of Lithuania, 2022). While there is no mandatory requirement to involve citizens specifically in budgeting matters, the principles of local self-government emphasize the importance of considering residents' positions and interests. Consequently, based on their own established procedures, some municipalities involve residents in decision-making on these matters in one form or another.

Article 42 of the Law on Local Self-Government stipulates that municipalities must provide opportunities for residents to participate in municipal affairs by:

- Informing residents;

- Consulting with residents;
- Evaluating and publicizing the results of consultations with residents;
- Involving residents in decision-making.

In essence, all municipalities in Lithuania have created opportunities for residents to participate in managing their affairs. However, the levels of involvement and engagement vary across municipalities. Moreover, some municipalities (a minority now) do not provide the opportunity to engage in participatory budgeting.

References

Ministry of Finance of the Republic of Lithuania. (2024). *Budget in brief*. Vilnius.

National Audit Office. (2024). *National Audit Office Information*. Vilnius.

Official Statistics Portal of the Republic of Lithuania. (2025).

Order by the Minister of the Interior of the Republic of Lithuania. (2024). *The description of the procedure for evaluating the assignment of municipal functions to either independent or state (state-delegated to municipalities) functions*. Vilnius.

State Audit Office Report No. VA-1. (2019). *Does the system of functions performed by municipalities create conditions for them to operate efficiently?* Vilnius.

The Constitution of the Republic of Lithuania. (1992).

The Constitutional Law on Referendums of the Republic of Lithuania. (2022).

The Electoral Code of the Republic of Lithuania. (2022).

The Law on Administrative Proceedings of the Republic of Lithuania. (2016).

The Law on the Approval of Financial Indicators of the State Budget and Municipal Budgets of the Republic of Lithuania for 2024 (2023).

The Law on the Budget Structure of the Republic of Lithuania. (2024)

The Law on Funding of Political Campaigns and Control of Funding Thereof of the Republic of Lithuania. (2004).

The Law on Local Self-Government of the Republic of Lithuania. (2023).

The Law on Methodology of Determination of Municipal Budget Revenue of the Republic of Lithuania. (2021).

The Law on the Territorial Administrative Units and Their Boundaries of the Republic of Lithuania. (1994).

Transparency International. (2024). *Nine out of ten municipalities in Lithuania implement participatory budgets*. https://transparency.lt/devynios-is-desimties-savivaldybiu-lietuvoje-igyvendina-dalyvaujamuosius-biudzetus/

CHAPTER 8

Philippines

Philip Arnold P. Tuaño, Ronald U. Mendoza, Tristan Canare, and Satyabhama Andrea C. Gulapa

8.1 Introduction

The Philippines is an archipelagic country in Southeast Asia, comprising 7,641 islands with a total area of roughly 300,000 square kilometres. In 2020, the Philippines had a population of approximately 110 million inhabitants. More than 60% of the country's population live in the coastal zone, and approximately 54% live in urban areas. The Philippines has a democratic government in the form of a constitutional republic with a presidential system. Local self-government is divided into three levels: provinces and independent cities, component cities and municipalities, and barangays.

P. A. P. Tuaño (✉) · R. U. Mendoza · T. Canare · S. A. C. Gulapa
Ateneo School of Government, Ateneo de Manila University, Manila, Philippines
e-mail: ptuano@ateneo.edu

P. A. P. Tuaño · S. A. C. Gulapa
Department of Economics, Ateneo De Manila University, Quezon City, Philippines

J. Nemec et al. (eds.), *Local Government and Fiscal Transfers*, Governance and Public Management,
https://doi.org/10.1007/978-3-031-95674-4_8

The decentralisation and devolution of powers to local government units (LGUs) have been central features of governance reform in the Philippines, notably since the mid-1980s. Enshrined in the Local Government Code of 1991, these processes aimed to transfer administrative responsibilities and resources from the national government to LGUs at the level of provinces, cities, municipalities, and barangays (local villages), fostering greater local autonomy and participation by citizens in political decision-making. By placing decision-making closer to citizens, decentralisation was expected to enhance governance efficiency, local service delivery, and democratic participation. However, the continuing dependence of LGUs on fiscal transfers—mainly through mechanisms such as the Internal Revenue Allotment (IRA), which provides a specific share of government revenues to LGUs, and the more recently National Tax Allotment (NTA), following the landmark Mandanas-Garcia Supreme Court ruling which brought a larger revenue share—raises critical questions about their effect on the quality of local democracy.

This chapter explores the impact of fiscal transfers on local democracy in the Philippines. It aims to investigate whether these transfers empower LGUs to pursue locally relevant policies or weaken their independence by reinforcing fiscal dependence. Moreover, it examines how the influx of resources following the Mandanas-Garcia ruling affects the dynamics between LGUs and the national government, influencing their capacity to promote inclusive and accountable governance.

The methodological framework is based on the decentralisation theory. For example, Brillantes (1987) enumerated the following significant criteria for establishing local autonomy or self-government:

- First, a set of locally elected officials must be responsible for the area. This legislative unit would represent the interests of the various geographic divisions and sectors, which would be critical for promulgating laws relevant to the needs of the local population.
- Second, self-government must have clearly defined areas of responsibility and mechanisms to ensure the delivery of public services such as education, healthcare, and local infrastructure.
- Third, the relationship between the national and local units must be clearly defined, with distinct boundaries established for areas of responsibility. This distinction should encompass the national government's review and approval processes concerning local decisions. Another example would be budgetary authority. It must be

clear whether local budgets require national approval or if certain aspects are subject to oversight by the central government, which brings the fourth criterion: that the area of self-government must have some authority to generate local revenue through taxation.

The main justification for decentralisation is that economic efficiency can be enhanced with "each public service being provided by the jurisdiction having control over the minimum geographic area that would internalise the benefits and costs" (Oates, 1972). In essence, greater decentralisation allows lower governments to respond to their constituents' local needs and preferences, leading to better efficiency and timely delivery of public services. With increased local autonomy, citizens are also able to "vote with their feet" to get the "public services-tax package" that they prefer (Tiebout, 1956), theoretically eliminating the rent-seeking nature of local politicians (Brennan & Buchanan, 1977).

8.2 Fiscal Federalism

8.2.1 Local Government Revenues and Expenditures

Figures 8.1, 8.2, and 8.3 visualise the trends and composition of fiscal data from all local government units in the Philippines for the past decade. A considerable increase in LGU income can be seen during the year 2022, following the implementation of the Mandanas-Garcia ruling. However, the same cannot be said for LGU expenditures, whose trend has remained consistent before and after the ruling (100 PHP–1.6 EUR).

8.2.2 Transfers to Local Governments

External sources comprise a significant portion of income for all provinces and municipalities, and Figs. 8.4 and 8.5 reveal that most of it is attributable to the IRA (renamed NTA following the year 2022), as compared to other external sources such as inter-local transfers and donations.

Since the early 1990s, fiscal transfers from the national government to LGUs have taken the form of the IRA, which allocates a fixed percentage of national internal revenues to local governments. These transfers ensure that LGUs have the financial resources to deliver essential services and pursue local development goals. In 2018, the Supreme Court expanded

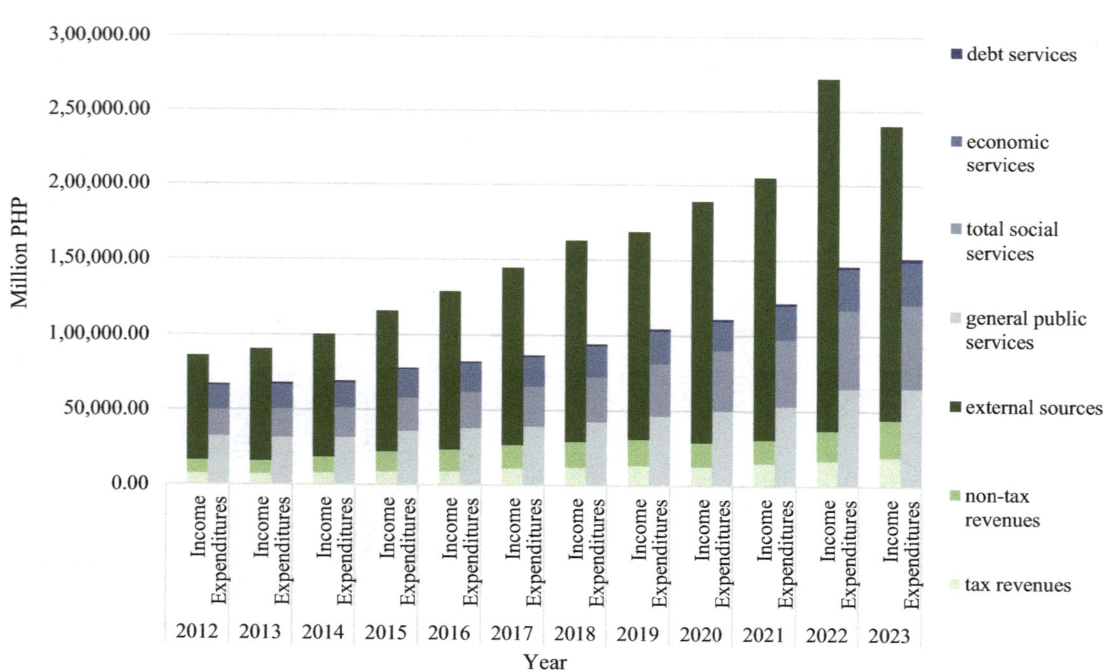

Fig. 8.1 Summary of fiscal data, provinces (*Source* Authors, based on data from the Bureau of Local Government Finance [2025])

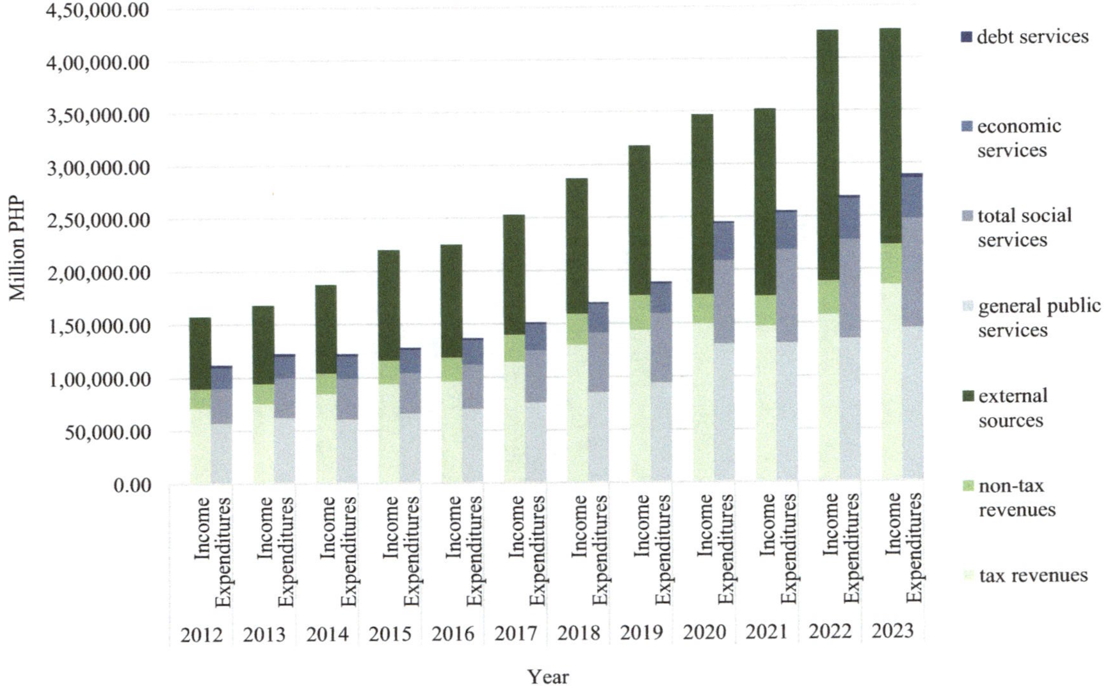

Fig. 8.2 Summary of fiscal data, cities (*Source* Authors, based on data from the Bureau of Local Government Finance [2025])

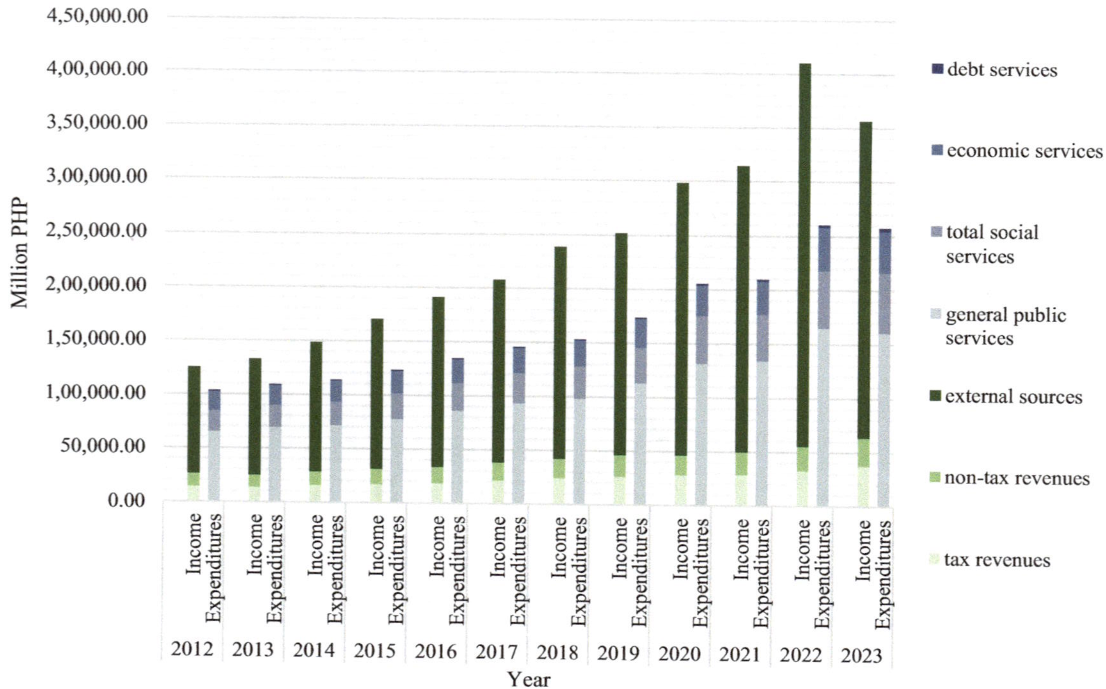

Fig. 8.3 Summary of fiscal data, municipalities (*Source* Authors, based on data from the Bureau of Local Government Finance [2025])

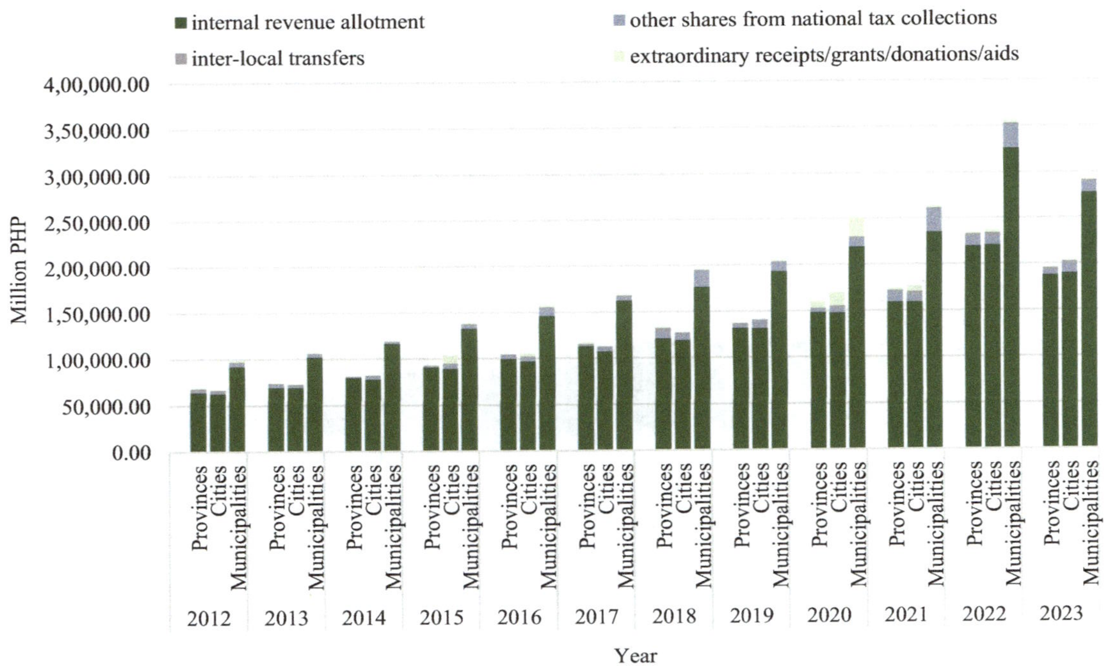

Fig. 8.4 Composition of LGU external sources (*Source* Authors, based on data from the Bureau of Local Government Finance [2025])

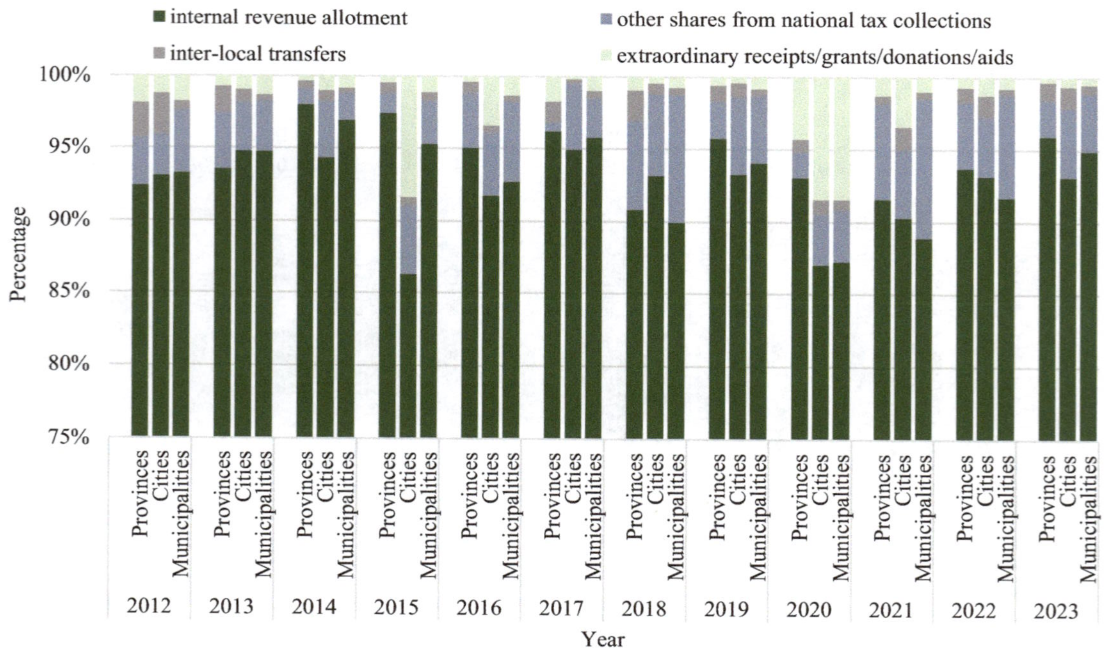

Fig. 8.5 Composition of LGU external sources (*Source* Authors, based on data from the Bureau of Local Government Finance [2025])

these fiscal entitlements through the Mandanas-Garcia ruling, which redefined the revenue base for the IRA to include national taxes collected by the Bureau of Customs, transforming the IRA into the NTA. This adjustment significantly increased the funds transferred to LGUs, providing new opportunities for local governance and presenting challenges in institutional capacity, spending efficiency, and intergovernmental relations, which was followed quickly by Executive Order No. 138 (EO 138) in 2021, which provided the main parameters for the transition of selected functions and responsibilities from national to the local governments. In particular, EO 138 called for designing and reviewing devolution transition plans (DTPs) (Gonzales, 2023; Juco et al., 2023).

Today, there are several components of intergovernmental fiscal transfers in the Philippines: (1) an unconditional, formula-based block grant called the internal revenue allotment (IRA) as mandated under Section 284 of LGC 1991; (2) a share in national wealth and certain taxes; and (3) ad hoc conditional grants. The formula for central-local sharing of revenues stipulates that local governments are set to receive 40% of national internal revenues in the third fiscal year before the allocation year. There are two stages for the allocation of the IRA: (1) distribution by levels of local governments (i.e. 23% to provinces, 23% to cities, 34% to municipalities, and 20% to barangays) and (2) division of the share of each level of government among individual local government units based on population (50%), land area (25%), and equal sharing (25%).

However, certain taxes collected by the Bureau of Customs (BOC) were excluded from the base when computing the IRA, prompting what is known as the Mandanas-Garcia ruling of the Supreme Court (SC). In 2018, the SC ruled on the petitions filed by Congressman Hermilando I. Mandanas and Congressman Enrique T. Garcia et al. about the National Government's manner of computing the IRA shares of the LGUs. The SC decided that the just share of LGUs from the national taxes is not only based on the national internal revenue taxes collected by the Bureau of Internal Revenue (BIR) but also on all national taxes, which became final and executory on 10 April 2019 (G.R. Nos. 199802 and 208,488). To carry out the decision of the SC, President Rodrigo Duterte released on 1 June 2021 Executive Order (EO) No. 138, mandating the full devolution of essential services from the national government agencies (NGAs) to local government units (LGUs).

Following the Mandanas-Garcia ruling, the IRA was renamed the National Tax Allocation (NTA), and the share of Philippine local government units from national tax revenues drastically increased since its implementation in 2022. Before this ruling, the Senate Economic Planning Office (SEPO) reported that the IRA amounted to only 15.40% (PHP 773.80 billion) of the 2021 national budget. In 2022, the NTA rose to PHP 959.04 billion, or 19.09% of the national budget, an estimated 3.69% increase from the previous year. With more fiscal space, programme allocations of LGUs are estimated to go up by 37.89%.

LGUs can utilise this unconditional, formula-based block grant to finance any necessary activities, subject to some imperatives. For instance, under Section 17(g) of the LGC, the IRA and other local resources shall first cover the cost of providing basic services and facilities. Section 287 of the LGC also mandates LGUs to appropriate at least 20% of their IRA to finance development projects. Commonly known as Local Development Fund (LDF), it is used to finance the priority projects of LGUs as embodied in their duly approved local development plans and Annual Investment Programs (AIP) (SEPO, 2022).

In the Philippines, ad hoc conditional grants are targeted funds the national government provides to local government units (LGUs) for specific purposes, such as supporting specific development projects or enhancing progress towards improved local governance. Unlike the Internal Revenue Allotment (IRA), which is an unconditional block grant, these conditional grants come with stipulations on their usage, aiming to address particular needs or policy objectives by the institution providing the grant. The grants are also dependent on the LGUs' matching counterparts.

One example of a conditional grant is the support provided by the municipal development fund, which has been administered by the Municipal Development Fund Office (MDFO) of the Department of Finance (DoF) until its closure in 2022. The MDFO provided technical support and grants to LGUs for projects that promote local economic development and improve public services. The fund was created in 1984 upon the recommendation of the DOF to be a system of channelling long-term (up to twenty years) development funds to LGUs; resources were channelled from proceeds of foreign loans, assistance, and grants (Llanto, 1997). Grants and technical assistance were provided together with low-interest loans.

Another type of conditional grant support is the Performance Challenge Fund (or PCF); LGUs receive grants under this fund if they receive a "Seal of Good Local Governance," or SGLG, which means that they can meet a certain level of effectiveness and efficiency in the delivery of public services and participation in their own constituency. These grants are used in conjunction with counterpart funds provided by the LGUs for projects that address environmental sustainability, disaster risk and management, local economic development, solid waste management, and participation and accountability. It has provided around PHP 6.8 billion from 2010 to 2020 (Diokno-Sicat et al., 2022).

During the COVID-19 pandemic, local governments also received additional resources from the national government for food and medical assistance, protective equipment and COVID testing kits, construction of temporary shelters and testing laboratories, and temporary shelters for people without housing. The above was provided under a national law that authorised the alignment of funds to address the pandemic, called the "Beyanihan to Heal as One Act." An estimated PHP 37 billion (around UD$600 million in 2024 nominal terms) was spent by LGUs for their COVID-19 response (Bureau of Local Government Finance, 2022b). However, not all were transfers from the national government.

Even though local governments have the authority to decide how to allocate the IRA funds, some of them become heavily reliant on it, leaving them with limited funds beyond this transfer. In contrast, other local governments can generate substantial revenue independently. This revenue independence is due to both higher fiscal capacity and greater collection efforts, although fiscal capacity likely plays a more significant role. Cities and municipalities vary widely in business presence and economic conditions, and those with more businesses and stronger economies benefit from a larger local tax base and greater fiscal capacity. A considerable proportion of cities' income is from tax revenue, a consistent trend that is not observed for both provinces and municipalities.

Furthermore, a study by Canare (2016) revealed that while a 1-peso increase in the IRA is associated with a 0.80 to 1.08 peso increase in total city government expenditures, the IRA has a smaller marginal effect on local government spending for LGUs that can generate more locally sourced revenues. In the Philippines, a business permit issued by the city or municipal government is required to start a business and must be renewed annually. Additionally, local governments charge various other business and licensing fees. They also collect real property taxes, which increase with land value. Therefore, fiscal capacity is key to a local government's revenue independence.

8.3 Case Study: Fiscal Transfers and Local Government Efficiency

Our earlier arguments suggest that fiscal transfers' effect on LGUs' development and governance outcomes is nuanced and subject to interactions with different factors. On one hand, fiscal transfers provide local governments with resources to improve their governance and make them responsive to local needs. On the other hand, fiscal transfers may create dependence, which is associated with adverse local development outcomes, including in the Philippines (Canare, 2021).

To illustrate, we used Philippine city local government fiscal data for the years 2015 to 2023 and the Cities and Municipalities Competitiveness Index (CMCI) Government Efficiency Score as a measure of governance quality at the city level for the same years.

Figure 8.6 shows the scatterplot, and the linear regression fit of the CMCI Government Efficiency Score on the NTA for Philippine cities from 2015 to 2023. A positive, albeit weak, correlation between the two variables is consistent with our earlier proposition that fiscal transfers can improve local government efficiency.

However, the relationship reverses and becomes stronger when NTA is replaced with NTA expressed as a share of total local government income, a measure of LGU dependency on transfers. As shown in Fig. 8.7, higher dependence on NTA is associated with a lower CMCI Government Efficiency Score.

Although this first-pass empirical analysis cannot infer causality, it provides a quantitative illustration of some of the points earlier made and underscores nuances on the effects of fiscal transfers. The implementation of the Mandanas ruling may even highlight these nuances. With more fiscal transfers, local governments will have more access to resources which they can use to improve service delivery. However, it can exacerbate fiscal dependence, particularly if the added NTA provides disincentives for LGUs to generate income, which can be more pronounced among local governments with weak governance and competences.

While this study highlighted the effects of regular transfers in strengthening good governance and politics at the local level, there is some

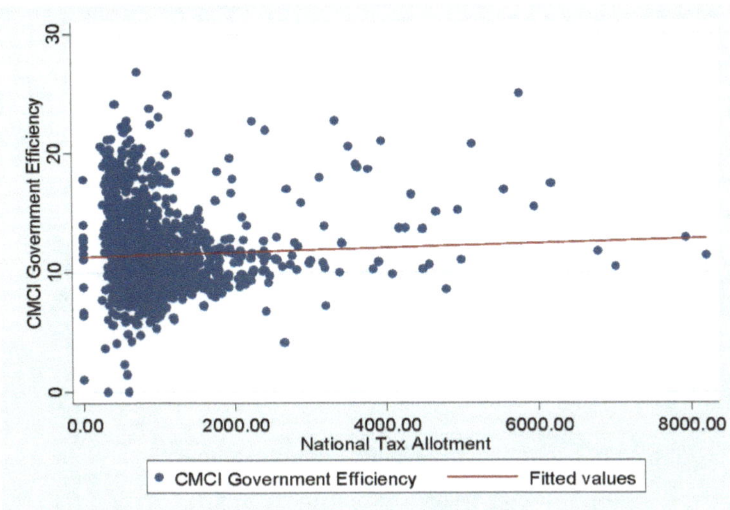

Fig. 8.6 CMCI government efficiency score and NTA, cities, 2015 to 2023 (*Source* Authors, based on own research [2025])

potential for conditional grants to affect the behaviour of local government units, given that, for example, the receipt of conditional grants depends on LGU performance on areas such as financial transparency, disaster preparedness, social protection, and environmental management, currently in the SGLG. However, according to Diokno-Sicat et al. (2022), the effectiveness of these funds is blunted by the stringent criteria for the SGLG that restricts poorer LGUs to the fund; around a fifth of all municipalities have never been eligible for a PCF grant.

8.4 Conclusions

In summary, decentralisation in the Philippines, while promising local autonomy and development, faces significant challenges, particularly in service delivery, political accountability, and institutional capacity. There are opportunities to trigger further reforms due to recent developments in decentralised finance. However, additional success in promoting decentralisation with stronger development outcomes will likely depend on several key parameters.

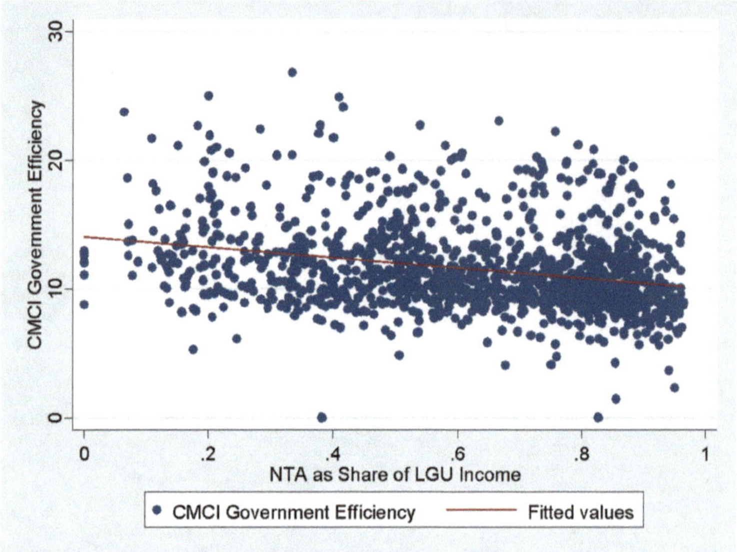

Fig. 8.7 CMCI government efficiency score and NTA as share of total LGU income (*Source* Authors, based on own research [2025])

Despite the intent to improve public services through decentralisation, many LGUs struggle to enhance service quality due to limited fiscal resources and inconsistent administrative capacities. Studies highlight a gap between policy aims and actual outcomes, with anecdotal successes largely concentrated in well-funded or more developed areas. Less affluent LGUs often lack the fiscal capacity to meet residents' needs, undermining the equitable impact of decentralisation policies (Diokno-Sicat & Maddawin, 2018).

Political dynasties, deeply embedded in local governance, influence LGU priorities, often favouring elite interests over broad-based development. Research by Mendoza and others indicates that dynastic control can reduce political accountability, leading to decision-making prioritising familial or factional gains. This lack of competitiveness in local politics stifles democratic participation as political positions become concentrated in specific families, thus limiting responsive governance and slowing reforms (Mendoza et al., 2022, 2023).

Strengthening political and administrative capacity is essential for LGUs to exercise fiscal autonomy effectively. However, institutional weaknesses, such as limited technical expertise and underdeveloped accountability mechanisms, hinder effective resource management. PIDS (2018) highlights that the success of decentralised governance relies heavily on institutional readiness; LGUs must be able to independently manage funds, engage in transparent governance, and adapt policies to local needs. Without these capabilities, LGUs struggle to meet national development goals, reducing the potential of decentralisation to enhance democratic participation and accountability.

Strengthening fiscal autonomy and addressing these structural issues will be crucial for LGUs to realise the full benefits of decentralisation and better serve their constituencies. Other factors that affect decentralisation include weak support from national government agencies and a lack of capacities of local governments, especially human resources. Suffice it to say that this brief paper has underscored where and how many of these challenges could be overcome in order to promote more successful decentralisation. This research also highlights the potential role of conditional grants to LGUs in improving local politics and development outcomes. However, these financial facilities should also examine balancing incentives for lower-income LGUs, technical assistance for capacity-building, and ensuring that objectives are attainable for all LGUs.

Annex: Country Profile: Philippines

Following the regime change in 1986, the Fifth Philippine Republic embarked on greater decentralisation efforts with the passing of the Republic Act No. 7160, or an Act Providing for a Local Government Code of 1991 (LGC 1991). This act allowed for "a more responsive and accountable local government structure instituted through a system of decentralisation whereby local government units shall be given more powers, authority, responsibilities, and resources." The Code allowed for greater decentralisation, especially in many areas of government functioning, including strengthened control by local government units in the areas of health provision (including the operation of local hospitals and clinics), social welfare (including disaster relief), agricultural development, and environmental management (including waste management and reforestation). LGUs were also given greater responsibilities for planning and development in their respective areas, and multisectoral councils were created to ensure participation of organised citizens' groups in the planning, implementation, and assessment of programs.

LGUs were provided significant resources through grants (called internal revenue allotment or IRA) and taxing powers. The IRA is the single, most significant revenue source for most LGUs, an unconditional block grant that allows LGUs full discretion in its utilisation. At the same time, local governments were given greater powers to collect taxes and undertake financial agreements, including real property taxes, business fees, and other license fees. Of course, the size of these revenues depends on the economic activity these LGUs could facilitate, presumably incentivising them to lay the foundation for sustained, inclusive growth and development. As will be reviewed later, however, success in this area has been uneven at best.

Nevertheless, the Mandanas-Garcia ruling by the Philippine Supreme Court in 2018 significantly reshaped the landscape of fiscal decentralisation in the Philippines. The ruling originated from a petition by two local politicians who argued that the IRA was incorrectly calculated. They contended that the IRA should be based on all national taxes collected, including those from the Bureau of Customs, not just the internal revenue taxes collected by the Bureau of Internal Revenue (BIR).

The Supreme Court agreed, ruling that the IRA (now termed the NTA) should indeed include all national taxes. This decision effectively increased the total funds allocated to LGUs, starting in 2022—estimated by some to reach up to 55% of the original amount (World Bank, 2021)—providing them with a larger share of national revenue to support local governance, development, and public service delivery. The increased fiscal allotment aims to empower LGUs by providing them with the financial means to address local needs more independently. However, it has also pressured LGUs, especially those with limited capacity, to manage these additional funds effectively and fulfil the expanded responsibilities (Table 8.1).

The Philippines is a republic with a presidential form of government wherein power is equally divided among its three branches: executive, legislative, and judiciary. The LGC 1991 defines the structure and powers of various LGUs, which are crucial in promoting local autonomy and governance. This legislation identifies five primary types of LGUs: provinces, component cities, chartered cities, municipalities, and barangays. Each of these possesses distinct powers that enable it to address the unique needs of its constituents.

Table 8.1 Municipal political power structures

Criteria	*Results*
The level of autonomy of municipal governments over their functional mandates: the question of whether municipal governance institutions can only perform mandated tasks or can choose from a predefined scope of tasks Indicator: yes, partly, no	Partly
The level of freedom of municipal governments to decide their own political organisation and electoral system (can they, for example, determine their own electoral districts, number of seats, electoral system, etc.) Indicator: yes, partly, no	No
The constitutional or legal mechanisms to assert the autonomy of municipal governments. Examples of specific constitutional or legal mechanisms that allow municipal governments to assert their autonomy include (a) constitutional clauses or other statutory regulations protecting local self-government; (b) recourse to the judicial system through constitutional courts to settle disputes with higher authorities; or (c) other constitutional or legal protections of municipal autonomy exist (e.g. higher-level governments are prevented from forcing municipal governments to merge) Indicator: yes, partly, no	Yes
Municipal governments' right to use the legal system against higher-level government (de jure and de facto—do they use such right?) Indicator yes (both de jure and de facto), partly, no	Yes
The level to which decisions made by municipal governance institutions are subject to administrative supervision for their responsibilities and if higher-level approval is needed to act in their own matters Indicator yes, no	Partly
Does the higher-level have the right to remove local executives [or other local officials] without judicial intervention? Indicator yes, no	Partly

Source Authors, based on own research (2025)

Provinces are the largest political subdivisions in the country and serve as the backbone of regional governance. They are endowed with significant legislative powers, allowing them to enact ordinances, resolutions, and regulations tailored to local needs. In addition to legislative authority, provinces hold administrative powers that enable them to oversee essential services such as public health, infrastructure development, and social services. Financially, provinces can levy taxes, fees, and charges, and they are entitled to a share of national taxes, enhancing their capacity to provide for their constituents.

Component cities, which remain under the jurisdiction of a province, also possess important powers. Like provinces, component cities have the authority to enact local ordinances and resolutions that govern their respective areas. They manage public services, including education, health, and local infrastructure, while also having the capacity to impose local taxes and collect various fees. Although they operate under provincial oversight, their governance structure allows for a degree of local autonomy that enables them to address specific community issues effectively.

On the other hand, chartered cities enjoy a higher degree of independence as they are not subject to provincial jurisdiction. This autonomy empowers chartered cities to enact legislation and manage public services independently. Their ability to generate revenue through taxes and fees is often broader than that of component cities, allowing them greater flexibility in addressing local challenges. This independence enhances their capacity to respond to the unique needs of their urban populations, making them vital centres of governance and development.

Municipalities, smaller subdivisions within provinces, share similar powers with component cities. They can create local ordinances and regulations, manage public services such as sanitation and safety, and impose local taxes. Despite their smaller scale, municipalities play a critical role in local governance by addressing the immediate needs of their communities through targeted services and initiatives. Finally, barangays, the smallest administrative units, possess the least power but are essential for grassroots governance. They can pass resolutions and ordinances, manage local programs, and collect limited taxes. This structure ensures that even the smallest communities have a voice in local governance, promoting civic engagement and participation.

The Philippines has a unified system of government, with a uniform political organisation and electoral system. Currently, it consists of 18 regions, 17 of which are administrative groups to which the President assigns a regional development council (RDC). At the same time, the Bangsamoro Autonomous Region in Muslim Mindanao (BARMM) has an elected government and parliament, and the Philippine Congress has delegated specific powers and responsibilities.

Republic Act No. 11054, also known as the Bangsamoro Organic Law, was enacted in 2018 to establish the BARMM. This law provides a framework for self-governance and autonomy for the Bangsamoro people, addressing long-standing issues related to the region's peace, justice, and development. The law emerged from peace agreements between the Philippine government and various Muslim groups, notably the Moro

Islamic Liberation Front (MILF), and reflects a commitment to promote inclusive governance and sustainable development in the area.

The Bangsamoro Organic Law outlines the Bangsamoro government's structure and powers, including an elected parliamentary system. It specifies the powers of the Bangsamoro Autonomous Government, including legislative, executive, and fiscal authorities, allowing for greater local control over resources, education, and social services. Additionally, the law provides revenue generation and sharing mechanisms, enabling the Bangsamoro region to fund its development initiatives and enhance local governance (Table 8.2).

The Omnibus Election Code of the Philippines outlines how chief executives are elected. The election for barangay officials has been held on the second Monday of May every six years since 1988. The electorate votes for a Punong Barangay or barangay captain—the highest chief executive for this administrative unit—along with seven barangay councillors that comprise the Sangguniang Barangay, and the chairman of the Youth Council, or Sangguniang Kabataan (SK). Similarly, the elected barangay officials will assume office on 30 June following the election and shall hold office for six years until their successors are elected.

According to the LGC 1991, an elective local official must be (1) a citizen of the Philippines; (2) a registered voter in the Barangay, municipality, city, province, or the district where they intend to be elected; (3) a resident therein for at least one year immediately preceding the day of the election; and able to read and write Filipino or any other local language or dialect.

Table 8.2 Structure and quality of subnational electoral systems

Criteria	*Results*
How are municipal councillors elected? Indicator—election mode	Local elections
For what term are municipal councils elected (years)? Indicator—years of mandate	3
What is the level of citizen participation in municipal elections? Indicator: Low—("Normal") voter turnout is below 35% of eligible (registered) voters Average—Voter turnout is between 35 and 60% of eligible (registered) voters High—Voter turnout is over 60% of eligible (registered) voters	High

Source Authors, based on own research (2025)

Candidates for the position of governor and vice-governor of highly urbanised cities must be at least twenty-three years of age on election day. In contrast, candidates for the mayor or vice-mayor of independent component cities and municipalities must be at least twenty-one years of age on election day. Candidates for the position of Punong Barangay or member of the Sangguniang Barangay must be at least eighteen (18) years of age on election day, and candidates for the Sangguniang Kabataan must be at least fifteen (15) years of age but not more than twenty-one (21) years of age on election day.

Article V addresses the election and composition of the Sangguniang Pampook, the regional assembly for autonomous regions in southern Philippines (Regions IX and XII). Section 31 specifies that each Sangguniang Pampook has 27 members, with 17 elected representatives and three sectoral representatives from youth, agricultural workers, and industrial labour. Furthermore, the President may appoint an additional seven representatives in each region should it be deemed that any sector is not adequately represented in the Sangguniang Pampook as a result of the elections (Table 8.3).

The Philippine party-list system is composed of three different groups: (1) national parties or organisations, (2) regional parties or organisations, and (3) sectoral parties or organisations. National and regional parties or organisations are different from sectoral parties in that they need not be organised along sectoral lines and need not represent any particular sector. These are jointly referred to as non-sectoral parties.

On the other hand, sectoral parties must either be (1) "marginalised and underrepresented" or (2) lacking in "well-defined political constituencies." Sectors that are "marginalised and underrepresented" include labour, peasants, fisherfolk, urban poor, Indigenous cultural communities, handicapped, veterans, and overseas workers. In contrast, sectors that lack "well-defined political constituencies" include professionals, older adults, women, and the youth. It is also imperative that the party's principal advocacy pertains to the special interest and concerns of the sector that they represent.

Any organised group of persons may register as a party, organisation, or coalition for purposes of the party-list system by filing with the COMELEC not later than ninety (90) days before the election. Registered parties must submit a list of nominees at least 44 days before elections, and only persons who have given their written consent may be named in the list.

Table 8.3 Nature of subnational political party systems

Criteria	*Results*
Which subjects can run in municipal elections? Indicator—define who can participate	1. a citizen of the Philippines; 2. a registered voter in the Barangay, municipality, city, province, or the district where they intend to be elected; 3. a resident therein for at least one year immediately preceding the day of the election; and 4. able to read and write Filipino or any other local language or dialect
How are party candidates for municipal council elections selected? Indicator—selected by party, elected by party, self-nomination, other	Selected by the party
Are there established rules for financing municipal political campaigns? Indicator—yes, no	No
Does the ruling national party have a dominant position in municipal elections? Indicator—yes, no	Yes

Source Authors, based on own research (2025)

Several local political parties operate exclusively at the regional, provincial, or city level. These parties focus on localised issues and typically compete in elections for regional or local positions such as governors, mayors, and councillors. Some examples include:

1. Hugpong ng Pagbabago—A regional party in the Davao Region, originally established to support local governance and leadership in Davao.
2. Asenso Manileño—A Manila-based party involved in city politics.
3. Padayon Pilipino—Active in Misamis Oriental and Cagayan de Oro.
4. Unang Sigaw—Based in Nueva Ecija, focused on provincial-level leadership.
5. Kambilan—Based in Pampanga, supporting provincial leadership and initiatives.
6. 1-Cebu—A provincial party operating in Cebu and Cebu City.

These parties are often established by influential political families, coalitions of local politicians, or regional leaders; the 1-Cebu party is closely affiliated with the Garcia political clan, whose members hold significant positions in the Cebu province in central Philippines. On the other hand, Asenso Manileño is a political party based in Manila City. Their numbers fluctuate as parties are created or dissolved based on political alignments and elections (Table 8.4).

As of 2022, the COMELEC reported a total of 65,831,806 registered voters across the country, 55,431,939 of which were those that actually voted during the national and subnational elections, amounting to a record high voter turnout of 84%. Citizen participation in governance has significantly grown in the Philippines since the enactment of the 1991 LGC. The above has been apparent through the consistent increase in registered voters and voter turnout and the inclusion of non-governmental organisations, people's organisations, cooperatives, and other citizens' groups in Local Development Councils (LDC) and Local Special Bodies. These include the local school board (responsible for local education issues), local health board (which provides advice on health programs), the local peace and order council, local housing board, the local children protection committee, and the local disaster risk management council. Overall, the LGC has institutionalised avenues for participatory governance, but continued efforts are needed to ensure genuine collaboration and empowerment of grassroots organisations.

Dynasties are historically and deeply entrenched within Philippine politics (Mendoza et al., 2019; Sidel, 1997; Teehankee, 2001), leading to

Table 8.4 Subnational political participation and accountability

Criteria	*Results*
Are all council meetings (required to be) open to the public? Indicator—yes, no	Yes
Are municipal records and documents (required to be) available to the public? Indicator—yes, no	Partly
Is the council (required to) engage in an open, participatory planning process? Indicator—yes, no	Yes
Are alternative participatory mechanisms, such as referendums or participatory budgeting, used? Indicator—yes, partly, no	Yes

Source Authors, based on the own research (2025)

significant socioeconomic repercussions on aspects like poverty, governance, and accountability (Cruz et al., 2017; Mendoza et al., 2023). Studies have also argued that this entrenchment of elite politics is mainly due to the country's weak institutional apparatus (Hutchcroft & Rocamora, 2003) and is further strengthened by the absence of strong political parties (Rivera, 2011).

Apart from these institutional factors, Porio (2017) argued that the expanding participation of civil society groups is actually helping local elites to strengthen their dominance through a process called "networked governance practices." In essence, the recent emphasis on citizen participation and accountability has not led to equalising and redistributing power; instead, it has paved the way for dynastic politicians to garner local support and reinforce their positions of authority. The state's efforts towards decentralisation have vested more power and fiscal authority for mayors and other local government officials, allowing them to craft initiatives that entail collaborative effort with civil society organisations and the private sector, but in doing so, perpetuating the clientelist partnerships between politicians and citizen groups, allowing dynasties to remain in power for an extended period of time.

References

Brillantes, A. B., Jr. (1987). Decentralization in the Philippines: An overview. *Philippine Journal of Public Administration, 31*(2), 131–148.

Brennan, Geoffrey, and James M. Buchanan. "Towards a tax constitution for Leviathan." *Journal of Public Economics 8*, no. 3 (1977): 255–273.

Bureau of Local Governance Finance. (2022b). *Detailed discussion and analysis of the preliminary report on COVID-19 receipts and expenditures of provinces, cities, and municipalities.* https://blgf.gov.ph/lgucovid19response/

Canare, T. (2016). The relationship between IRA and local government expenditures: Evidence from a cross-section of Philippine cities. *Philippine Political Science Journal, 37*(3), 167–189. https://doi.org/10.1080/01154451.2016.1236476

Canare, Tristan. 2021. "Decentralization and development outcomes: What does the empirical literature really say?." *Hacienda Publica Espanola* 237: 111–151.

Cruz, C., Labonne, J., & Querubín, P. (2017). Politician family networks and electoral outcomes: Evidence from the Philippines. *The American Economic Review, 107*(10), 3006–3037. http://www.jstor.org/stable/44871776

Diokno-Sicat, J., & Maddawin, R. B. (2018). *A survey of literature on Philippine decentralization* (Discussion Papers DP 2018–23). Philippine Institute for Development Studies. https://ideas.repec.org/p/phd/dpaper/dp_2018-23.html

Diokno-Sicat, J., Mariano, M. A., Castillo, A. F., & Maddawin, R. B. (2022). Local government conditional grants: The seal of good local governance and the performance challenge fund. *Philippine Journal of Development, 46*(1), 1–18.

Gonzales, A. L. (2023, December 25). *PBBM orders national gov't agencies to analyze devolution initiative*. Philippine News Agency. https://www.pna.gov.ph/articles/1215927

Hutchcroft, Paul D., and Joel Rocamora. 2003. "Strong demands and weak institutions: The origins and evolution of the democratic deficit in the Philippines." *Journal of East Asian Studies 3*, 2: 259–292.

Juco, M., Maddawin, R., Palomar, R. H., Ruiz, M. G., & Diokno-Sicat, C. J. (2023). *Baseline study on the state of devolution in the (pre-Mandanas) Philippines*. https://doi.org/10.62986/dp2023.09

Llanto, G. (1997). *Financing local infrastructure through a municipal development fund*. Infrastructure Finance Regional Workshop Report Submitted to USAID Indonesia, Research Triangle Institute.

Local Government Code (LGC), Republic Act No. 7160. (1991).

Mendoza, R. U., Beja, E. L., Jr., Venida, V. S., & Yap, D. B., II. (2019). Political dynasties in the Philippine Congress. In R. Mendoza, E. Beja, J. Teehankee, A. La Viña, & M. Villamejor-Mendoza (Eds.), *Building inclusive democracies in ASEAN* (pp. 7–38). World Scientific Publishing Co Pte Ltd.

Mendoza, R. U., Mendoza, G. A. S., Teehankee, J. C., Tuaño, P. A. P., & Yap, J. K. (2023). Interrogating the links between dynasties and development in the Philippines. *Asian Journal of Comparative Politics, 8*(3), 765–786. https://doi.org/10.1177/20578911231182490

Mendoza, R. U., Yap, J. K., Jaminola, L. M., & Yu, E. C. (2022). Political dynasties, business, and poverty in the Philippines. *Journal of Government and Economics, 7*, Article 100051. https://doi.org/10.1016/j.jge.2022.100051

Oates, Wallace E. 1972. "Fiscal Federalism. New York: Harcourt Brace Jovanovich".

Philippine Institute of Development Studies (PIDS). (2018). *Critical perspectives on federalism for regional development*. https://www.pids.gov.ph/publication/books/critical-perspectives-on-federalism-for-regional-development

Porio, E. (2017). Citizen participation and decentralization in the Philippines. In W. Berenschot, H. Schulte-Nordholt, & L. Bakker (Eds.), *Citizenship and democratization in Southeast Asia* (pp. 31–50). Brill. https://doi.org/10.1163/j.cttlw76ws5.6.

Rivera, Temario. 2011. "In search of credible elections and parties: The Philippine paradox." In *Chasing the wind: Assessing Philippine democracy*, ed. F.

Miranda, T. Rivera, M. Ronas and R. Holmes. Quezon City: Commission on Human Rights.

Senate Economic Planning Office (SEPO). (2022). *Internal Revenue Allotment (IRA) in 2022.* https://serp-p.pids.gov.ph/publication/public/view?slug=ira-in-2022

Sidel, J. T. (1997). Philippine politics in town, district, and province: Bossism in Cavite and Cebu. *The Journal of Asian Studies, 56*(4), 947–966. https://doi.org/10.2307/2658295

Teehankee, J. C. (2001). Emerging dynasties in the post-Marcos House of Representatives. *Philippine Political Science Journal, 22*(45), 55–78. https://doi.org/10.1080/01154451.2001.9754225

Tiebout, Charles M. 1956. "A pure theory of local expenditures."*Journal of Political Economy 64*, 5: 416–424.

World Bank. (2021). *Philippines: Mandanas ruling provides opportunities for improving service delivery through enhanced decentralization.* https://www.worldbank.org/en/news/press-release/2021/06/10/philippines-mandanas-ruling-provides-opportunities-for-improving-service-delivery-through-enhanced-decentralization

CHAPTER 9

Slovak Republic

Beáta Mikušová Meričková, Nikoleta Jakuš Muthová, and Janka Holíková

9.1 Introduction

Slovakia is a small country in the middle of Europe, a member of the European Union since 2004. It is one of the most fragmented countries in Europe, with almost 3,000 municipalities and a population of 5.5 million. The average Slovak local government—the municipality has an area of approximately 17 square kilometres. Only two cities, Bratislava and Košice, have more than 100,000 inhabitants (approximately 430,000 in Bratislava and 250,000 in Košice).

The current form of the local government system in Slovakia is based on the changes in the former Czechoslovakia after 1989. In 1990, the Act on Local Self-Government (no. 518/1990 Coll.) was adopted, creating

B. M. Meričková (✉) · N. J. Muthová · J. Holíková
Matej Bel University, Banská Bystrica, Slovakia
e-mail: beata.mikusovamerickova@umb.sk

N. J. Muthová
e-mail: nikoleta.jakusmuthova@umb.sk

J. Holíková
e-mail: janka.holikova@umb.sk

J. Nemec et al. (eds.), *Local Government and Fiscal Transfers*,
Governance and Public Management,
https://doi.org/10.1007/978-3-031-95674-4_9

a modern local self-government responsible for the competences of the former national committees. Slovakia signed the European Charter for Local Self-Government in 1999 with reservations, which were step by step removed, and from 2007, Slovakia is bound by all its provisions. A Slovak municipality is a legal entity with a comprehensive set of responsibilities and the right to independently manage its property and income under the conditions established by law. The state delegates to municipalities the performance of specified tasks of local state administration and is expected to cover the costs of such a delegated performance of state administration.

9.2 Fiscal Federalism

9.2.1 Local Government Revenues

Local government revenues in Slovakia consist of tax revenue, non-tax revenue, transfers and grants, financial operations revenue, and capital revenue. The structure of local government revenue for Slovakia is shown in Fig. 9.1.

Municipalities primarily receive their funds from taxes and transfers from the state budget. A significant portion of tax revenue comes from a share of the personal income tax collected. Transfers from the state budget are used to finance devolved responsibilities, such as primary education.

9.2.2 Local Government Expenditures

Local government expenditures (accounting structure) consist of employee compensation, payables, intermediate consumption, transfers, capital expenditure and transfers, interest repayment, financial operations, and debt repayments (Fig. 9.2). From the functional classification point of view, the main expenditure area is education.

Municipalities are the primary and closest point of contact between citizens and the state. Their expenditures are primarily driven by employee compensation and payables, which cover the salaries of primary school teachers and the numerous councillors—more than 20,000 across fewer than 3,000 municipalities.

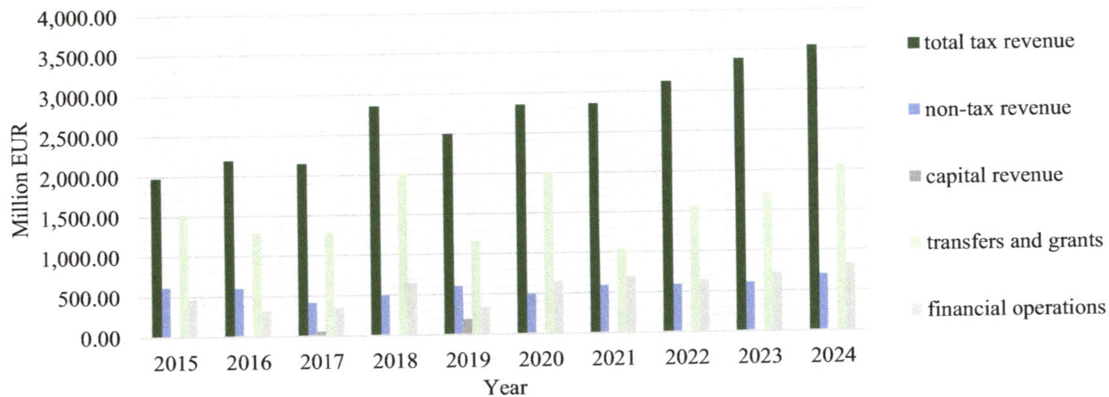

Fig. 9.1 Local government revenues (*Source* Authors, based on data from INESS [2024a])

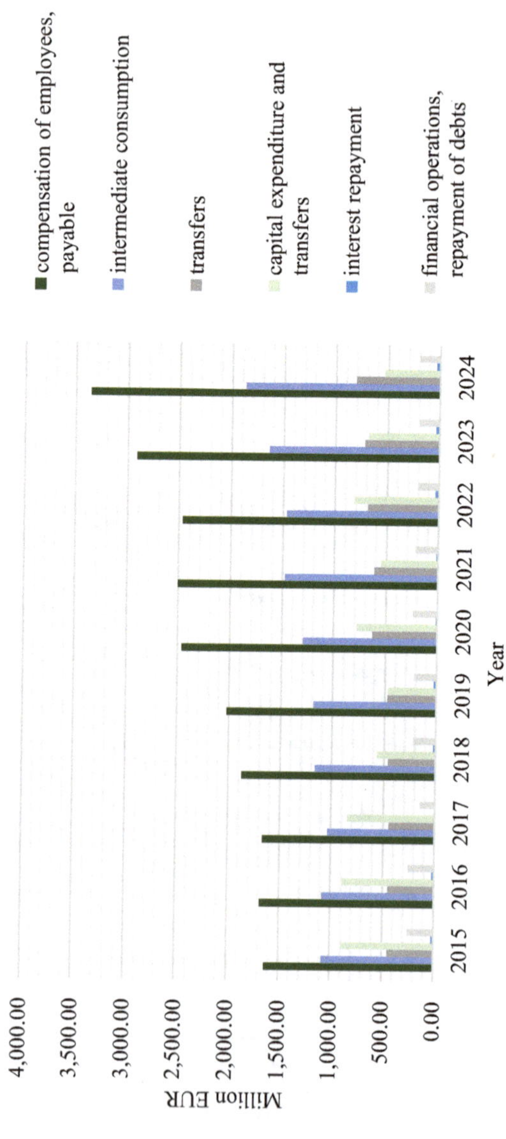

Fig. 9.2 Local government expenditure (*Source* Authors, based on data from INESS [2024b])

9.2.3 *Transfers to Local Governments*

The system of transfers includes the payment of the state for the execution of state administration's delegated performance, which is (or should be) funded by the state from the national budget, and the set of conditional and non-conditional transfers earmarked for specific activities or serving other purposes (balancing local budgets, investment support, and others).

Table 9.1 and Fig. 9.3 show the amount of domestic current transfers from the state budget to cover the costs of devolved government and domestic current transfers from the state budget, excluding those intended to cover the costs of devolved government, based on the OpenData portal information.

It is necessary to stress that the data in Table 9.1 do not fully correspond with the official data provided by the Ministry of Finance in the final state account—Tables 9.2 and 9.3, which provide data about transfers to municipalities by the functional classification and by respective central state bodies.

Transfers for delegated responsibilities represent a major part of the total sum of transfers. Municipalities cannot use current transfers from the state budget to cover the costs of delegated responsibilities for other purposes. Mederly et al.'s (2019) study describes the method of financing delegated competences in Slovak municipalities in detail. We provide some examples.

The state finances most of the costs of operating elementary schools and the activities of school authorities in education. Since 1 January 2004, the financing of these schools has been based on the principle of normative financing based on the number of pupils.

Regarding the delegated competences in building regulations, according to the current legislation, every municipality is a building authority (even the smallest municipality, with tens of inhabitants). A simple methodology finances these delegated competences: the number of inhabitants of the municipality multiplied by the monetary coefficient determined by the Ministry of Transport and Construction of the Slovak Republic. The financing of the delegated competencies in local and purpose-built roads is carried out similarly, as the Ministry of Transport and Construction determines the amount of the monetary coefficient.

In the field of performance and the financing of delegated competences in registry offices, the agenda is regulated by a separate law determining the rights and obligations concerning reporting life events from citizens

Table 9.1 Transfers to local government (2015–2023) in millions €

	2015	*2016*	*2017*	*2018*	*2019*	*2020*	*2021*	*2022*	*2023*
Domestic current transfers from the state budget to cover the costs of delegated government	576.94	632.33	699.67	748.50	854.42	974.71	1040.58	1092.39	1327.56
Share of total general government revenue	12.12%	13.80%	14.58%	13.66%	14.41%	15.66%	16.05%	15.33%	15.53%
Domestic current transfers from the state budget, excluding transfers to cover the costs of delegated government	374.44	355.68	319.98	352.24	438.03	549.27	585.22	526.62	923.81
Share of total general government revenue	7.87%	7.76%	6.67%	6.43%	7.39%	8.82%	9.03%	7.39%	10.81%
Total domestic current transfers	951.38	988.01	1019.65	1100.74	1292.45	1523.98	1625.79	1619.02	2251.38
Share of total general government revenue	19.98%	21.57%	21.25%	20.09%	21.79%	24.48%	25.08%	22.73%	26.34%
Total public revenue	4760.58	4580.66	4797.50	5477.80	5930.31	6224.69	6483.66	7124.34	8548.98

Source Authors, based on Opendata (2024)

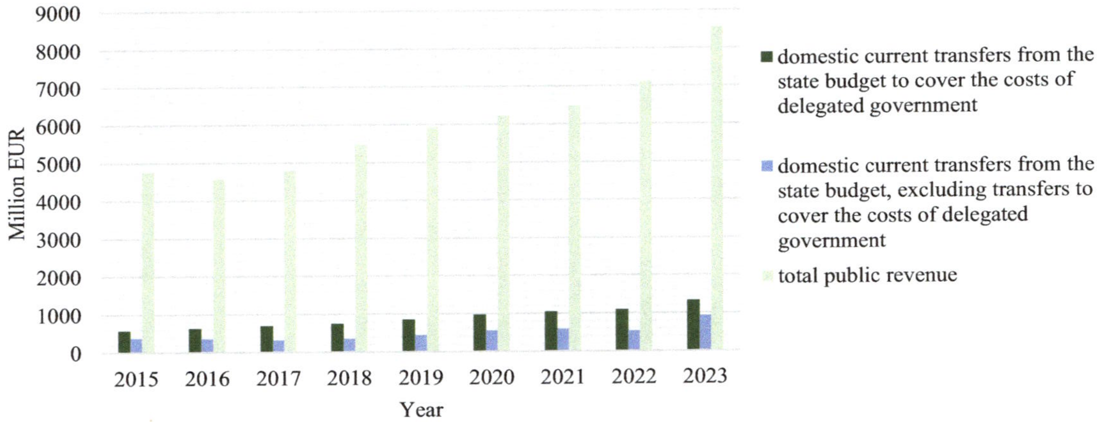

Fig. 9.3 Transfers to local government (*Source* Authors, based on Open data [2024])

Table 9.2 Transfers from the state budget to local government, classified by COFOG (Classification of the Functions of Government)

In thousands of €	*2021*	*2022*	*2023*	*2023*
Education	1,213,265	1,265,978	1,448,692	1,457,990
Economic affair	149,171	113,439	10,252	430,028
Social protection	160,779	107,528	80,642	221,791
Housing and community amenities	27,276	41,366	0	188,611
Environmental protection	51,838	52,787	0	156,636
General public services	146,631	105,775	140,22	152,462
Public order and safety	3,789	10,575	600	8,180
Recreation, culture, and religion	10,630	4,444	0	3,657
Health	16	x	0	513
Total	1,763,395	1,701,892	1,554,208	2,619,868

Source Authors, based on the Ministry of Financedata (2024)

and public authorities. The registry offices that perform these tasks are located in approximately one-third of the municipalities in Slovakia. The financing method primarily considers the number of inhabitants and, to a lesser extent, the number of implemented operations. The grant covers the registrar's salary and insurance, goods and services, and an allowance for clothing expenses. The Ministry of the Interior, which is in charge of this agenda, keeps detailed statistics on the operations carried out by individual registry offices.

The one-time nature of delegated competences in elections and referendums, a regularly recurring activity, corresponds to the method of financing, which is significantly different from ensuring the performance of other delegated competences. Municipalities receive advances for this competence from the Ministry of the Interior, which they subsequently account for; the Ministry reimburses them in full for all costs associated with the tasks defined in the law.

The performance and financing of the delegated responsibilities in the area of the environment include a wide variety of activities financed by the Ministry of the Environment, which determines the amount of the monetary coefficient per citizen of the municipality.

Except for the transfers expected to cover the costs of delegated responsibilities, different state bodies provide specific transfers, for example, transfers to cover municipalities' investment needs, transfers connected with environmental burdens, and similar. Comprehensive

Table 9.3 Transfers from the state budget to local government in Slovakia

In thousands of €	*2021 S* *1*	*2022 S* *2*	*2023 R* *3*	*2023 S* *4*
Ministry of Education, Science, Research, and Sport of the SR	11,683	1,245,324	1,448,692	1,433,501
Ministry of Investments, Regional Development, and Informatization of the SR	95,579	87,039	0	394 699
Ministry of Labour, Social Affairs, and Family of the SR	204,588	113,464	80,640	227,224
Ministry of Interior of the SR	1,321,234	120,553	13,774	201,883
Ministry of Environment of the SR	53,486	59,021	0	180,786
General Treasury Administration	7,856	1,893	0	92,805
Ministry of Transport of the Slovak Republic of the SR	32,970	36,020	10,252	40,219
Office of the Government of the Slovak Republic	11,750	18,556	850	20,187
Ministry of Agriculture and Rural Development of the SR	7,008	14,970	0	12,417
Office for Territorial Planning and Construction	x	x	0	8,797
Ministry of Culture of the SR	3,013	3,922	0	7,205
Ministry of Defence of the SR	0	150	0	145
Ministry of Economy of the SR	1,498	980	0	X
Statistical Office of the Slovak Republic	12,714	x	x	x
Ministry of Health of the Slovak Republic	16	x	x	x
Total	1,763,395	1,701,892	1,554,208	2,619,868

Source Authors, based on the Ministry of Financedata (2024)

information about the detailed structure of these transfers is not publicly available.

9.3 Case Studies

This part includes two case studies documenting the negative impacts of transfers on local democracy in Slovakia. The first focuses on the issue of the balance between the costs of delegated responsibilities and the amount of transfers required to cover them (vertical fiscal imbalance element). The second documents that the existing equalisation mechanisms are not effective (horizontal fiscal imbalance element).

9.3.1 *Case 1: Transfers to Cover the Costs of Delegated Responsibilities*

Through our primary qualitative research, we examine the issue of vertical fiscal imbalance. The core input for this part was the questionnaire, delivering the subjective perception of the topic by selected local governments of the Slovak Republic. We set the following research questions:

RQ1: Do local governments consider the revenues for the performance of delegated competences sufficient—covering the full costs of delegated responsibilities?
RQ2: Do local governments know the actual costs of exercising devolved competences (they know how much money they would realistically need)?
RQ3: What is the actual mismatch between revenue and expenditure to exercise devolved competences (vertical fiscal imbalance)?

Our survey was conducted online between September and October 2022. Eighty-eight local authorities participated in the survey. Table 9.4 presents the structure of the municipalities according to selected characteristics.

In the second step, we used secondary statistical data to quantitatively analyse public revenues and expenditures to objectively confirm the presence of a vertical fiscal imbalance, i.e. a mismatch between revenues and expenditures in the provision of devolved competences.

The opinion of municipalities about the level of the coverage and the costs (RQ1 and RQ2)

Table 9.4 Structure of the sample

		Percentage in % of responses
Number of inhabitants	1–999	39.3
	1,000–2,499	28.3
	2,500–4,999	14.6
	5,000–9,999	6.7
	10,000–49,999	8.9
	50,000–99,999	2.2
	More than 100 000	0

Source Authors, based on own research (2022)

Through our questionnaire, we mapped municipalities' opinions about the level of cost coverage and the extent to which municipalities know the costs for the two chosen delegated competences: the registry and planning and building authority. Tables 9.5 and 9.6 present the results.

Regarding RQ1, Tables 9.5 and 9.6 show the wildly varying intervals of the estimates of the cost coverage rate for the performance of two selected delegated competences (last columns). In one case, the municipality claimed that only 1% of costs are covered, while the other extreme is the opinion that 100% are covered.

Regarding RQ2, the tables show that the approaches to cost calculations differ and that some municipalities do not try to calculate the costs. Only in a very few cases could the municipalities understand that the full costs consist of personnel costs, i.e. expenditure on salaries and deductions of employees performing the delegated exercise of the state administration in building regulations, material and service costs, possible capital costs, and overheads. In many smaller municipalities, the employees are responsible for more delegated responsibilities, and these municipalities cannot define the personnel costs separately. Many municipalities feel that

Table 9.5 Costs for delegated competences in the registry offices

Method of exercising competence		*Municipality knows the exact costs*		*Method of calculation*			*Cost recovery rate*
Separately	*Joint office*	*yes*	*no*	*None*	*Calculates direct costs*	*Calculates/ knows the full costs*	*%*
Municipalities up to 999 inhabitants							
1	13	5	20	22	3	0	1–100
Municipalities from 1,000 to 2,499 inhabitants							
18	0	10	8	13	4	1	10–100
Municipalities from 2,500 to 4,999 inhabitants							
10	0	9	1	7	2	1	11–95
Municipalities from 5,000 to 9,999 inhabitants							
6	0	5	1	3	2	1	45–90
Municipalities from 10,000 to 49,999 inhabitants							
6	0	4	2	5	1	0	50–80
Municipalities with over 50,000 inhabitants							
1	0	1	0	0	0	1	95

Source Authors, based on own research (2022)

Table 9.6 Costs for delegated competences in the section of the construction administration

Method of exercising competence		*Municipality knows the exact costs*		*Method of calculation*			*Cost recovery rate*
Separately	*Joint office*	*yes*	*no*	*Separately*	*Joint office*	*yes*	*no*
Municipalities up to 999 inhabitants							
14	11	10	15	15	1	2	1–80
Municipalities from 1,000 to 2,499 inhabitants							
12	6	5	13	17	0	1	2–80
Municipalities from 2,500 to 4,999 inhabitants							
5	5	4	6	10	0	0	18–80
Municipalities from 5,000 to 9,999 inhabitants							
5	1	3	3	5	0	1	3–80
Municipalities from 10,000 to 49,999 inhabitants							
4	2	5	1	2	2	2	25–85
Municipalities with over 50,000 inhabitants							
1	0	1	0	0	0	1	75

Source Authors, based on own research (2022)

it is inefficient and uneconomic for the staff to keep track of the timesheet and allocate attendance according to the areas carried out. When a joint service model is used, municipalities pay a fee to cover the costs of such office, according to the population size—in this case, the direct costs are well visible.

The results from our analysis document two basic facts:

1. municipalities mostly do not know (and many of them probably do not even need to know) the total amount of the costs of delegated competences, and.
2. the state finances only part of the costs incurred by municipalities in exercising delegated competences.

We expected such results. With municipalities' excessive territorial fragmentation and non-existent cost accounting, which would be needed to allocate overheads to specific activities, knowing the costs is impossible (e.g. Oplotnik et al., 2012). However, such a minimal capacity (and willingness) to calculate exact costs, even among larger municipalities, was surprising. Regarding the cost coverage levels, we came to the same conclusion as similar studies (e.g. Alibegović et al., 2013). However, again, the excessive and unrealistic dispersion of municipalities' opinions on the level of coverage of the costs of delegated competences, which includes extremely high and extremely low values, was surprising.

9.3.2 *Case Study 2: Transfers and Vertical Fiscal Imbalance (RQ3)*

The theory of fiscal federalism suggests that transfers can be used as equalisation mechanisms to compensate municipalities for lower revenue base and/or higher expenditure needs (Bird, 1999; Brennan & Buchanan, 1980; Dollery, 2002; Meloni, 2016; Musgrave, 1959; Oates, 1972; Tanzi, 2000; Tiebout, 1956, and many other) and to assure that municipalities can deliver all expected tasks. To calculate the vertical fiscal imbalance levels, we analysed the data on revenues of Slovak local governments in 2021 provided by the DataCentre of the Slovak Republic based on cooperation with academia.

Inspired by the research studies by Meloni (2016) and Jia et al. (2020), we use the following method in this paper to calculate the measure of vertical fiscal imbalance (Ebel & Yilmaz, 2002):

$$VFI = \frac{TR}{R} \tag{9.1}$$

The left part of the formula presents the vertical fiscal imbalance as the share of transfers in total revenue. Using a transfer dependency indicator, the ratio of transfers to total revenue, we analyse the vertical fiscal imbalance in individual local governments in the Slovak Republic in 2021 (RQ3—What is the actual mismatch between revenue and expenditure for the exercise of devolved competences [vertical fiscal imbalance]).

Table 9.7 shows the average vertical fiscal imbalance rate values for individual municipalities in self-governing regions. Vertical fiscal imbalance was calculated for every municipality in the region, and the value in the table is the average for all municipalities in the region. We have evaluated the vertical fiscal imbalance in 2,911 municipalities allocated in eight regions. The values of the monitored indicator's maxima and minima indicate a significant variability of the vertical fiscal imbalance rate among individual municipalities within the self-governing regions.

Table 9.7 Summary of the issue of vertical fiscal imbalance of local governments in the conditions of self-governing regions of the Slovak Republic in 2021

Region	*Number of evaluated municipalities*	*Mean in %*	*Standard deviation*	*Median in %*	*Maximum in %*	*Minimum in %*	*Registered unemployment rate in %*	*Number of inhabitants*
Bratislava region	87	22.03	17.94	22.12	91.61	0.14	4.38	1,043 700
Trnava region	250	25.49	17.50	20.88	89.05	2.79	4.16	564,826
Trenčín region	275	25.72	19.86	20.53	99.75	0.45	4.26	575,459
Nitra region	350	28.13	22.43	22.22	99.77	1.27	4.80	675,811
Banská Bystrica region	513	25.47	23.54	17.73	99.97	1.01	9.01	625,221
Žilina region	312	26.30	22.52	23.28	99.62	0.50	5.32	689,893
Prešov region	663	31.88	30.75	19.76	99.95	0.99	10.75	808,482
Košice region	461	26.48	27.69	15.87	99.99	0.50	9.98	1,020,393

Source Authors, based on own research (2022)

Based on Table 9.7, we can identify the Prešov region as the region with the highest average rate of vertical fiscal imbalance, which is at 31.88%, with a standard deviation of 30.75%. We also observe that for about half of the local governments in the Prešov region, the vertical fiscal imbalance rate is 19.76%. The relatively high average vertical fiscal imbalance of the Prešov region is the highest among other local government regions, resulting from a combination of several factors. An important factor in revenue generation is the population's unemployment. The registered unemployment rate in the Prešov region territory is 10.75%, which is the highest value among the self-governing regions of the Slovak Republic. Another important factor influencing the vertical fiscal imbalance is the region's population, which is much smaller than the Košice or Bratislava regions, i.e. the municipalities get less money from the government as the transfers are calculated based on the number of inhabitants.

On the other hand, the Bratislava region has the lowest average vertical fiscal imbalance rate, at 22.03%, with a standard deviation of 17.94%. Approximately half of the local governments in the Bratislava region have a vertical fiscal imbalance rate of 22.12%. The rate of vertical fiscal imbalance of the Bratislava region is closely linked to demography in terms of the region's population, which is the largest among other municipal regions and is also strongly determined by the situation in the labour market. This can be considered relatively good—expressed in the form of the rate of registered unemployment, which, as of 2021, is 4.38% in the Bratislava region, i.e. one of the lower values compared to other regions of the Slovak Republic.

The vertical fiscal imbalance in the conditions of local governments of the Slovak Republic for 2021 is, on average, 27.42%, while the standard deviation is 25.06%. We consider the main reasons determining the different levels of vertical fiscal imbalance rates for individual local governments in the Slovak Republic to be a combination of economic and non-economic factors, and we agree with the idea of Mederly et al. (2019) that each local government has a unique combination of factors affecting its vertical fiscal imbalance rate.

Drawing on the research study by Aldasoro and Seiferling (2014), we also find that a significant factor is the demographics of a given local government, in particular, the size of the population and its age structure in terms of the representation of the working-age population and the population over 65 years of age, which significantly determines the amount of own-source revenues of a given local government. In addition to demographics, the overall characteristics of the local government, such as its geographical location, tourism opportunities, the management of the local government in the person of the mayor or mayoress, unemployment, and various other economic and non-economic indicators, play an important role in the vertical fiscal imbalance.

The obvious conclusion is that the well-known factors causing fiscal imbalances are insufficiently reflected by the existing transfer system, as too significant differences between municipalities are clearly documented.

9.4 Conclusions

The chapter explored how the mechanisms associated with intergovernmental transfers work in the Slovak intergovernmental fiscal system and their impact on local democracy and autonomy.

Slovak municipalities spent approximately 7% of the country's GDP, meaning that Slovakia remains a centralised country from the perspective of local government spending. Its tax revenues still represent only a tiny share of municipal financial resources—indeed, among the lowest in the OECD—while its share of central government transfers is among the highest of OECD countries (for more, see, for example, Plaček et al., 2020). The share of central government transfers in municipal budget revenues is somewhat high and seems to be increasing (almost 20% in 2015 and more than 26% by 2023).

The first case documented that the state (with a maximum probability) does not cover the full costs of executing delegated responsibilities. The under-financing impacts local democracy, as municipalities need to reallocate their resources to pay for services delivered on behalf and for the state. What is surprising is the fact that neither actor (the state nor the municipalities) shows genuine interest in knowing the actual situation. Maybe it is not a surprise at the state level, which can use "unpaid" money for other purposes, but surprising at the municipal level.

The second case documents that Slovak local governments, which depend on transfer payments from the state budget, as transfers account, on average, for almost one-third of the total revenues of individual local governments, are very unequal from the point of vertical imbalance calculations. The degree of vertical fiscal imbalance varies considerably across local governments in the Slovak Republic, as it results from a combination of several economic and non-economic factors specific to a given local government and insufficient capacity of the transfer system to deliver its equalisation function. Too high financial inequalities between municipalities undoubtedly negatively influence local democracy in Slovakia.

Both investigated aspects have been known for a long time; however, the indicated malfunctioning aspects were and are still not addressed. Neither is a concrete action nor a prospective reform proposal.

Acknowledgements The preparation of this chapter was co-supported by the grant project VEGA 1/0003/24 Inter-municipal cooperation in providing local public services.

Annex: Country Profile: Slovakia

See Table 9.8.

The local self-government autonomy in Slovakia can be considered partly formal. Local governments have the right to decide which tasks (residual competences) they will handle unless these have been assigned to other levels of government.

From the perspective of local self-government's freedom to decide on its political organisation and electoral system, local self-government in Slovakia enjoys extensive organisational autonomy. Mayors and local councillors are directly elected. In organising local elections, local authorities have considerable discretion in certain areas, such as multi-mandate

Table 9.8 Municipal political power structures

Criteria	*Results*
The level of autonomy of municipal governments over their functional mandates: the question of whether municipal governance institutions can only perform mandated tasks or can choose from a predefined scope of tasks Indicator: yes, partly, no	Yes
The level of freedom of municipal governments to decide their own political organisation and electoral system (can they, for example, determine their own electoral districts, number of seats, electoral system, etc.) Indicator: yes, partly, no	Yes
The constitutional or legal mechanisms to assert the autonomy of municipal governments. Examples of specific constitutional or legal mechanisms that allow municipal governments to assert their autonomy include (a) constitutional clauses or other statutory regulations protecting local self-government; (b) recourse to the judicial system through constitutional courts to settle disputes with higher authorities; or (c) other constitutional or legal protections of municipal autonomy exist (e.g. higher-level governments are prevented from forcing municipal governments to merge) Indicator: yes, partly, no	Yes
Municipal governments' right to use the legal system against higher-level government (de jure and de facto—do they use such right?) Indicator yes (both de jure and de facto), partly, no	Yes
The level to which decisions made by municipal governance institutions are subject to administrative supervision for their responsibilities and if higher-level approval is needed to act in their own matters Indicator yes, no	No
Does the higher-level have the right to remove local executives [or other local officials] without judicial intervention? Indicator yes, no	No

Source Authors, based on own research (2025)

constituencies and the proportional system, within the limits set by legislation, including the recommended size of constituencies.

In Slovakia, there are legal mechanisms that enforce local autonomy. With the establishment of the Constitution of the Slovak Republic (Act No. 460/1992 Coll.) in 1993, the constitutional foundation of local self-government was strengthened. For example, Article 67(3) in Title Four of the Constitution states, "The State may interfere in the activities of a municipality and a higher territorial unit only in the manner provided by law". Decisions of local governments can be protected in courts, including the Constitutional Court, and may be challenged by the prosecutor's office.

Regarding the criterion of the right of lower territorial units to use the legal system against higher territorial units (de jure and de facto), it should be noted that since the establishment of local governments in 1990 by Act No. 369/1990, Coll., the Act on Municipal Establishment, direct supervision by state institutions or public administration has been minimal. Administrative supervision is primarily concerned with ensuring compliance with the law and cannot suspend a decision; only a court has that authority.

In Slovakia, decisions made by sub-national institutions are not subject to administrative oversight and do not require approval from a higher level. Local governments have total decision-making freedom. They can, for example, determine their "organisational structure, number of employees, remuneration, delegation of tasks, and subordination issues".

Higher authorities cannot remove local or other officials in Slovakia. One way to recall a mayor is by involving the municipality's inhabitants, who can express their dissatisfaction with the mayor's actions through a local referendum. Organising a petition allows Residents to initiate a local referendum (Act No. 369/1990 Coll., Section 11a, paragraph 1). According to Sect. 11a, the municipal council must call a local referendum on the mayor's recall if at least 30% of eligible voters sign the petition.

Act No. 180/2014 determines municipal councillors' election. According to Act No. 180/2014 on the conditions for exercising the right to vote and amending and supplementing certain acts, a municipality resident with permanent residence has the right to vote for municipal self-government bodies Section (Section 163). Residents with permanent residence in the municipality where they are standing for election and who have attained the age of 18 by election day may be elected as a member of a municipal council or district (Section 164). Residents with permanent residence in the municipality where they are standing for election and who have attained the age of 25 by election day may be elected as mayor of the municipality (Section 165). Local governments have the right to decide on the organisation of local elections, subject to specific principles (e.g. multi-member constituencies, proportional system) and limits set by legislation (e.g. recommended size of electoral districts). They can set the number of councillors according to local/city council decisions within the "ranges" defined in legislation and delimit electoral districts based on the number of councillors. This early post-socialist tradition has not been changed by the new legislation that consolidated electoral rights and rules in Slovakia (Act No. 180/2014). Mayors of municipalities are elected by direct suffrage. Voters cast their votes for individual candidates, and the candidate with the most votes wins. A second round of elections is held if no candidate obtains an absolute majority (over 50%) of the votes. Councillors are elected using a majority system. In smaller municipalities, there is often a single-constituency system where each voter can vote for as many candidates as there are seats. In larger towns, the town may be divided into multiple constituencies (Table 9.9).

At the local and regional government levels, the mandate of municipal councillors is four years.

Table 9.9 Structure and quality of municipal electoral systems

Criteria	*Results*
How are municipal councillors elected? Indicator—election mode	Direct election, Majority Electoral Systems
For what term are municipal councils elected (years)? Indicator—years of mandate	4
What is the level of citizen participation in municipal elections? Indicator: Low—("Normal") voter turnout is below 35% of eligible (registered) voters Average—Voter turnout is between 35 and 60% of eligible (registered) voters High—Voter turnout is over 60% of eligible (registered) voters	Average

Source Authors, based on own research (2025)

The level of citizen participation in municipal elections: The highest voter turnout in local elections was 1990 63.75%. Since then, voter turnout has generally oscillated around 50%, but it is important to clarify that it has not always been precisely around that figure. For example, the turnout in the last municipal election in 2022 was 46.19% (Table 9.10).

In Slovakia, party candidates for municipal council elections, which include regional (self-governing regions) and municipal (local) elections, are generally selected through internal party processes. In the case of an independent candidate, the process is self-nomination. The candidate does not rely on a political party to select or nominate them. Instead, they independently decide to run for office and must meet certain legal requirements, such as gathering a specified number of signatures from voters to qualify for the election.

Act No. 181/2014 Coll. regulates the financing of municipal political campaigns, with Section 6 addressing the financing of independent candidates and Section 7 addressing the financing of candidates from political parties.

The ruling national party in Slovakia does not necessarily have a dominant position in municipal elections. While the national ruling party can have a strong influence due to its resources, visibility, and political power, municipal elections often reflect local dynamics and issues, leading to

Table 9.10 Nature of municipal political party Systems

Criteria	*Results*
Which subjects can run in municipal elections? Indicator—define who can participate	Political parties and movements, coalitions of political parties, independent candidates, group of independent candidates
How are party candidates for municipal council elections selected? Indicator—selected by party, elected by party, self-nomination, other	Selected by party, self-nomination
Are there established rules for financing municipal political campaigns? Indicator—yes, no	Yes
Does the ruling national party have a dominant position in municipal elections? Indicator—yes, no	No

Source Authors, based on own research (2025)

Table 9.11 Municipal political participation and Accountability

Criteria	*Results*
Are all council meetings (required to be) open to the public? Indicator—yes, no	Yes
Are municipal records and documents (required to be) available to the public? Indicator—yes, no	Yes
Is the council (required to) engage in an open, participatory planning process? Indicator—yes, no	No
Are alternative participatory mechanisms, such as referendums or participatory budgeting, used? Indicator—yes, partly, no	Partly

Source Authors, based on own research (2025)

different outcomes. During the last municipal elections held in 2022, the ruling party, OĽaNO (Ordinary People and Independent Personalities), won less than 1% of the mayoral seats, while independent candidates won 46.45%, and HLAS—Social Democracy, a newly formed political party, won 9.09% of the mayoral seats.

Act No. 369 Coll. on the municipal system states that the municipal council's deliberations are, in principle, open to the public. However, the council must always declare a deliberation closed to the public if the subject involves information or matters protected under special laws (Table 9.11).

The municipality's obligation to publish information primarily arises from Act No. 211/2000 Coll. on free access to information and on the amendment and supplementation of certain acts (Act on Freedom of Information), as amended.

Slovak legislation does not explicitly grant citizens, civic associations, or non-profit organisations the right to participate in the development of participatory budgeting. However, it also does not exclude the possibility of such cooperation.

References

Aldasoro, I., & Seiferling, M. (2014). Vertical fiscal imbalances and the accumulation of government debt. *International Monetary Fund Working Papers, 14*(209). https://doi.org/10.5089/9781498338051.001.

Alibegović, D. J., Slijepčević, S., & Vila, Z. K. (2013). Can local governments in Croatia cope with more responsibilities? *Lex Localis, 11*(3), 471–495.

Bird, R. M. (1999). *Fiscal federalism*. Urban Institute Press.

Brennan, G., & Buchanan, J. M. (1980). *The power to tax: Analytic foundations of a fiscal constitution*. Cambridge University Press.

Dollery, B. E. (2002). *Fiscal decentralization and public sector reforms in developing countries*. Cambridge University Press.

Ebel, R. D., & Yilmaz, S. (2002). *On the measurement and impact of fiscal decentralization* (Policy Research Working Paper No. 2809). The World Bank. https://documents1.worldbank.org/curated/pt/309771468764353136/pdf/multi0page.pdf

INESS. (2024a). *Price of the state: How much public sector collects?* Cenastatu.sk. https://www.cenastatu.sk/kv-d-dvv-p/2023/dn/. Accessed November 12, 2024.

INESS. (2024b). *Price of the state: How much public sector spends?* Price of the State. http://www.priceofthestate.org/km-sr-vm/2017/dn/. Accessed November 12, 2024.

Jia, J., Liu, Y., Martinez-Vazquez, J., & Zhang, K. (2020). *Vertical fiscal imbalance and local fiscal indiscipline: Empirical evidence from China*. International Center for Public Policy (Working paper 20–06, p. 75). https://icepp.gsu.edu/files/2020/04/paper2006.pdf

Mederly, P., Krajčír, Z., Sládečková, J., Pilát, E., Plai, Ľ., Čerňanská, J., Marušinec, J., Lenčéšová, S., Ubreži, T., Pipišková, I., & Brennerová, R. (2019). *Výkon a financovanie prenesených kompetencií*. ZMOS. https://npmodmus.zmos.sk/download_file_f.php?id=1193191. Accessed November 14, 2024.

Meloni, O. (2016). Electoral opportunism and vertical fiscal imbalance. *Journal of Applied Economics, 19*(1), 145–167.

Musgrave, R. A. (1959). *The theory of public finance: A study in public economy*. McGraw-Hill.

Oates, W. E. (1972). *Fiscal federalism* (1st ed.). Edward Elgar.

Open Data. (2024). *Slovak open data portal*. https://data.slovensko.sk/

Oplotnik, Ž. J., Brezovnik, B., & Vojinović, B. (2012). Local self-government financing and costs of municipality in Slovenia. *Transylvanian Review of Administrative Sciences* [special issue], *8*(37), 128–142.

Plaček, M., Ochrana, F., Půček, M. J., & Nemec, J. (2020). *Fiscal decentralization reforms: The impact on the efficiency of local governments in Central and Eastern Europe* (Vol. 19). Springer Nature.

Tanzi, V. (2000). *Policies, institutions and the dark side of economics*. Edward Elgar.

Tiebout, C. M. (1956). A pure theory of local expenditures. *Journal of Political Economy, 64*(5), 416–424.

CHAPTER 10

South Africa

Ajiv Maharaj and Purshottama Sivanarain Reddy

10.1 Introduction

South Africa forms the southern basin of Africa, with a roughly V-shaped coastline which stretches for about 2,798 kilometres. The east coast of the country fronts onto the warm Indian Ocean, while the west coast fronts onto the colder South Atlantic Ocean, with the two oceans meeting at the southernmost tip of Africa known as Cape Agulhas. In addition, just outside the boundaries of the country are eSwatini (Swaziland) and Lesotho, two landlocked independent states (Republic of South Africa, 2022). South Africa is home to a population of 60.8 million people, with about 41 million (67%) living in urban areas. The urban landscape of South Africa can be divided into three primary urban regions. The largest urban agglomeration is in Gauteng Province, which is largely a continuous urban settlement consisting of three metropoles, namely Tshwane

A. Maharaj
University of KwaZulu-Natal, Durban, South Africa
e-mail: Ajiv.Maharaj@durban.gov.za

P. Sivanarain Reddy (✉)
University of Kwa Zulu-Natal, Durban, South Africa
e-mail: Reddyp1@ukzn.ac.za

J. Nemec et al. (eds.), *Local Government and Fiscal Transfers*,
Governance and Public Management,
https://doi.org/10.1007/978-3-031-95674-4_10

(formerly Pretoria), Ekurhuleni (formerly East Rand), and Johannesburg. This major urban agglomeration has a combined populace of almost 15 million people, as per the 2022 National Census (Statistics South Africa, 2023). In addition, it is by far the most dominant economic region of the country, accounting for 34% of the national economy, while only making up 1.4% of the land area. The second and third economic areas are equivalent to each other in terms of size, and consist of the Durban-Pietermaritzburg region, which makes up almost 13% of the national economy, and Cape Town, which accounts for approximately 11–12%. Additionally, there are three metropolitan cities which are much smaller than those highlighted above. Collectively, the metropolitan areas account for less than 5% of the whole surface area of the country, but constitute more than 60% of the economy.

South Africa is a republic which can be described as a constitutional democracy, following its first democratic election on 27 April 1994, and the adoption of the Constitution on 8 May 1996, amended thereafter on 11 October 1996. The Constitution (1996) signifies the highest law of the country, and no state action or law can surpass the constitutional provisions. Internationally, the South African Constitution has been highly acclaimed and is viewed as very advanced.

The Constitution (Clause 40.1) makes provision for three governmental levels—national, provincial, and local—which are distinctive, interdependent, and interrelated. Constitutional provision has been made for an independent judiciary, and intergovernmental relations and co-operative government principles have been detailed in Clause 41. This denotes that the three governmental levels and associated organs of state at all levels must factor in the powers, functions, and governmental institutions in the other spheres within their all-encompassing constitutional status. Each sphere has legislative/executive/legislative authority pertaining to the powers/functions attributed to the respective spheres. Additionally, the governmental levels must discharge their functions and exercise their powers such that they do not impinge on the institutional, functional, and geographical integrity of another sphere, and more importantly, must co-operate in good faith and mutual trust (Republic of South Africa, 1996).

Clause 151 of the Constitution defines the local government as comprising municipalities, covering the entire country. Municipal executive and legislative powers are devolved in a municipality's municipal council, which subject to national and provincial legislation, and on its own initiative, has the right to govern the local government affairs of the local citizenry. However, constitutionally, the provincial and national governments may not hinder or compromise a municipality's capacity or right to perform its functions or exercise its powers. Local government is tasked with providing accountable and democratic government for local communities, ensuring sustainable service provision to communities; promoting socio-economic development, a healthy, safe environment, and community involvement in matters of local government.

Clause 155 of the Constitution lists three distinct groups of municipalities:

a. Category A: A municipality that has exclusive municipal executive and legislative authority in its area.
b. Category B: A municipality that shares municipal executive and legislative authority in its area with a category C municipality within whose area it falls.
c. Category C: A municipality that has municipal executive and legislative authority in an area that includes more than one municipality.

10.2 Fiscal Federalism

Chapter 13 of the Constitution lays the basis for the government's financial system and establishes the National Revenue Fund. Clause 215 indicates that the national, provincial, and municipal budgets and the resultant budgetary processes must enhance transparency, political accountability, and the financial management of debt efficaciously, as well as the economy and the public sector generally. Provision has been made in the Chapter for revenue raised nationally, provincially, and locally and for the equitable division of revenue nationally, and constitutes the foundation of Division of Revenue Act (DORA) (2003), which guarantees predictability, certainty, and transparency. This Act empowers municipalities to budget efficaciously and engage in a system of three-year budgeting. In terms of this Act, information is provided on municipal grants and allocations on a three-year basis. Other requisite information serves as the basis for individual transfer programmes and strategic contexts for the co-ordination of other several transfers (Sections 11 and 13).

10.2.1 Local Government Revenues

Figure 10.1 illustrates the revenue sources for South African local governments from 2015 to 2024 (1 Rands–5 EUR). The three primary revenue sources are grants and subsidies; local tax; and local fees. This data highlights the growing reliance on grants and local fees, which reflects challenges in municipalities' financial self-sufficiency and collection rates, due to factors like affordability and changes in consumption patterns (Republic of South Africa, National Treasury, 2023a, 2023b, 2023c).

In terms of the Local Government: Municipal Systems Act (Act 32 of 2000), municipalities are allowed to levy property rates as a form of property tax (Republic of South Africa, 2000a). Municipalities levy property rates based on the value of immovable properties within their jurisdiction. Municipal rates are a substantial revenue source, and are calculated on the municipal valuation of properties, as determined by national law, other taxes, and levies/duties apposite to local government or relevant municipal category and jurisdiction. However, municipalities cannot impose other taxes such as income tax, general sales, customs duty, or value-added tax. Municipalities can charge a fee for services provided to residents and businesses which include inter alia electricity, waste removal, sanitation, and water supply. The rates for these services are often structured to

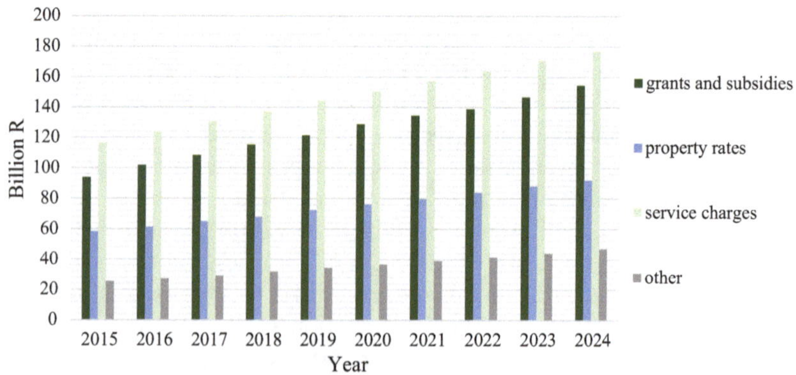

Fig. 10.1 Local government revenues (*Source* Authors, based on data from National Treasury, Republic of South Africa [2024])

cover the costs of providing and maintaining the services. Municipalities are allowed to generate funding through interest on investments, and trading entities. Municipalities are also encouraged to explore alternative revenue sources to reduce dependence on traditional taxes and charges. This may include revenue generated from municipal entities, investments, or other commercial activities. Municipalities can also apply for loans for capital or current expenditure; however, loans for the former can only be raised for bridging purposes in any particular year when required.

The governmental system in South Africa has entrusted municipalities with the responsibility of rudimentary service provision such as water and sanitation, waste management, electricity, local roads, and management of traffic. While some of these functions can be operated on a commercial basis and bring a return in the form of revenue for services provided, others, such as roads, parks, and traffic, are public goods which do not provide a direct revenue. However, municipalities are required to manage their finances prudently to ensure long-term sustainability, which includes effective financial planning, expenditure control, and debt management. The legal framework for municipalities to generate revenue is detailed in the Local Government: Municipal Systems Act (Act 32 of 2000). It outlines the principles and mechanisms for revenue collection, including property rates, service charges, and fees for municipal services.

In terms of budgets and financial planning, municipalities are required to prepare annual budgets, outlining their revenue projections and expenditure plans. The budgeting process involves public participation to ensure transparency and accountability details. The accounting principles and framework for the management of municipal finances are detailed in the Public Finance Management Act 1 of 1999. The Act promotes sound public financial management by developing guidelines for the utilisation and allocation of public funds, in the broader context of accountability and transparency.

10.2.2 Local Government Expenditure

Figure 10.2 illustrates the total local government expenditure from the 2019/20 to 2023/24 financial years, as contained in the National Treasury Local Government Expenditure Budget Reviews for 2023/24. While there was a steady growth in the overall financial expenditure by local governments between 2019/20 and 2022/23, local government expenditure decreased in 2023/24. It is further evident that operating expenditure has grown significantly more than capital expenditure. Capital expenditure represents the investment of local governments into infrastructure and fixed assets, while operating expenditure represents spending on salaries and wages, bulk purchases (water and electricity), and operations. The current pattern of expenditure underlies the persistent service delivery challenges faced by many cities and towns in the country.

The aggregate spending at the end of the 2023/24 financial year (30 June 2024) was 90.5%, or R562.2 billion of the total adjusted expenditure budget of R621.4 billion. Aggregated local fees and other revenue were 93.2% or R574.6 billion of the total adjusted revenue budget of R616.9 billion. Capital expenditure was R60.7 billion or 77.2% of the adjusted capital budget of R78.6 billion. The adjusted operating expenditure budget was R542.7 billion, of which R501.5 billion, or 92.4%, was spent by 30 June 2024.

However, in 2023/24 financial year, 63% of the total local government expenditure was incurred in the eight metro cities, while a further 16.7% was incurred in the secondary cities, leaving just 21.3% being spent in

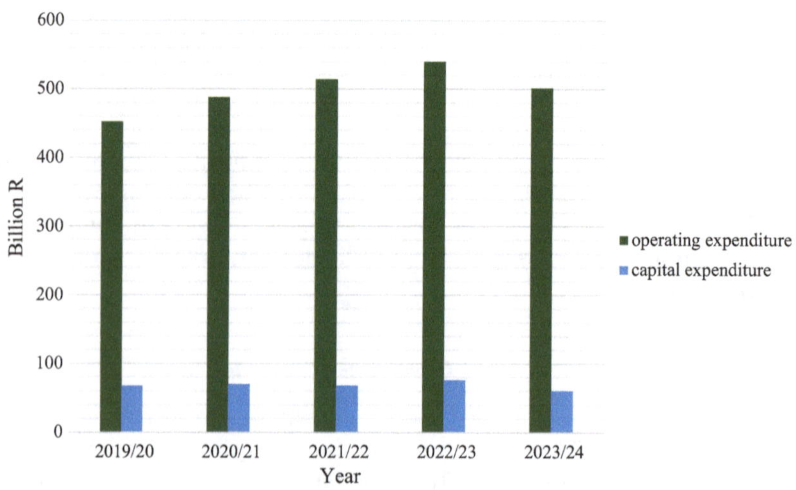

Fig. 10.2 Local government expenditure (*Source* Authors, based on data from National Treasury, Republic of South Africa [2024])

all other local governments in the country. In addition, 59.7% of capital expenditure occurred in the eight metro cities while a further 25.4% was spent in secondary cities, leaving just 14.9% having been spent in all other local governments in the country. As is evident from expenditure patterns, the metro cities and secondary cities account for the overwhelming majority of expenditure. However, despite this, there is little differentiation in the approach towards these cities in terms of their powers and functions.

10.2.3 Transfers to Local Government

Two core transfers are used to co-finance local governments in South Africa—the "equitable share" (non-conditional grant) and the "conditional grant". Through DORA, municipalities receive funding which is tabled in parliament annually along with the Minister of Finance's Budget Speech. Since its first publication in 2003, the local government's equitable share has remained relatively unchanged at 9% of the national budget. It is worth bearing in mind that an "equitable" share does not mean an "equal" share of the national budget, as the share of the budget is relative to the mandate being delivered as well as other powers and functions in terms of raising own revenue. The equitable share formula allocates funds based on the municipality's population, financial needs, and capacity.

In addition to the equitable share, local governments receive conditional grants which are allocated for specific purposes, such as infrastructure development, healthcare, education, and other priority areas. These grants are provided with specific conditions attached, thereby guaranteeing that funds are utilised for their envisioned purposes.

10.3 Local Democracy and Transfers to Local Governments

10.3.1 Equitable Share

The main aim of the DORA Act is the equitable division of revenue, a critical aspect for a country with significant economic disparities. Constitutionally, each governmental sphere—given that it receives an equitable share of revenue raised nationally as detailed in the legislation—must provide rudimentary services and additionally discharge its roles and responsibilities as per the legislation. The equitable share is an unconditional allocation, as eloquently testified by the Act (Republic of South Africa, 2023).

The appropriateness of the allocation methodology is questionable in the extent to which it adequately considers differing socio-economic contexts and different municipalities' abilities to efficiently utilise funds. The criteria used for the distribution of funds do not adequately address the varying needs and capacities of different municipalities. Furthermore, there is limited transparency in the processes behind the allocation decisions, and public participation and scrutiny are generally limited.

Given South Africa's unequal past, the need to respond to social and service delivery challenges is paramount. However, South African local government is certainly limited in terms of both the budget and its mandate (and the commensurability between them). The share of national spending for local government has continued unchanged in the low range of between 7 and 9% of national spending. The current system of municipalities depending on local taxes and fees is becoming increasingly unsustainable nationally, and the percentage of people that cannot afford to pay the costs of municipal services is increasing (SACN, 2021). Additionally, if the municipality fails to contain its costs, the resultant effect will be severe financial unviability. The SACN (2021) adds that municipalities cannot charge rates/taxes across municipal jurisdictions uniformly, as some communities are unable to pay. This implies that the private sector and a distinct section of the population will be responsible for financing service delivery for the masses. All these specifics are not well reflected in the equitable share allocation formula; horizontal and vertical equalisation is thus imperfect via this transfer.

This poorly designed system of fiscal support, partly delivered with the idea that "local government failure is naive if not downright immoral", discourages municipalities from expanding their own revenue base, and consequently could result in greater future dependency on grants. The resultant effect will be a negative downward trajectory if the rudimentary aspects are not addressed.

Intergovernmental fiscal relations which are centralised and siloed, and a top-down planning approach, has implied that municipalities do not have a voice in the distribution of the budget nationally.

10.3.2 Conditional Grants

Regarding the conditional grants, while the aim of these provisions is to strengthen local governance capacities, in the process they also impose conditions which may become constraints that hinder local democracy and effective local service delivery. For example, the South African Cities Network (SACN, 2021) identifies that cities tend to package capital project proposals to meet grant requirements rather than based on the actual service delivery needs within the local area (SACN, 2021).

Conditional grants (or other types of transfers) also do not well reflect the specificities of South Africa's intergovernmental relations. A regulatory environment is required by co-operative governance that is appropriate and clear relative to the functions of local, provincial, and national government. It is a pre-requisite for co-operative government, as well as for efficacious execution of the varied functions in each governmental sphere, that concurrent and exclusive functions for the local or provincial governmental spheres are detailed in Schedules 4/5 of the Constitution. The distribution of powers and functions was negotiated in the early 1990s, the resultant effect of which is that certain arrangements do not seem as logical or practical as they might have done three decades ago. For example, constitutionally, provinces can assume the responsibility for municipal functions when a municipality cannot discharge its mandate. This tends to create some confusion around the issue of municipal autonomy, given the inconsistencies between well-functioning and struggling municipalities. Additionally, it is envisaged constitutionally that several powers (notably transport and housing) would transfer to be managed by well-capacitated municipalities. There has been partial devolution, and in this regard, municipalities have not been given the requisite funding, responsibilities, scope, accountability, and a clear performance framework.

The National Land Transport Act 5 of 2009 (Republic of South Africa, 2009) forms the basis for the powers and functions allocated to the various spheres of government in the transportation mandate. However, this mandate is typical of functional fragmentation, with national government responsible for national roads, provinces responsible for arterials, main roads and district level roads, and municipalities responsible for local roads (Institute for Transportation and Development Policy (ITDP), 2021). Moreover, as towns and cities have grown and boundaries of municipalities have expanded, many of these main roads have become routes that only service the local municipal area and hence should have been reclassified and allocated to municipalities to manage. Instead, due to the budget tied to a road (fixed asset), provincial government has neglected to hand over such assets to local government. The result is that towns and cities have become a maze of roads which are managed by different entities, each with their own norms and standards of development and maintenance. In towns, roads managed by local municipalities are typically better maintained, as provinces spread their resources over a vast area and focus on more rural and under-resourced areas.

The White Paper on Transport Policy (1996), responsible for the review of transport policy, identified the breakdown of responsibility and authority as a critical weakness in the country's transport infrastructure. Provision was made for the creation of integrated transport authorities through the National Land Transport Act 22 of 2000, which was later repealed. These transport authorities provided for the integration of transport functions at local level, where municipalities were sufficiently capacitated to taken on this function. Shortly thereafter, in 2004, the country's first integrated transport authority was promulgated and launched in the eThekwini Metropolitan Municipality. Despite this, twenty years later the provincial and national departments have not delegated the respective functions to the municipality, and the transport authority exists only in name.

The Constitution provides for local government to ensure an environment which is safe and healthy. However, the functions of policing and healthcare are assigned to provincial government, with policy and oversight at a national level. Therefore, local government does not receive any funding from tax collection for these functions. In addition, functions relating to social services such as homelessness, substance abuse, and care for the vulnerable are deemed to be provincial and national functions. Functions such as primary and secondary education, skills development, housing and human settlements, art, culture, heritage, environmental authorisation, libraries, and early childhood development are all functions that are placed at the provincial sphere with no funding provided to local governments for such functions, which are typically local in nature.

While a municipality does not receive funding for issues such as homelessness or social housing, the reality of local democracy necessitates that local government intervene in such issues due to its profound impact in the local space. This has led to the term "unfunded mandates" in local municipal colloquia. Financial officers in local government are often averse to municipalities taking on unfunded mandates, while politicians, civil society, and more progressive municipal officers work to address such issues through bringing them to the attention of the appropriate governmental sphere, as well as, in many instances, through direct intervention. Provincial and national spheres are further removed from local communities and hence are less responsive to the dynamics and challenges that occur on the ground, while local democracy demands a direct response that is more closely linked to their reality.

Moreover, despite the wide array of local governments, from large metropolitan cities to small hamlets and everything in-between, a "one-size-fits-all" approach to local government has been largely adopted (SACN, 2021). This *relates to the legislative, policy, and fiscal environments, which have remained either unresponsive to the great differences in the capacities of local governments, or where provisions do exist for the graduation of municipalities to assume greater functions but remain unimplemented.

10.3.3 Policy Recommendations

Transport authorities that are duly established or equivalently coordinated structures, at municipal, provincial, mega-city, or city-region levels, should be vested with the requisite powers, functions, and resources for coordinating public transport across modes, and in planning, implementing, and monitoring public transport to ensure efficient application of subsidies and addressing public transport needs. This chapter underscores the importance of coordinated planning, capacity building, and the integration of transportation modes within municipalities, so as to enhance public transport services, address urban sprawl, and ensure sustainable development.

Local government powers and functions must be reviewed to enhance service delivery and public accountability in local communities. Local governments are often overlooked in key legislation, and this should be corrected through the review process. The role of local government should be central in addressing issues such as housing, homelessness, and transport. Along with the devolution of authority should come the appropriate resources for the execution of such functions.

The division of revenue between the different governmental spheres and state-owned entities needs to be reviewed to ensure that greater resource allocation is provided to local government, which is at the coalface in terms of interacting with local communities.

Local government does not help its own cause when there are negative findings by the Auditor General (2022) and when municipalities are in financial distress. Therefore, the allocation of municipal powers and functions is based on the good standing and capacity of the respective municipality. However, where such municipalities have a demonstrated capacity to assume such functions, they should be empowered to deliver on their mandate, and foster local democracy.

A differentiated approach to local government should be embraced at the provincial/national governmental spheres structured on the priorities of the specific municipality and their respective capacities and track record.

Amid the local and other governmental spheres, intergovernmental relations should be structured along specific goals and key performance indicators, with a regular independent evaluation of the outcomes. Addressing structural challenges and high-profile initiatives should be the structural cornerstone of intergovernmental relations, to ensure that results are achieved.

10.4 Conclusion

The South African Constitution's vision of a flourishing local democracy remains largely unrealised as the national and provincial governmental spheres have largely retained the functions and powers that are better served at local level. This has been coupled with a chronic underfunding of local government, which has assumed by far the smallest proportion of the national fiscus. The policy and legislative context of local government is generally defined by provincial and national government, and local government remains the stepchild in the family of government. To fulfil the ideal of a flourishing local democracy, local government requires better devolution of critical functions, along with support and funding to deliver on functions that are important to citizens and their communities.

Regarding fiscal decentralisation, local governments generate their own revenues but also rely heavily on the system of intergovernmental transfers. These transfers do not reflect the socio-economic realities and needs of South Africa and have different negative impacts on local democracy.

The financial health of municipalities continues to deteriorate, partly because increased economic pressures meant that consumers are not paying their bills, but also because of poor financial management. Municipalities do not explore different ways of generating their own revenue through, for instance, commercial trading. They tend to be conservative, relying heavily on taxes, fees, and transfers. Municipalities are also losing money because they are not billing and collecting revenue, are using unfair and uncompetitive procurement practices, and/or are paying for goods and services that they either do not receive or do not use. Poorly managed local government finances directly affect municipalities' capacity to discharge their constitutional mandate to their local communities, thereby putting additional pressure on a public purse which is already heavily constrained. The fact that local public financial management quality is problematic is certainly influenced also by the system of fiscal transfers, which do not motivate municipalities to perform.

Annex: Country Profile: South Africa

South Africa's Electoral System

South Africa's electoral system has undergone significant evolution, transitioning from a history of exclusion to a model that emphasises inclusivity and proportional representation. Prior to 1994, South Africa's political landscape was marred by apartheid policies that systematically disenfranchised the majority of its population. The first non-racial elections in 1994 marked a pivotal shift towards democracy, introducing a proportional representation (PR) system designed to ensure inclusivity and fairness in representation. This system was chosen to accommodate the country's diverse populace and to promote coalition-building among various political groups (Helen Suzman Foundation, 2025).

South Africa employs a closed-list proportional representation system for its National Assembly and provincial legislatures. The National Assembly comprises 400 seats, equally divided between national and regional (provincial) lists:

- National List: 200 members are elected from party lists on a nationwide basis.
- Regional Lists: The remaining 200 members are elected from party lists within each of the nine provinces, with the number of representatives per province proportional to its population.

Seats are allocated to political parties based on the percentage of votes they receive, ensuring that the composition of the legislature reflects the electorate's preferences. This method promotes a multi-party system and aims to provide equitable representation for both majority and minority groups. In response to evolving democratic needs, South Africa has undertaken reforms to its electoral system. A landmark development was the Constitutional Court's ruling in June 2020, which declared the Electoral Act unconstitutional for not allowing independent candidates to contest national and provincial elections. This led to the enactment of the Electoral Amendment Act in April 2023, permitting independent candidates to run for seats in the National Assembly and provincial legislatures. The Act also established the Electoral Reform Consultation Panel to explore further enhancements to the electoral framework (Helen Suzman Foundation, 2025).

South Africa's electoral system has been instrumental in shaping its democratic landscape, striving to balance inclusivity with effective representation. Ongoing reforms reflect a commitment to enhancing democratic processes and addressing emerging challenges. As the nation continues to evolve, its electoral system will undoubtedly play a crucial role in promoting a representative and accountable governance structure.

Local Government Electoral System

South Africa's local government electoral system operates under the framework of the Constitution of South Africa, which defines local government as a sphere of government that is distinct from national and provincial governments but is still part of the broader governance system (Municipalities.co.za, 2024). The electoral system used for local government elections is largely based on a mixed system, which blends proportional representation with ward-based representation.

Mixed-Member Proportional Representation

Local government elections in South Africa are held every five years. The system is a combination of a ward-based and proportional representation system. This means that voters cast two votes: one for a local candidate and another for a political party.

Ward-based representation: South Africa is divided into a number of electoral wards. Each ward elects a representative to the local council.

These representatives are known as ward councillors, and they are elected through a first-past-the-post voting system, meaning that the candidate with the most votes in each ward is elected.

Proportional representation: The second vote is for a political party, and this determines the proportional allocation of seats on the council. The total number of seats on the council is allocated to the political parties based on the percentage of votes they receive, ensuring a representation that aligns with the voters' preferences across the municipality. This system helps to balance the local interests of individual wards with broader party representation.

The combination of these two systems aims to achieve a balance between the advantages of direct local representation through wards and the more inclusive, broad-based representation offered by proportionality. This ensures that both geographically concentrated and widely spread political interests are fairly represented in the local government (Municipalities.co.za, 2024).

Structure of Local Government in South Africa

The Local Government Structures Act (2000) establishes the South African system of local government, which is structured into three categories, each with distinct powers and responsibilities (Republic of South Africa, 2000b):

> Category A: Metropolitan Municipalities. These municipalities are found in the largest urban areas, including cities such as Cape Town, Johannesburg, and Durban. Metropolitan municipalities have a high level of autonomy and are responsible for services in their entire urban area, including electricity, water, waste management, and housing. They are governed by a mayoral executive system, where the executive mayor is directly elected by the council.
>
> Category B: Local Municipalities. These municipalities are smaller than metropolitan municipalities and cover a more rural or mixed urban and rural area. Local municipalities are responsible for services such as roads, sanitation, and local development. Local municipalities have both ward councillors (elected through the first-past-the-post system) and proportional representation councillors. The council is headed by a mayor, who is elected by the councillors.

Category C: District Municipalities. District municipalities are responsible for coordinating services across multiple local municipalities within a specific geographic area. They provide services like water and sanitation to local municipalities that may not have the resources or infrastructure to manage these services on their own. District municipalities work closely with local municipalities to ensure service delivery and development. District municipalities are also governed by a mayor, elected by the council.

The structure of local government in South Africa allows for a division of responsibilities that balances the need for localised governance with the need for co-ordination and shared services across different municipalities. Local governments are further supported by various sector-specific departments, such as the Department of Co-operative Governance and Traditional Affairs (COGTA), which helps ensure that municipalities meet the needs of their residents.

In the hierarchical system of governance, local governments report to the Department of Co-operative Governance and Traditional Affairs (COGTA) at provincial level on operational and governance matters. In contrast, the financial reporting system is established through the National Treasury. In addition, local government also reports to provincial and national departments on a line function basis, e.g. the National Department of Water Affairs provides oversight on inter alia the municipality's water distribution services.

The lack of alignment and integration across the different spheres of government remains a challenge. There have been numerous interventions and initiatives to try to foster intergovernmental co-operation. Forums exist at various levels politically and administratively to facilitate integration. However, the approach has differed based on the department or entity pursuing this integration. National Treasury pursues a more differentiated approach based on the size and capacity of the Municipality. A city budget forum is employed for the metro cities with dedicated relationship managers, as well as support in the form of technical assistance, based on the needs of the city.

However, COGTA has pursued an undifferentiated approach for all municipalities, called the District Development Model (DDM), which has a political and an administrative component. This model has established hierarchical co-ordination forums which bring all government departments and the municipality into meetings with each other. However, despite this being in operation for four years, these forums are not established to achieve any target or mission, other than to ensure co-ordination. The result has been hugely wasteful engagements in which dozens and sometimes hundreds of government officials sit in meetings for days undertaking broad and general reporting. After years of such engagements, the model has little if anything to show for the hundreds of hours that officials have spent in meetings. These forums also have no bearing on financial transfers to local government, and hence bring little value, other than satisfying the need for mundane rhetoric around existing political matters. Within the political hierarchy, the national sphere is often treated as the most important and influential, followed by provincial and then local. Politicians at a local level, whether they be mayors of metro cities or of rural villages, are seen as the most "junior" or least influential in the hierarchy. Consequently, the model has been used as a mechanism whereby the directives of more "senior" politicians at national and provincial levels can control the narrative and directives of the more "junior" local government (Table 10.1).

This is represented by the Local Autonomy Index 2.0, where the resulting score for South Africa is 2.0, reflecting a moderate to low degree of local autonomy and indicates a reasonably strong local governance system, with a legal framework that favours autonomy and citizen participation in public management. Local authorities have the ability to make relevant decisions for their communities, although dependence on transfers from the central government and limitations on functional autonomy present challenges to be considered. These include areas that are typically local in nature such as housing/human settlements and transport, which are vested at the provincial government rather than the local.

Local authorities in South Africa are only endowed with a limited scope of functions, which relate to water and sanitation, electricity distribution, local roads, local parks and gardens, local bylaws, and local economic development. Fundamental aspects of local autonomy such as housing provision, healthcare, education, social welfare, ports and harbours, passenger and freight rail, policing, rivers and environment, agriculture, etc. are reserved for provincial and national government. Although functions in areas such as local infrastructure and local development remain with the local authority, these activities are frequently limited by specific mandates established by the national government. While there is some flexibility for local authorities to address local demands and adapt

Table 10.1 Municipal political power structures. Adapted by Author from UNIL, Université de Lausanne. (2020)

Criteria	*Results*
The level of autonomy of municipal governments over their functional mandates: the question of whether municipal governance institutions can only perform mandated tasks or can choose from a predefined scope of tasks Indicator: yes, partly, no	Partly
The level of freedom of municipal governments to decide their own political organisation and electoral system (can they, for example, determine their own electoral districts, number of seats, electoral system, etc.). Indicator: yes, partly, no	No
The constitutional or legal mechanisms to assert the autonomy of municipal governments. Examples of specific constitutional or legal mechanisms that allow municipal governments to assert their autonomy include (a) constitutional clauses or other statutory regulations protecting local self-government; (b) recourse to the judicial system through constitutional courts to settle disputes with higher authorities; or (c) other constitutional or legal protections of municipal autonomy exist (e.g. higher-level governments are prevented from forcing municipal governments to merge) Indicator: yes, partly, no	Yes, partly
Municipal governments' right to use the legal system against higher-level government (de jure and de facto—do they use such right?) Indicator yes (both de jure and de facto), partly, no	No, partly
The level to which decisions made by municipal governance institutions are subject to administrative supervision for their responsibilities and if higher-level approval is needed to act in their own matters Indicator yes, no	No, partly
Does the higher-level have the right to remove local executives [or other local officials] without judicial intervention? Indicator yes, no	Yes, partly

Source Authors, based on own research (2025)

policies to the specific needs of each region, in general, these activities are subject to national and provincial regulations, which reduces full autonomy in decision-making and policy execution. The Local Government Structures Act (117 of 1998) and the Municipal Systems Act (Act 32 of 2000) establish the framework for the transfer of powers from the national government to local authorities. The Municipal Finance Management Act (56 of 2003) spells out the financial management of local authorities in accordance with rules and processes set out by national government.

Local government does not possess the authority to decide on an electoral system or the right to determine electoral districts or voting stations. Municipalities in South Africa have a standard political structure established by national legislation, which prevents them from creating electoral districts or modifying the electoral system. Local elections are conducted through a proportional representation system, using closed party lists as well as independent candidates. The number of seats available in municipal chambers is determined based on the municipality's population, which restricts the organisational freedom of the local authorities. Legislation imposes restrictions on the creation of local electoral districts and the alteration of electoral systems, as this is undertaken at the national level. Thus, local authorities do not possess any authority in adapting their electoral processes to the particularities of their communities, which remaining strictly under the authority of national government.

In South Africa, there are legal mechanisms that enforce local autonomy. The Constitution of the Republic provides some protection to local autonomy, and ensures that municipalities have some capacity to legislate on matters of local interest, as long as they are aligned with the guidelines of the national government. Thus, the South African legal system is largely centralised with some autonomy provided to municipalities.

The right of municipal governments to use the legal system against higher-level government is limited. The Intergovernmental Relations Framework Act (13 of 2005) provides the mechanism by which local governments can challenge decisions of provincial and national government. Generally, this removes the ability of local government to use the legal system to challenge decisions by a higher sphere of government.

In South Africa, decisions made by subnational institutions are subject to administrative oversight by national and provincial government, particularly as they relate to financial and regulatory oversight. This oversight primarily occurs to ensure compliance with national laws and to guarantee the proper management of public funds, but municipal autonomy in local matters is generally respected. The Municipal Finance Management Act (56 of 2003) provides the framework and mechanism for financial management as well as oversight.

The level to which decisions made by municipal governance institutions are the subject to administrative supervision for own responsibilities and if higher-level approval is needed to act in own matters. In South Africa, higher authorities have no right to remove local officials or other officials. The removal of local elected politicians generally occurs through the parties they represent. The removal of municipal executives cannot occur without an appropriate judicial process. Any dismissal must respect legal rights and procedures, which protect local leaders from arbitrary political interventions by the central government (Table 10.2).

The election of subnational councillors: Municipal councillors are directly elected by citizens in each municipality, using a proportional representation system through closed party lists. This method ensures public participation in the selection of representatives. The electoral system is managed by the Independent Electoral Commission (IEC), which is a national body.

The years of mandate of subnational councillors at local and regional government level: The term of office for members of municipal councils and parish councils lasts for five years. This duration allows for administrative continuity that benefits medium-term planning while promoting political accountability through regular elections. The Municipal Electoral Act (27 of 2000) and Municipal Systems Act (32 of 2000) establish the five-year term for members of local government bodies, aligning with national electoral cycles. This arrangement provides a balance between stability and renewal, enabling elected officials to implement their policies and projects while ensuring that the public has the opportunity to evaluate and decide on their leadership at regular intervals. Thus, the system

Table 10.2 Structure and quality of subnational electoral systems. Adapted by Author from UNIL, Université de Lausanne. (2020)

Criteria	*Results*
How are municipal councillors elected? Indicator—election mode	Elected directly through secret ballot
For what term are municipal councils elected (years)? Indicator—years of mandate	5 years
What is the level of citizen participation in municipal elections? Indicator: Low—("Normal") voter turnout is below 35% of eligible (registered) voters Average—Voter turnout is between 35 and 60% of eligible (registered) voters High—Voter turnout is over 60% of eligible (registered) voters	Average

Source Authors, based on own research (2025)

contributes to the effectiveness of local governance and the maintenance of citizens' trust in democratic institutions.

The level of citizen participation in subnational elections: Participation in local elections in South Africa tends to be moderate, ranging between 35 and 60% of registered voters. In the 2021 local government election, 46% of registered voters participated. This was relatively low given that the registration levels were lower than the actual population eligible to vote. This level of participation is influenced by citizens' interest and engagement in local issues, which is generally lower than in national elections. However, this rate reflects a reasonable presence of society in local governance. The Constitution and Municipal Electoral Act (27 of 2000) ensures the right to vote and promotes electoral participation. These legal provisions aim to encourage active citizenship and inclusion in decisions that affect community life, recognising the importance of citizens' involvement in local democratic processes. Thus, the South African electoral system seeks to strengthen democracy and ensure that the voices of the population are heard (Table 10.3).

Which subjects can run in subnational elections? In local elections, political parties, party coalitions, and independent candidates can run, allowing for diverse competition. This diversity enables candidates from different backgrounds and perspectives to compete, promoting plural representation in municipal councils. The Municipal Electoral Act (27 of

Table 10.3 Nature of subnational political party systems. Adapted by Author from UNIL, Université de Lausanne. (2020)

Criteria	*Results*
Which subjects can run in municipal elections? Indicator—define who can participate	Political parties, movements, party coalitions, independent candidates
How are party candidates for municipal council elections selected? Indicator—selected by party, elected by party, self-nomination, other	Selected by the parties and self-proclaimed
Are there established rules for financing municipal political campaigns? Indicator—yes, no	No
Does the ruling national party have a dominant position in municipal elections? Indicator—yes, no	Yes

Source Authors, based on own research (2025)

2000) establishes the eligibility rules for parties, movements, and independent candidates in local elections. This legislation ensures that all groups and individuals have the opportunity to participate in the electoral process, contributing to a more inclusive and representative democracy. Thus, the South African electoral system strengthens political plurality, allowing the voices of different segments of society to be heard and considered in local government decisions.

In South Africa, political parties select their candidates for local councils, although there is also room for independent candidacies. This system allows parties a certain autonomy in choosing candidates while also providing opportunities for individuals who wish to participate without party affiliation.

The financing of subnational political campaigns: The Constitution of the Republic of South Africa (1996) only addresses the funding of political parties at national and provincial levels. Section 236 of the Constitution deals with the funding of political parties and provides as follows: "To enhance multi-party democracy, national legislation must provide for the funding of political parties participating in national and provincial legislatures on an equitable and proportional basis". The Constitution does not provide for the public funding of political parties represented in local government.

The ruling national party in South Africa has maintained a dominant position in subnational elections. However, with the ruling national party losing its outright majority in the last national elections, it is anticipated that it may lose a number of local authorities in the planned 2026 local government elections. Party competition in local authorities is common, allowing different parties to establish a support base in specific areas, depending on regional dynamics. There is no specific legislation favouring national parties, which contributes to a more equitable electoral environment (Republic of South Africa, Department of Communications and Information Systems, 2022). Thus, the South African political system promotes party diversity and representation at the local level, reflecting the needs and interests of the communities (Table 10.4).

Municipal council meetings are open to the public, allowing citizens to follow and observe discussions, but they are not allowed to participate in the discussions. This transparency is essential for ensuring the accountability of elected representatives and promoting trust in local government. Thus, the local democratic system is strengthened, promoting a more open and participatory governance environment.

Table 10.4 Subnational political participation and accountability. Adapted by Author from UNIL, Université de Lausanne. (2020)

Criteria	*Results*
Are all council meetings (required to be) open to the public? Indicator—yes, no	Yes
Are municipal records and documents (required to be) available to the public? Indicator—yes, no	Yes
Is the council (required to) engage in an open, participatory planning process? Indicator—yes, no	Yes
Are alternative participatory mechanisms, such as referendums or participatory budgeting, used? Indicator—yes, partly, no	Partly

Source Authors, based on own research (2025)

Municipal documents and records are available to the public, and transparency in administrative information is encouraged. This facilitates social oversight and promotes citizen participation in local decision-making. The Municipal Systems Act (32 of 2000) and the Promotion of Access to Information Act (PAIA) of 2000 establish the right to access administrative documents and regulate transparency in making local documents available to the public. This legislation ensures that citizens can access relevant information about municipal management, contributing to greater accountability of government officials and strengthening local democracy. By allowing the public to access these documents, a greater environment of trust and engagement in public administration is created.

The Municipal Systems Act (32 of 2000) requires that citizens are given the opportunity to participate in the development of Integrated Development Plans (IDP) which represent a municipality's overall five-year plan. These local plans are subject to provincial oversight.

While municipalities are required to consult citizens in the adoption of the budget, there is no provision for referendums on local matters. In some South African local authorities, mechanisms such as participatory budgets are adopted, allowing citizens to decide on the use of a portion of financial resources for local projects. However, in general, budgets are decided on by local officials and politicians, and members of the public are then consulted regarding an already prepared budget.

References

Auditor General of South Africa. (2022). *General report on local government audit outcomes MFMA 2021–22*.

Helen Suzman Foundation. (2025). *The South African electoral system*. https://hsf.org.za/publications/hsf-briefs/the-south-african-electoral-system

Institute for Transportation and Development Policy (ITDP). (2021). *Transport Journal: The role of BRT in post-pandemic South Africa*.

Municipalities.co.za. (2024). *The local government handbook, South Africa 2024: A complete guide to local government in South Africa*. Yes Media.

Republic of South Africa. (1996). *The constitution of the Republic of South Africa*. https://www.gov.za/documents/constitution

Republic of South Africa. (2000a). *Local government: Municipal systems act 32 of 2000*. Government Gazette, Cape Town.

Republic of South Africa. (2000b). *The local government: Municipal structures act 117 of 1998*. Government Gazette, Cape Town.

Republic of South Africa. (2003). *Division of revenue act 7 of 2003*. Government Gazette, Cape Town.

Republic of South Africa. (2009). *The national land transport act 5 of 2009*. Government Gazette, Cape Town.

Republic of South Africa. (2022). *Notice 1050 of 2022: Transport white paper on national transport policy 2021*. Government Gazette, Cape Town.

Republic of South Africa. (2023). *The division of revenue act 05 of 2023*. Government Gazette, Cape Town.

Republic of South Africa, Department of Communications and Information Systems. (2022). *South Africa Yearbook 2021/22*. https://www.gov.za/about-government/government-system/structure-and-functions-south-african-government

Republic of South Africa, National Department of Transport. (1996). *White paper on transport policy*. Government Gazette, Cape Town.

Republic of South Africa, National Department of Transport. (2000). *The national land transport act 22 of 2000*. Government Gazette, Cape Town.

Republic of South Africa, National Treasury. (2023a). *Chapter 6 of the 2023 budget review: Division of revenue and spending by provinces and municipalities*.

Republic of South Africa, National Treasury. (2023b). *Chapter 6 of the 2023 budget review: Statistical annexure of the 2023 Budget Review*.

Republic of South Africa, National Treasury. (2023c). *Local government adopted operating and capital budgets for 2023/24 MTREF*.

South African Cities Network (SACN). (2021). *Beyond 2021: Local government outlook*.

Statistics South Africa. (2023). *South African national census of 2022*. https://www.statssa.gov.za/?p=16716.

UNIL, Université de Lausanne. (2020). *Local autonomy index 2.0 and coding scheme: Codebook LAI 2.0*.

CHAPTER 11

Sweden

Iwona Sobis

11.1 Introduction

Sweden is a unitary state, constitutional monarchy, and parliamentary democracy. The country has a Nordic welfare system that provides universal access to healthcare and higher education for its citizens. Sweden has one of the highest GDP per capita rates globally, ranking 12th overall. The country also ranks highly in quality of life, health, education, economic competitiveness, income equality, gender equality, and human development. Since January 1, 1995, Sweden has been a member of the European Union. However, following an earlier referendum, the country opted out of the eurozone. Sweden is also a member of the United Nations, the Nordic Council, the Council of Europe, the World Trade Organization, the Organisation for Economic Co-operation and Development (OECD), and, since March 7, 2024, NATO. Sweden signed the European Charter of Local Self-Government in 1998, which was in force from 1999.

Sweden is located on the Scandinavian Peninsula, covering 450,295 square kilometres with a population of 10,564,484 as of July 2024

I. Sobis (✉)
School of Public Administration, University of Gothenburg, Gothenburg, Sweden

J. Nemec et al. (eds.), *Local Government and Fiscal Transfers*, Governance and Public Management,
https://doi.org/10.1007/978-3-031-95674-4_11

(SCB, 2024). Stockholm is the capital. The population density is 26 people per km^2 (approximately 67 people per mil^2), with most residents concentrated in the southern regions, especially in major cities like Stockholm (1,719,600 residents), Gothenburg (637,880 residents), and Malmö (336,618 residents) (see: World Population Review, 2024). Swedish local governments-municipalities are divided into three groups: (a) large cities with populations of at least 200,000, (b) medium-sized towns and municipalities with populations of at least 50,000, and (c) small towns/urban areas and rural municipalities with populations of at least 15,000. In 2023, eleven municipalities in Sweden had fewer than 4,000 residents (SKR/SALAR, 2024; SCB, 2024), with Dorotea being the smallest municipality, having only 2,339 residents in 2024.

11.2 Fiscal Federalism

11.2.1 Local Government Revenues

In Sweden, local income taxes are the primary source of revenue for municipalities and regions. The Constitution and the Local Government Act ensure a significant degree of political and financial autonomy for local self-governments (LSGs) at both municipal and regional levels. This empowerment enables individual municipalities and regions to effectively manage their revenues and align them with expenditures to provide essential public services. Chapter 14, Article 5 of the Swedish Constitution states, "According to law, local authorities may be obliged to contribute to costs incurred by other local authorities if necessary to achieve an equal financial base".

Approximately 70% of the total revenue for LSGs is derived from income taxes imposed by municipalities and county councils/regions. In comparison, around 16% comes from state general and earmarked grants at the municipal level. Additionally, roughly 10% is generated through municipal charges and fees. Regions also receive significant amounts of conditional grants from the central government, accounting for about 9%, to fund delegated responsibilities. The allocation of these grants is contingent on individual LSGs meeting specific criteria (see Sweden-Fiscal Powers, 2020).

Figure 11.1 presents the overall revenues of LSGs; Fig. 11.2 details municipal revenues; and Fig. 11.3 outlines regional revenues, including their approximate volume and structure. These graphs cover the period from 2015 to 2023 (100 SEK–9.25 EUR).

When the state government imposes new responsibilities on individual local self-governments that affect their operations, corresponding financing grants are allocated to facilitate the fulfilment of these duties. State-directed grants impact local democracy in two ways: (1) the size of transfers from the state can diminish the accountability of individual LSGs, and (2) these targeted grants, which focus on specific activities and geographic locations, can enhance local democracy. The second aspect mainly affects LSGs as they grapple with long-standing structural problems, often leading to the electoral success of representatives from populist parties and movements in these circumstances.

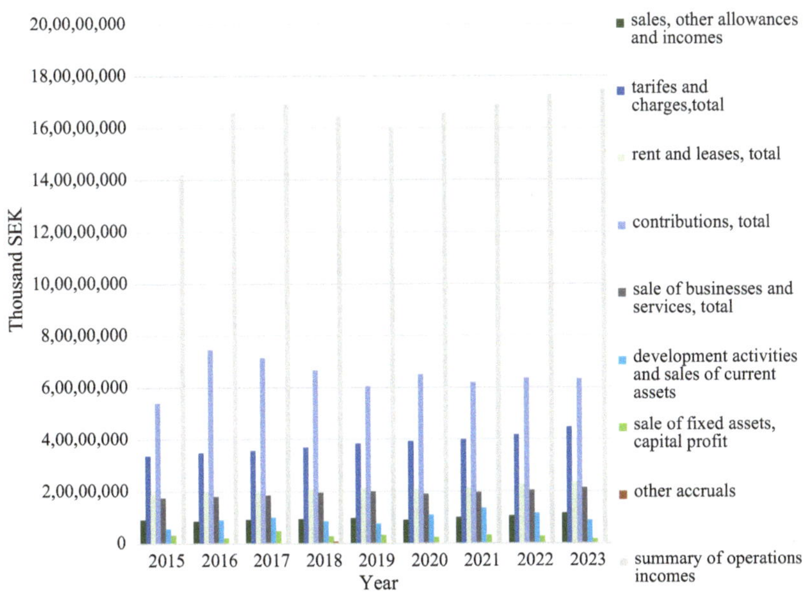

Fig. 11.1 Incomes of local self-governments for 2015–2023 (*Source* Author, based on Official Statistics Sweden [2024])

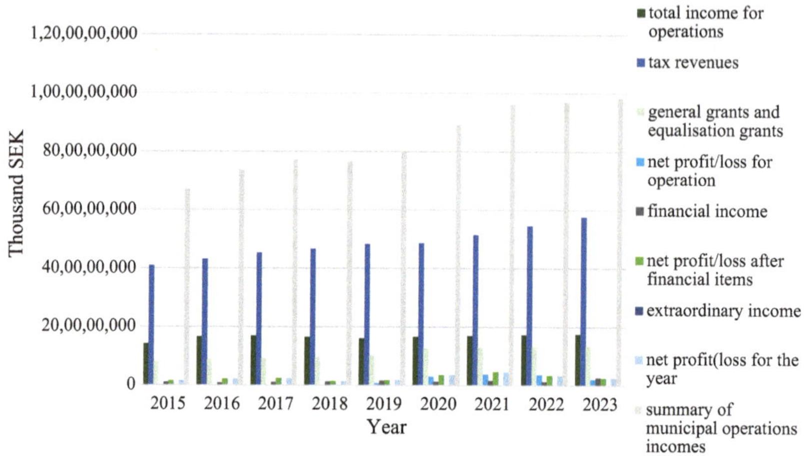

Fig. 11.2 Local self-government revenues on municipal level, current prices by item, for 2015–2023 (*Source* Author, based on SCB/Official Statistics Sweden [2024])

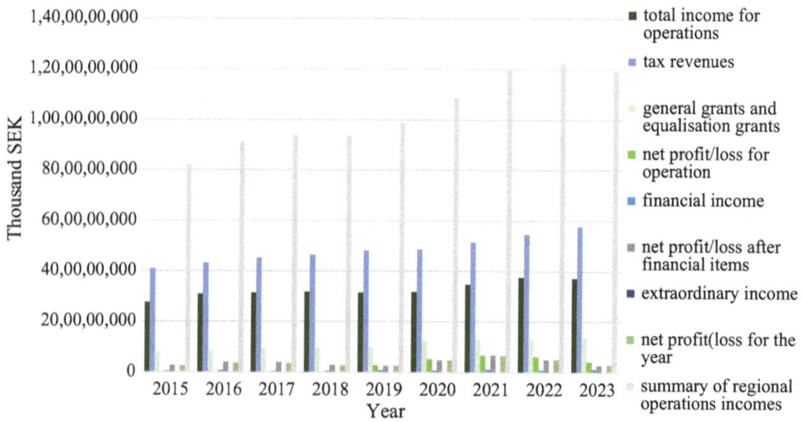

Fig. 11.3 Revenues of local self-government at regional level, current prices by item for 2015–2023 (*Source* Author, based on SCB/Official Statistics Sweden [2024])

11.2.2 Local Government Expenditures

Municipalities bear significant responsibility for delivering public services and social welfare, including education (from preschool to upper secondary school), elderly care, social services, local planning and building, infrastructure, environmental protection, and fire department services. Regional councils primarily focus on healthcare and dental care for young people. Both municipalities and regions operate within the framework of the Local Government Act, while specific laws, such as the Health and Medical Services Act, also govern counties/regions.

Although the central government can exert some influence over decisions made by local self-governments, these entities maintain extensive freedom to organise their activities when delivering mandated public services. This flexibility includes decisions related to availability, volume, quality, and user costs, all in adherence to regulatory requirements. According to "Sweden – Fiscal Powers" (Legal Notice, April 2020), the central government allocates approximately 50% of Swedish public expenditures, while about 50% are managed by municipalities and regions.

Figure 11.4 presents the general costs of municipalities from 2015 to 2023; Fig. 11.5 details municipalities' expenditures, and Fig. 11.6 outlines regional expenditures.

Swedish municipalities and counties/regions are in solid financial positions because their expenditures closely match their revenues, except during the COVID-19 pandemic.

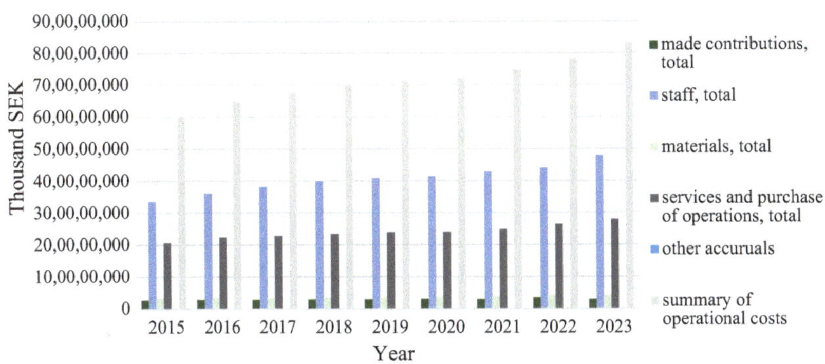

Fig. 11.4 Municipalities costs, current prices by item for 2015–2023 (*Source* Author, based on SCB/Official Statistics Sweden [2024])

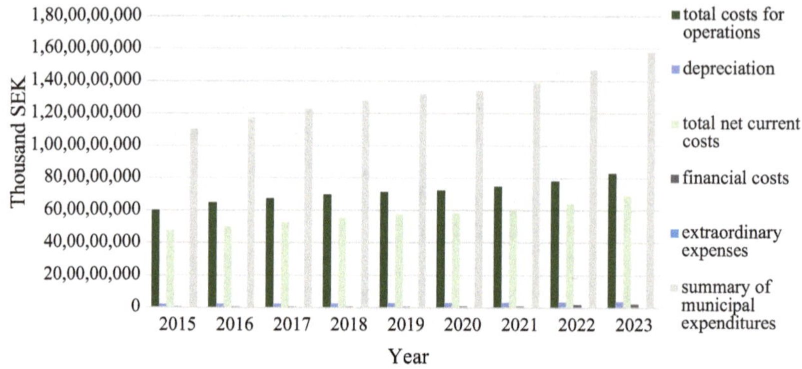

Fig. 11.5 Municipal expenditures for 2015–2023 (*Source* Author, based on SCB/Official Statistics Sweden [2024])

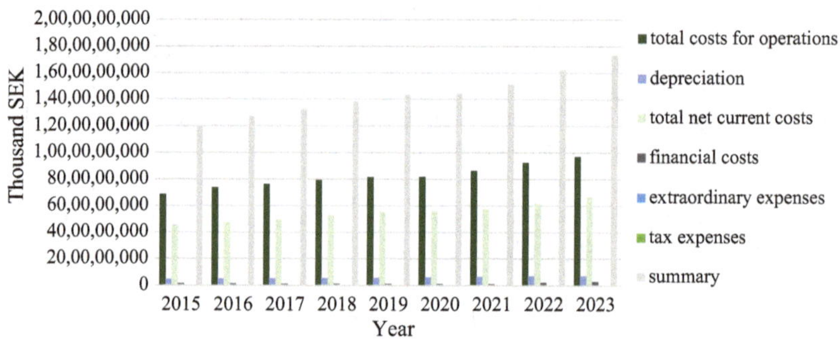

Fig. 11.6 Regional expenditures for 2015–2023 (*Source* Author, based on SCB/Official Statistics Sweden [2024])

11.2.3 Transfers to Local Governments

The Swedish system of state financial transfers to local self-governments is a means of central government supervision and control over municipalities and counties/regions. The public reforms implemented after 2000 aimed to enhance the powers and independence of LSGs at both levels. In 2005, an equalisation system was introduced to ensure the provision of public services in areas where the costs significantly exceed the financial capabilities of municipalities or regions. Thus, state transfers to municipalities and regions should be regarded as a financial equalisation system that enables them to provide essential public services, such as housing, education, healthcare, social care, and public transportation.

The state financial transfer system consists of five components: (1) income equalisation, (2) cost equalisation, (3) structural grants, (4) introduction grants, and (5) regulatory grants/fees. Income equalisation is the most significant component of the equalisation system, accounting for 69% of the redistribution. Its introduction is based on unfavourable demographics and other structural factors affecting municipalities. Some municipalities have greater tax revenue potential, while others face higher costs. Therefore, the equalisation system aims to address these structural differences, ensuring that each LSG has the same conditions to fulfil its obligations (Ekonomifakata, 2023-12-28).

Moreover, the Swedish Agency for Public Management identifies three types of grants provided by the state to local self-governments:

1. **General State Grants**: These are allocated to Swedish local self-governments through the municipal financial equalisation system. They aim to balance the financial conditions of municipalities and counties/regions. LSGs decide how to spend the funds allocated by the central government.
2. **Directed State Grants** (also known as target state grants or earmarked state transfers): These grants are voluntary, meaning that municipalities and counties/regions must apply for them by specifying a particular purpose to receive financial support from the central government. The funds cannot be spent on activities outside the specific initiatives mentioned in the application. The targets of LSGs may vary, but they must always support specific local activities.
3. **Cost Reimbursements**: These are related to specific costs incurred by municipalities or counties/regions due to decisions made by state authorities. Municipalities or counties/regions must fulfil orders from state authorities, regardless of whether they receive compensation for carrying out the governmental order or service (Statskontoret 2023, p. 24f).

The Riksdag usually approves state subsidies proposed by Riksdag/ the Swedish Parliament. However, the allocation of financial resources to LSGs is influenced by the country's current situation, such as mass migration, the COVID-19 pandemic, rising unemployment in certain municipalities, and other challenges. The final financial subsidies are determined during parliamentary debates, which may lead to increases, decreases, or even temporary funding suspensions.

To illustrate the pattern of state financial transfers to LSGs in Sweden during the period from 2015 to 2023, data were collected from (1) the annual reports of the Swedish Agency for Public Management (Statskontoret) on the state's governance of municipalities for the years 2016–2024, (2) budget proposals for the years 2015–2023 under expenditure area 25: General grants to municipalities, and (3) Official Statistics Sweden. Although these data sources are complementary, they present only approximate values due to occasional contradictions. The presentation of data in these public documents does not provide a clear picture of state financial transfers to municipalities and counties/regions. Some reports combine data for municipalities and regions, while others present the funds separately by category (general grants, directed grants, and cost reimbursements). Additionally, specific amounts of transferred money may be reported in thousands, millions, or billions, sometimes in tables or graphs.

Despite these challenges, careful analysis of public documents allows for the identification of major trends in state financial transfers to LSGs from 2015 to 2023. Figure 11.7 shows all state grants transferred to the public sector in Sweden during this time.

Table 11.1 and Fig. 11.8 illustrate the amounts of money allocated to municipalities and counties/regions by the central government during 2015–2023.

State financial transfers to the municipal sector increased from 2015 to 2018 due to significant immigration, which compelled the central government to support municipalities and counties/regions in providing refugees with essential living conditions, housing, education, healthcare, and other services. Consequently, it can be assumed that targeted transfers and cost reimbursements incurred by municipalities and counties/regions for the unplanned reception of refugees required additional state funding.

In 2019, state grants decreased due to the massive influx of immigrants. However, the COVID-19 pandemic emerged as a new challenge for the central government and local authorities. From 2019 to 2021, state financial transfers to local self-governments once again rapidly

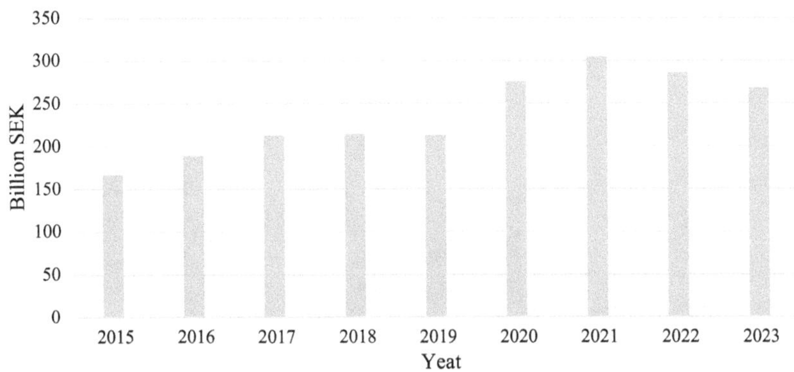

Fig. 11.7 State grants paid to the municipal sector during 2015–2022 (*Source* Author, based on Official Statistics Sweden [2024])

Table 11.1 Swedish State Grants paid to municipalities and county councils (Regions) by category (in Billions of SEK) for 2015–2023, with the share of the total amount presented in parentheses (in percent)

Receiver	*Category of state grants*	*2015*	*2016*	*2017*	*2018**	*2019**	*2020*	*2021*	*2022*	*2023*
Municipalities	Cost reim-bursements	14 (13)	33 (26)	40 (28)	28	15	14	9	11	7
	Directed grants	15 (14)	22 (18)	25 (17)	30	28	34	46	44	42
	General grants	75 (72)	70 (56)	78 (54)	81	87	113	110	113	114
	Total	105 (100)	125 (100)	144 (100)	139 (100)	130 (100)	160 (100)	165 (100)	168 (100)	163 (100)
County Councils (Regions)	Cost reim-bursements	28 (45)	27 (42)	30 (43)	18	18	37	37	39	40
	Directed grants	8 (13)	26 (40)	29 (42)	18	20	32	56	35	21
	General grants	27 (42)	26 (40)	29 (42)	43	44	45	45	44	44
	Total	63 (100)	64 (100)	69 (100)	79 (100)	82 (100)	114 (100)	138 (100)	118 (100)	105 (100)

*The years 2018 and 2019 represent the estimated data based on the diagrams from the report of Statskontoret (2021, pp. 34-35f)

Sources Own calculations of author based on data from the Statskontoret report (2024)

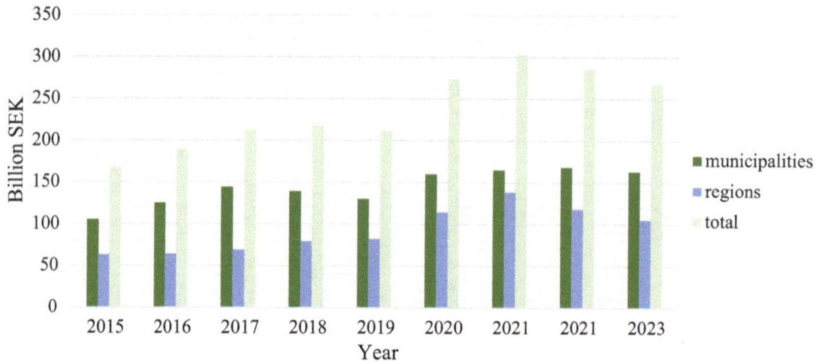

Fig. 11.8 Proportion of the municipalities' and regions' revenues consisting of state grants 2015–2023 (*Sources* Own calculations of author based on data from the Statskontoret report [2024])

increased. The situation began to normalise after 2022. Table 11.2 highlights the increase in general grants within the framework of the financial equalisation system.

Due to the varying scope of responsibilities and operational activities, municipalities and counties/regions receive different grants. These specially designated state grants differ in distribution models and amounts. The report from Statskontoret/the Swedish Agency for Public Management explains, "Financial governance means that the state tries to bring about the desired behaviour of the municipalities through taxes, subsidies, and grants" (Statskontoret 2016:24, p. 29). The central government's subsidies and grants are considered "soft policy instruments", which are neither conditional nor mandatory. Their purpose is to inform and guide municipalities in a particular direction.

The state exercises detailed control over how tasks imposed on municipalities must be carried out. Some governmental authorities exert coercive control by issuing regulations or exercising supervision. This mandatory control often operates in conjunction with softer control tools, such as general advice, guidelines, or information about state financial grants. Consequently, part of the state financial transfers to municipalities and counties/regions functions as soft policy mechanisms that support state governance.

Table 11.2 General grants transferred to Swedish municipalities, 2015–2022 (in Millions of SEK)

	2015	*2016*	*2017*	*2018*	*2019*	*2020*	*2021*	*2022*
General state grants	90,773	89,680	94,657	99,808	105,939	120,809	148,511	151,223
Equalisation allowance for LSS* costs	3,713	3,713	3,891	4,070	4,446	4,600	4,683	4,893
Contributions to municipal economic organisations	5	5	7	7	7	8	7	7
Temporary support to individual municipalities and regions (e.g., due to migration)	....	....	7,000	7,000	5,000	3,000	250	375
Support for smaller municipalities in terms of population or to counteract unemployment	....	....	....	500	500	....	....	300
Total	94,491	93,398	105,555	111,385	115,892	128,417	153,451	156,798

*LSS (1993:387) Lagen om stöd och service till vissa funktionshindrade In English: The Act on support and services for certain disabled persons

Source Author, based on data from Budgetproposition/Budget Proposals for the years of 2015, 2016, 2017, 2018, 2019, 2020, 2021, 2022, 2023

In 2015, public administration was characterised mainly by state governance based on results, and state-directed grants were distributed according to this governance model. The state unilaterally decided most grants, but some were regulated through agreements between the state and the Swedish Association of Local Authorities and Regions (SALAR) (In Swedish: Svenska Kommuner och Landstig/Regioner SKL or SKR). This approach faced significant criticism for its excessive focus on results, extensive follow-ups, and demanding documentation requirements that hindered everyday operations in providing public services. Most state-directed grants addressed education, healthcare, and elderly care.

In 2015, the central government also transferred temporary financial support of SEK 9.8 billion to the municipal sector. The distribution of these funds was influenced, among other factors, by the number of newly arrived refugees that each municipality received. In 2016, state-directed grants to the municipal sector increased to approximately SEK 30 billion compared to 2015 due to the rise in refugees in 2014–2015. However, general state grants decreased by SEK 9 billion in 2016 compared to the previous year, following the withdrawal of the temporary support of SEK 9.8 billion (see Statskontoret 2016:24, p. 41). The significant population increase over a short period necessitated adaptations to local public services in education, housing, healthcare, and social security. The increases in state-directed grants and cost reimbursements proved essential, as evidenced by the state-earmarked grants for education rising by approximately 30% in 2017 compared to 2016 (Statskontoret 2017, p. 11).

From 2019 to 2021, lockdowns caused by the COVID-19 pandemic required additional financial transfers from the central government to local self-governments (LSGs). In 2020, the state disbursed grants totalling SEK 276 billion, of which around SEK 50 billion were allocated explicitly due to the pandemic. This was significantly more funding than the central government had provided to the public sector in the past decade. The graphs below illustrate this trend: Fig. 11.9 shows the structure of state financial transfers to municipalities, while Fig. 11.10 presents the corresponding data for regions. Both graphs cover the period from 2015 to 2023.

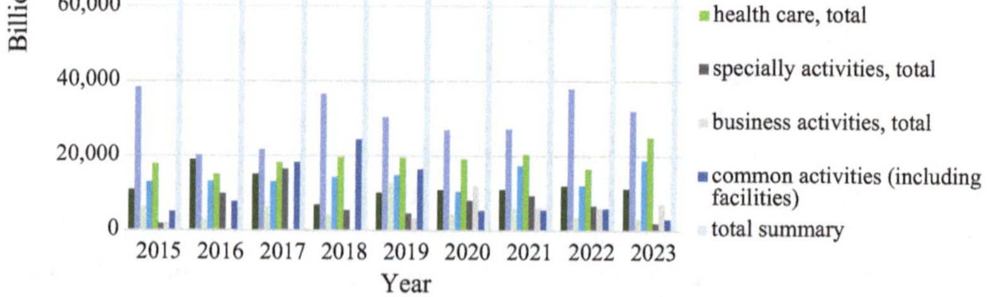

Fig. 11.9 Left grants to municipalities by activity and year (*Source* Author, based on SCB/Official Statistics Sweden [2024])

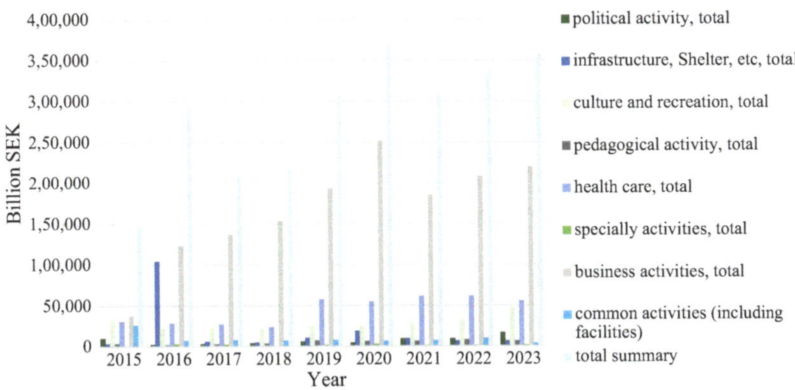

Fig. 11.10 Left grants to the regions/counties by activity and year (*Source* Author, based on SCB/Official Statistics Sweden [2024])

11.3 Case Study: Targeted Social Sector Grants to Municipalities and Their Negative Impacts on Local Democracy in Sweden

Bjørnskov et al. (2007) and Lander et al. (2021) argue that local autonomy and fiscal decentralisation can significantly enhance social outcomes, particularly in healthcare and education. This perspective suggests that citizens trust local politicians to represent their community's interests, fostering a sense of being heard and strengthening democracy, empowerment, and greater satisfaction with local public services.

Sweden, known for its generous welfare state—especially for seniors—faced new challenges by the end of the 1980s due to global socio-economic and financial crises. The governing authorities at the time drew inspiration from New Public Management (NPM), which was popularised by leaders like Ronald Reagan in the USA and Margaret Thatcher in the United Kingdom. Christopher Hood (1991) described this governance model, emphasising that decentralisation, privatisation, and marketisation of public services could alleviate the prevailing crisis. The concept of NPM was further popularised in Sweden by Roland Almqvist (2006).

Subsequent central governments introduced numerous reforms; one initiative was often replaced before completion by another. The authorities continuously experimented with various governance models, including needs budgeting, framework budgeting, zero-based budgeting, responsibility budgeting, performance management, efficiency follow-up, the customer-performer model, cooperation, balanced scorecards, process control, lean management, and value-based steering to improve the socio-economic and financial situation in the country (see Brorström, 2009; Brorström et al., 2014).

The reforms driven by NPM also impacted Swedish elderly care. However, studies by Szebehely (2006), Nyström et al. (2014), Hansson et al. (2018), and Sobis (2013a, 2013b, 2023) have shown that these reforms did not achieve the promised high quality of health, medical, and social services for seniors. When challenges arose, staff in these sectors often requested additional financial resources to improve conditions. It is hard to disagree with the cynics' saying: "If you don't know what it's about, it's about money", especially since Swedish politicians have consistently conveyed to their constituents that society is in a perpetual financial crisis.

The purpose of this subchapter is to examine state financial transfers to municipalities and counties/regions in the areas of healthcare, medical care, and social care for older adults in order to explain the consequences of the transfer mechanisms for local democracy in Sweden during the period from 2015 to 2023. This case is of particular interest because the elderly population in Sweden has been steadily increasing over the last two decades, while the number of economically active residents has become insufficient to meet the needs of older adults. Ensuring equal treatment for seniors has become a formidable challenge. Although the senior population is not homogeneous, this section will focus on state financial transfers to municipalities and counties/regions as outlined in the central government's budget, specifically position 9 on Health Care, Medical Care, and Social Care, sometimes in position 16 on Education, to identify which municipal and regional tasks and activities have been prioritised.

Between 2015 and 2023, agreements between the central government and SALAR became a common approach to managing health, medical, and social care for older adults. These agreements aimed to gather and support knowledge for municipal and regional activities while developing national knowledge management in this area. On the one hand, the agreements sought to establish state subsidies and inform local self-governments that such targeted grants could improve their financial situation if they applied for them through the Swedish Agency for Public

Management. On the other hand, the agreements served as controlling mechanisms for LSG activities. In the early years, some health, medical, and social care agreements for older adults were performance-based. However, after 2015, the amount of such grants gradually decreased, shifting from management by results to management by objectives. Since 2016, the central government has been able to impose new obligations on municipalities and counties/regions, including documented goals and guidelines for their minority policy work, including an obligation for municipalities to provide care services in minority languages, such as Finnish, Meänkieli, and Sami (Statskontoret 2017, p. 38, 66).

Another noteworthy new state grant for municipalities constitutes an exception within the state budget. This new targeted grant appears not under Expenditure Area 9: Health Care, Medical Care, and Social Care in the central government budget but somewhat under Expenditure Area 16: Education. This grant focuses on upper-secondary-level education aimed at individuals temporarily employed in elderly care or healthcare (Statskontoret 2017, p. 15). Table 11.3 illustrates the state financial transfers to municipalities and regions in health, medical, and social care for older adults during 2015–2023.

11.4 Conclusions

The analysis of state financial transfers to municipalities and counties/regions clearly indicates a growing number of targeted government subsidies. Financial resources from these targeted state grants and cost reimbursements have increased faster than general grants. These transfers constitute a significant source of income for local self-governments (LSGs). Such a trend contradicts the principles of the European Charter of Local Self-Government.

These targeted grants have negative consequences on local democracy and local management. They complicate current planning within municipalities and create additional administrative burdens. In the long term, making state-targeted grants dependent on costs can undermine the effectiveness of state management, as well as local democracy and autonomy. The main problem is that targeted grants in the analysed sectors "tell" local governments which tasks and activities should be prioritised, force local governments to realise activities financed by the central government and no other services, which might be more important in a concrete

Table 11.3 The state financial transfers to municipalities and regions in the areas of health, medical, and social care for the elderly, 2015–2023

Year(s)	*State Grants in EA9 *and A16***	*Purpose*	*Municipalities (in SEK million)*	*Regions (in SEK million)*
2015	Increased staffing within elderly care (Directed time limited grant)	Increase staffing within municipal care for older adults	1,000 million SEK	…
2016–2018	Increased staffing within elderly care (Directed time limited grant)	Increase staffing within municipal care for older adults	2,000 million SEK per 1 year (6,000 million SEK)	…
2016	Initiatives for increased competence and knowledge investment for basic staff in elderly and disability care	Give elderly and disability care better conditions to increase knowledge through various skills development efforts	178 million SEK	…
2017–2020	Education is combined with a trainee job or other work (2015:504) (Directed time limited grant for EA16 on education) **	The grant has been extended to also include training for temporary employees in healthcare or elderly care	…	…
2018	Work with National Study on Ageing and Care (Directed investment/project grant time limited)	Based on the so-called the standard cost of elderly care in the municipal equalisation system	County councils and municipalities 1,995 million SEK (unclear rules for distributing grants between municipalities and regions)	
2018	Research in elderly care (Directed investment/ project grant)	…	…	36 million SEK per 1 year (210 million SEK)

(continued)

Table 11.3 (continued)

Year(s)	*State Grants in EA9 *and A16***	*Purpose*	*Municipalities (in SEK million)*	*Regions (in SEK million)*
2019	Elderly care (Directed time limited grant for 2019)	Distributed based on the number of older adults in each municipality, the municipalities were allowed to use the funds in the part of elderly care that they judged they needed	500 million SEK	…
2020–2023	Elderly care (Directed time limited grant to 2023)	Means to increase competence among elderly care staff	462 million SEK per 1 year	…
2020	Agreement between the state and SALAR on elderly care—technology, quality, and efficiency with older adults in focus (Directed time limited grant to 2022)	This agreement aims to give the municipalities better conditions to improve care for older adults through digitalisation. Distribution key: different, primarily predetermined amount per municipality based on the number of residents aged 80 or older	200 million SEK per 1 year	…
2021–2023	The elderly care lift (Directed time limited grant, 2023)	Means to increase competence among elderly care staff	3,393 million SEK per 1 year	…
2021–2023	The elderly care (Directed time limited grant, 2023)	The aim was to increase medical competence in elderly care	…	300 million SEK per 1 year (900 million SEK)

(continued)

Table 11.3 (continued)

Year(s)	*State Grants in EA9 *and A16***	*Purpose*	*Municipalities (in SEK million)*	*Regions (in SEK million)*
2021	The elderly care (Directed time limited grant 2023)	Means to counteract loneliness among older adults and for increased quality in care and care for people with dementia	610 million SEK	...
2022–2023	Elderly care lift (Directed time limited grant to 2023)	Means to increase competence among elderly care staff	1,700 million SEK per 1 year (3,400 million SEK)	...

*EA 9—Expenditure area 9: Health care, medical care and social care (in Swedish: UO 9—Utgiftsområde 9): Hälsovård sjukvård och socialomsorg)
**EA 16—Expenditure area 16: Education
Source Author, based on data from Statskontoret (2016:24)

territory, and motivate municipalities to undertake tasks prioritised by the central government.

Moreover, this case highlights the difficulty in obtaining a comprehensive understanding of Swedish financial transfers to municipalities and regions despite the extensive literature on the topic. With this, the system of targeted grants decreases the transparency of local government and sectoral finance. The lack of a uniform framework for information and statistical data on state financial transfers necessitates a new policy approach. Criticism primarily centres on the design of the government's financial transfers, emphasising the need for a deeper understanding of how taxpayer money is allocated. It is essential to evaluate whether the distribution of the three types of transfers has yielded the anticipated positive effects on LSGs autonomy and local democracy in addressing the needs of residents. Perhaps it is time to consider allowing municipalities and regions to retain a more significant portion of their tax revenues rather than sending them to the central government to enhance social services overall and improve elderly care specifically.

The final important, negative impact of this system of targeted grants relates to the fact that municipalities must actively apply for state-targeted grants. Such a system creates the risk that unnecessary inequalities in service access between citizens of different municipalities may occur. Even in cases where the service financed from such a grant is needed, municipalities may not apply, not to bear the administrative burden of the application and reporting processes.

In elderly care, the current support system appears poorly designed based on available knowledge, and its effects remain unclear. The government should consider providing more general financial support, as operational stability is paramount. According to Statskontoret (2018:47)/Swedish Agency for Public Management (2018:47), municipalities have adopted various strategies for organising elderly care. Therefore, the state should primarily offer general subsidies, supplementing them with targeted subsidies only in exceptional cases. This recommendation is critical, as the local autonomy and democracy of Swedish LSGs are under serious threat. Indications suggest that the central government has gradually shifted towards centralising the public services sector over the past decade, compromising LSG autonomy.

Regarding policy recommendations, it is challenging to propose new solutions that state authorities have not yet identified in official reports such as SOU (2017:35) and SOU (2018:47), which suggest that the number of targeted state grants should decrease. General grants should serve as the primary means of supporting municipalities and regions. This position is echoed in reports by the Swedish Association of Local Authorities and Regions (SKL/SALAR May 2018a, 2018b; December 2018).

Annex: Country Profile: Sweden

See Table 11.4.

The level of autonomy of subnational governments over their functional mandates in Sweden has a formal character. Local and regional self-government (LSG) was first included in the Swedish Constitution in 1974 (the original Constitution was established in 1862). According to Chapter 14 on Local Authorities, local self-government is considered integral to democratic governance, playing a crucial role in the country's politics and economy. Sweden's public sector operates as a two-tier system of territorial self-government within a multi-level governance structure. It consists of the state level and two types of local self-governments: (a)

Table 11.4 Subnational political power structures

Criteria	*Results*
The level of autonomy of municipal governments over their functional mandates: the question of whether municipal governance institutions can only perform mandated tasks or can choose from a predefined scope of tasks Indicator: yes, partly, no	Yes
The level of freedom of municipal governments to decide their own political organisation and electoral system (can they, for example, determine their own electoral districts, number of seats, electoral system, etc.) Indicator: yes, partly, no	Yes
The constitutional or legal mechanisms to assert the autonomy of municipal governments. Examples of specific constitutional or legal mechanisms that allow municipal governments to assert their autonomy include (a) constitutional clauses or other statutory regulations protecting local self-government; (b) recourse to the judicial system through constitutional courts to settle disputes with higher authorities; or (c) other constitutional or legal protections of municipal autonomy exist (e.g., higher-level governments are prevented from forcing municipal governments to merge) Indicator: yes, partly, no	Yes
Municipal governments' right to use the legal system against higher-level government (de jure and de facto—do they use such right?) Indicator yes (both de jure and de facto), partly, no	Yes
The level to which decisions made by municipal governance institutions are subject to administrative supervision for their responsibilities and if higher-level approval is needed to act in their own matters Indicator yes, no	No
Does the higher-level have the right to remove local executives [or other local officials] without judicial intervention? Indicator yes, no	No

Sources Author, based on own research (2025)

290 municipalities (in Swedish: Kommuner) and (b) 21 county councils (in Swedish: Landsting), also referred to as regional governments. Gotland is a unique case as it holds regional responsibilities, manages regional development, and has the right to refer to itself as a region. There is no hierarchical relationship between municipalities and counties/regions, as both subnational levels have self-governing authority, overseeing distinct areas of responsibility. Since joining the European Union in 1995, Sweden, as an EU member state, has ratified the European Charter of Local Self-Government, impacting local authorities' regulations, activities, and community services. Kommunallag (2017:725)/The Local Government Act of (2017:725) defines the framework for local autonomy, specifying competencies and revenue sources for local entities.

The Act clearly outlines the scope of duties for both municipalities and counties/regions. LSGs can decide on additional tasks if local authorities consider them beneficial or necessary for the community. They can fund these tasks independently or apply for grants from the central government. Occasionally, the central government assigns additional duties to LSGs due to socio-economic or political factors, which may limit local autonomy.

Local self-government's freedom to decide its political organisation and electoral system is significant. Swedish LSGs enjoy considerable autonomy due to the Constitution, the Instrument of Government, and Kommunallag (1991:900)/the Local Government Act (1991:900), which provide regional and local authorities with greater flexibility to organise internally. Subnational governments have several options for service delivery: (a) they can produce services directly, (b) they can outsource services through inter-municipal cooperation or partnerships with foundations or non-governmental organisations, or (c) they can contract private companies. According to the relevant statutory provisions, LSGs have complete discretion to initiate activities within their competencies. Political organisations, electoral systems, and the election of mayors and local councillors must comply with specific regulations. However, local authorities' discretion may be limited when they perform tasks on behalf of the central government.

The constitutional or legal mechanisms to assert the autonomy of subnational governments include the Swedish Constitution, the Instrument of Government (1974:152) (in Swedish, Regeringsform), as well as its amendments through the Swedish Constitutional Collection i.e., (SFS 2010:1408; 2011:109); the Local Government Act/Kommunallag (2017:725; SFS, 2019:835, Chapter 5, §5); Election Act/Vallag/ (2005:837; SFS 2018:28). These laws protect the country's democratic system and the autonomy of LSGs.

The right of lower territorial units to use the legal system against higher territorial units (de jure and de facto): According to Kommunallagen (2019:835)/the Local Government Act (SFS, 2019:835, Chapter 13, §1), municipalities and regions, as well as residents, may appeal to the Supreme Administrative Court to "challenge the legality of a decision or measure taken within the framework of supervision by another authority" (see: Report, CG(2022)43–12final, 2022, p. 25).

The extent to which decisions made by subnational governance institutions are subject to administrative supervision for their responsibilities and whether higher-level approval is required for independent actions. The Constitution and the Local Government Act assign local authorities' responsibility for their tasks. Local authorities do not need higher-level approval to act independently. However, the Swedish Agency for Public Management (in Swedish, Statskontoret) and central government agencies are tasked by the central government with overseeing municipalities and county councils/regions for legal and regulatory compliance (see: Report, CG(2022)43–12final, 2022, p. 25). Administrative supervision also applies to tasks assigned to LSGs by central authorities.

The right of higher levels to remove local executives or other local officials without judicial intervention does not exist. The answer to this question is definitely "no" (Table 11.5).

Subnational councillors are elected through a proportional representation system in direct elections, meaning parties receiving the most votes in subnational elections also secure the most seats in municipal and regional councils. This is a majority-based electoral system.

Elections to the Riksdag (Swedish Parliament), municipal, and regional assemblies occur on the same day, the second Sunday of September, every four years. Each mandate is for a four-year term.

Voter turnout is high in Sweden, consistently above 80% since the 1950s. In 2018, 87.1% of the population participated in the national

Table 11.5 Structure and quality of subnational electoral systems

Criteria	*Results*
How are municipal councillors elected? Indicator—election mode	Direct election, Majority Electoral Systems
For what term are municipal councils elected (years)? Indicator—years of mandate	4
What is the level of citizen participation in municipal elections? Indicator: Low—("Normal") voter turnout is below 35% of eligible (registered) voters Average—Voter turnout is between 35 and 60% of eligible (registered) voters High—Voter turnout is over 60% of eligible (registered) voters	High

Source Author, based on own research (2025)

elections, while turnout in regional and municipal elections was 83.8% and 84.1%, respectively. Four years later, 2022 turnout decreased slightly to 84.2% for the national level, 80.2% for the regional level, and 80.5% for municipal elections (SCB, 2023, February 27). Several factors contribute to this high voter turnout, including respect for electoral law, trust in democratic institutions, and the organisation of national parliamentary elections alongside local and regional elections. It is also notable that elections are popular among young people. Secondary school students, in particular, participate in meetings organised by schools with representatives from various political parties. Through these meetings, young people develop their political preferences and understand the importance of a democratic system that empowers them to make independent voting choices. Additionally, Sweden has a high percentage of women in elected positions compared to other EU member countries (see Report, CG(2022)43--12final, 2022, p. 3) (Table 11.6).

In Sweden, the electoral system is party-based, meaning voters cast their ballots for a party and can also select a specific candidate from that party. To become a candidate in subnational council elections, a person must: (a) be at least 18 years old, (b) have lived in Sweden for at least three years to qualify for municipal assembly elections, (c) be a member of a political party, and (d) be nominated by a political party. According to Kungörelse (1974:152)/Proclamation (1974:152) with amendments

Table 11.6 Nature of subnational political party systems

Criteria	*Results*
Which subjects can run in municipal elections? Indicator—define who can participate	The electoral system is based on parties
How are party candidates for municipal council elections selected? Indicator—selected by party, elected by party, self-nomination, other	Selected by party, self-nomination
Are there established rules for financing municipal political campaigns? Indicator—yes, no	Yes
Does the ruling national party have a dominant position in municipal elections? Indicator—yes, no	No

Source Author, based on own research (2025)

from SFS (2010:1408) and SFS (2011:109), Chapter 3, Article 1, “Party denotes any association or group of voters which runs for election under a particular designation”. Thus, there is no clear legal definition of what constitutes a political party.

In both regional and municipal elections, candidates are chosen through the internal selection process of their party. According to Vallagen (2005:837)/the Electoral Act (2005:837), Chapter 2, §1, any party that wishes to register its designation must notify the central electoral authority in writing. §9 further specifies that a party can register all its candidates for a particular election, with written submissions required to the central election authority or the county administrative board. Each candidate must also submit a signed declaration agreeing to the nomination. The central electoral authority subsequently issues a voting card to each voter, which must be delivered to their home address no later than 18 days before election day. Mandates are allocated based on the number of personal votes received by candidates. If no candidate or insufficient candidates receive enough personal votes, mandates are distributed according to the order on the party’s ballot, provided only one ballot type is used. The process becomes more complex if multiple ballot types are used in the constituency (Vallagen 2005:837, Chapter 14, §9–§10).

Kommunallagen (2017:725)/the Local Government Act (2017:725), Chapter 4 on Party Support, §29, states that municipalities and regions provide financial contributions and other forms of support to political parties to enhance their role in municipal democracy. This support is available to parties that have obtained a mandate in the county council, as defined in Vallagen (2005:837)/the Electoral Act (2005:837), Chapter 14 on Party support may also be given to parties that lost their representation, but only for one year after their representation. The county council determines the extent and form of party support. This support must be impartial and not favour any party. §31 further mandates that recipients of party support submit an annual report demonstrating that the funds were used as stipulated in §29. This is reinforced by SFS (2018:90), which requires transparency in political financing (§3 and §6). Neither Kommunallagen (2017:725)/the Local Government Act (2017:725) nor SFS (2018:90) specifies rules for financing subnational political campaigns. However, §9–§10 of SFS (2018:90) bans anonymous contributions, while §11 lays out detailed reporting requirements, including income from sales, lotteries, fundraising, and donations from individuals, companies, organisations, and other sources.

These funding sources likely support subnational political campaigns. Financial reports from political parties are submitted to the Chamber of Deputies, which publishes them as required by SFS (2018:90) to ensure transparency in party financing.

In Sweden, the ruling national party has no dominant influence over subnational elections. These elections operate according to local dynamics and political preferences specific to each area. The ruling party's influence on local elections is primarily constrained by legal frameworks, including the Constitution, the Instrument of Government, and the Local Government Act, which all ensure autonomy for municipalities and regions. Power in municipalities and regions shifts regularly based on election results. A clear trend has emerged: an increasing number of political parties are represented at the national and local levels, making it challenging for traditional blocs to form majority governments independently. The 2014 elections notably demonstrated that inter-bloc governments outnumbered conservative and left-wing governments. This trend continued after the 2022 elections, where half of Sweden's municipalities are now governed by inter-county coalitions, resulting in a greater variety of party coalitions managing municipalities and regions (SKR/SALAR, 2023, pp. 51–59) (Table 11.7).

According to Kungörelse (1974:152)/Proclamation (1974:152), with amendments in SFS, (2011:109), Part 8, Article 9, sessions of the Chamber are open to the public. However, a meeting may be held behind closed doors if stipulated by the rules outlined by the Riksdag Act.

Table 11.7 Subnational political participation and accountability

Criteria	*Results*
Are all council meetings (required to be) open to the public? Indicator—yes, no	Yes
Are municipal records and documents (required to be) available to the public? Indicator—yes, no	Yes
Is the council (required to) engage in an open, participatory planning process? Indicator—yes, no	No
Are alternative participatory mechanisms, such as referendums or participatory budgeting, used? Indicator—yes, partly, no	Yes

Source Author, based on own research (2025)

Yes, the principle of transparency was established in Sweden as early as 1766 to allow citizens insight into governmental activities. This principle still applies today. Kommunallagen (1991:900)/the Local Government Act (1991:900), Chapter 3, §18, along with Offentlighets- och sekretesslag (2009:400)/the Public Access to Information and Secrecy Act (SFS 2009:400), upholds the principle of openness, which extends to municipalities, county councils, and municipal companies (such as joint-stock companies, commercial companies, economic associations, and foundations) where municipalities or county councils exert a decisive influence.

Swedish legislation does not mandate the involvement of citizens, civic associations, or non-profit organisations in an open, participatory planning process for local matters.

In Sweden, consultative referendums have been possible since 1922, and binding referendums have been available through specific constitutional mechanisms since 1979 (see The Constitution of Sweden, 2013, p. 4). Though they are not commonly used, both referendums and participatory budgeting can be implemented at the municipal or regional level. Instead, Kommunallagen (2017:725)/the Local Government Act (2017:725) has introduced opportunities for citizens to submit petitions, and voluntary citizen dialogues between elections have become the most widely used mechanism across municipalities and counties/regions (see Report, CG(2022)43–12final, 2022, p. 12).

Regarding participatory budgeting (PB), this remains a voluntary institution in Sweden. The first PB projects were introduced in 2007 under pressure from the EU, the Swedish central government, and the Swedish Association of Local Authorities and Regions (SALAR), which offered various incentives to encourage local authorities to experiment with PB. However, only 12 out of 290 municipalities adopted the approach. Following the pilot projects, no municipality continued with PB, which remains an underdeveloped practice. Local politicians generally prefer representative democracy (see Sobis 2022).

References

Almqvist, R. (2006). *New public management: Om konkurrensutsättning, kontrakt och kontroll*. Liber.

Bjørnskov Christian, Dreher Axer and FischerJustina A.V. (2007). The Bigger the Better? Evidence of the Effect of Government Size on Life Satisfaction Around the World Public Choice 130(3):267–292. https://doi.org/10.1007/s11127-006-9081-5

Brorström, B. (2009). *Styrning i offentlig förvaltning teori, trender och tillämpningar*. Högskolan Borås.

Brorström, B., Haglund, A., Solli, R., & Malmer, S. (2014). *Förvaltningsekonomi: En bok med fokus på organisation, styrning och redovisning i kommuner och landsting*. Studentlitteratur AB.

Budgetproposition/Budget proposal. (2015). (Online) Available from: https://www.regeringen.se/contentassets/f479a257aa694bf097a3806bbdf6ff19/utgiftsomrade-25-allmanna-bidrag-till-kommuner/. (October 20, 2024).

Budgetproposition/Budget proposal. (2016). (Online) Available from: https://www.regeringen.se/contentassets/49618bcb4fd94b6081d9696f55bc7f8d/utgiftsomrade-25-allmanna-bidrag-till-kommuner.pdf. (October 20, 2024).

Budgetproposition/Budget proposal. (2017). (Online) Available from: https://www.regeringen.se/contentassets/e926a751d9eb4c978c4d892c659ebc8e/utgiftsomrade-25-allmanna-bidrag-till-kommuner/. (October 20, 2024).

Budgetproposition/Budget proposal. (2018). (Online) Available from: https://www.regeringen.se/contentassets/79f6d27416794f0bb146c792e02b65fc/utgiftsomrade-25-allmanna-bidrag-till-kommuner.pdf. (October 20, 2024).

Budgetproposition/Budget proposal. (2019). (Online) Available from: https://www.regeringen.se/rattsliga-dokument/proposition/2018/11/prop.-2018191. (October 20, 2024).

Budgetproposition/Budget proposal. (2020). (Online) Available from: https://www.regeringen.se/contentassets/c689564aa19c4d29bcebb1c037a2e37b/utgiftsomrade-25-allmanna-bidrag-till-kommuner.pdf. (October 20, 2024).

Budgetproposition/Budget proposal. (2021). (Online) Available from: https://www.regeringen.se/contentassets/bc0f4b1a4ce844f2aa59949d09c93f29/utgiftsomrade-25-allmanna-bidrag-till-kommuner.pdf. (October 20, 2024).

Budgetproposition/Budget proposal. (2022). (Online) Available from: https://www.regeringen.se/contentassets/cdd922ce835e4da0a87edcb38aafef65/utgiftsomrade-25-allmanna-bidrag-till-kommuner.pdf. (October 20, 2024).

Budgetproposition/Budget proposal. (2023). (Online) Available from: https://www.regeringen.se/contentassets/def2026cac0b4ef7acf4afeb988326ed/utgiftsomrade-25-allmanna-bidrag-till-kommuner.pdf. (October 20, 2024).

Constitution of Sweden. (2013, August). Regeringskansliet, Ministry of Justice. Stockolm: Elanders. (Online) Available from: https://www.government.se/contentassets/7b69df55e58147638f19bfdfb0984f97/the-constitution-of-sweden/. (October 11, 2024).

Council of European Municipalities and Regions (CEMR). (2020). *Sweden—Fiscal powers*. https://portal.cor.europa.eu/divisionpowers/Pages/Sweden-Fiscal-Powers.aspx

Election Act. (2005:837). https://www.government.se/contentassets/4e2fdee5a8e342e88289496d34701aec/the-elections-act-2005837.pdf

Ekonomifakta. (2023, December 28). *Kommunala utjämningssystemet*. https://www.ekonomifakta.se/sakomraden/offentlig-ekonomi/kommunal-ekonomi/kommunala-utjamningssystemet_1210647.html. (February 2, 2024).

Hansson, A., Svensson, A., Hedman, A. B., Larsson, L. G., Forsman, B., & Alsén, P. (2018). Flawed communications: Health professionals' experience of collaboration in the care of frail elderly patients. *Scandinavian Journal of Public Health, 46*(7), 680–689. https://doi.org/10.1177/1403494818797014. (10 March 2023).

Health and Medical Services Act. (2017:30)/Hälso- och sjukvårdslag (2017:30). https://www.riksdagen.se/sv/dokument-och-lagar/dokument/svensk-forfattningssamling/halso-och-sjukvardslag-201730_sfs-2017-30/ (February 2, 2024).

Hood, Christopher. (1991). "A Public Management for all Seasons?" *Public Administration, 69*(1), 3–19.

Kammarkollegiet. (2010). *Insyn i hur politiska partier finansierar sin verksamhet*. https://www.kammarkollegiet.se/om-oss/kammarkollegiets-uppgifter/insyn-i-hur-politiska-partier-finansierar-sin-verksamhet

Kommunallag. (1991:900)/Local Government Act (1991:900). Online) Available from: https://www.riksdagen.se/sv/dokument-och-lagar/dokument/svensk-forfattningssamling/kommunallag-1991900_sfs-1991-900/. (February 2, 2024).

Kommunallag. (2017:725). https://www.riksdagen.se/sv/dokument-och-lagar/dokument/svensk-forfattningssamling/kommunallag-2017725_sfs-2017-725/

Kungörelse. (1974:152). om beslutad ny regeringsform/Proclamation (1974:152) on the adoption of a new form of government. (Online) Available from: https://www.riksdagen.se/sv/dokument-och-lagar/dokument/svensk-forfattningssamling/kungorelse-1974152-om-beslutad-ny-regeringsform_sfs-1974-152/ (February 2, 2024).

Lag. (1993:387). Om stöd och service till vissa funktionshindrade—LSS / Act (1993:387) on support and services for certain disabled people. (Online) Available from: https://translate.google.com/?hl=sv&sl=sv&tl=en&text=Lag%20(1993%3A387)%20om%20st%C3%B6d%20och%20service%20till%20vissa%20funktionshindrade&op=translate. (February 2, 2024).

Lander, A., Keuffer, N., & Bastianen, A. (2021). *Self-rule index for local authorities in the EU, Council of Europe and OECD countries, 1990–2020*. European Commission, Directorate-General for Regional and Urban Policy. https://local-autonomy.andreaslander.ch/

LSS. (1993: 387). Lagen om stöd och service till vissa funktionshindrade. In English: The Act (1993: 387) on support and services for certain disabled persons. https://www.riksdagen.se/sv/dokument-och-lagar/dokument/svensk-forfattningssamling/lag-1993387-om-stod-ochservice-till-vissa_sfs-1993-387/

Nyström, M. E., Strehlenert, H., Hansson, J., & Hasson, H. (2014). Strategies to facilitate implementation and sustainability of large system transformations: A case study of a national program for improving quality of care for elderly people. *BMC Health Services Research, 14*, 401. https://doi.org/10.1186/s12913-014-0401-0

Report, CG(2022)43–12final (26 oktober 2022). *Monitoring of the application of the European Charter of Local Self Government in Sweden*. (Online) Available from: https://rm.coe.int/monitoring-of-the-application-of-the-european-charter-of-local-self-go/1680a863e7 (January 30, 2024).

SCB. (2023). *Valdeltagande i Sverige*. https://www.scb.se/hitta-statistik/sverige-i-siffror/manniskorna-i-sverige/valdeltagande-i-sverige/. (October 7, 2024).

SCB. (2024). *Sveriges minsta kommuner krymper: Dorotea ny minsting*. https://www.scb.se/pressmeddelande/sveriges-minsta-kommuner-krymper--dorotea-ny-minsting

SFS. (2009). *Offentlighets- och sekretesslag (2009:400)*. https://www.riksdagen.se/sv/dokument-och-lagar/dokument/svensk-forfattningssamling/offentlighets-och-sekretesslag-2009400_sfs-2009-400/

SFS. (2010:1408). *Regeringsform. (Governance form)*.. https://rkrattsdb.gov.se/SFSdoc/11/110109.PDF

SFS. (2011:109). *Regeringsform. (Governance form)*. Online) Available from: https://www.riksdagen.se/sv/dokument-och-lagar/dokument/svensk-forfattningssamling/kungorelse-1974152-om-beslutad-nyregeringsform_sfs-1974-152/

SFS. (2018). *Lag (2018:90) om insyn i finansiering av partier*. https://www.riksdagen.se/sv/dokument-och-lagar/dokument/svensk-forfattningssamling/lag-201890-om-insyn-i-finansiering-av-partier_sfs-2018-90/. (October 14, 2024).

SFS. (2018:28). *Lag om ändring i vallagen* (2005:837). https://filedn.com/ljdBas5OJsrLJOq6KhtBYC4/forarbeten/sfs/2018/sfs-2018-28.pdf

SFS. (2019:835). Act amending the Local Government Act (2017:725). https://svenskforfattningssamling.se/sites/default/files/sfs/2019-11/SFS 2019-835.pdf

Sobis, I. (2013a). Comparison of public and private home care services for elderly in Gothenburg Region. *International Review of Public Administration, 11*(3–4), 25–55.

Sobis, I. (2013b). Nothing but trouble: Studies on the effects of reforms in elderly care in Sweden and Poland. *The NISPAcee Journal of Public Administration and Policy, 6*(1), 31–60. https://doi.org/10.2478/nispa-2013-0002

Sobis, I. (2022). Participatory budgeting in Sweden. In M. S. De Vries, J. Nemec, & D. Špaček (Eds.), *International trends in participatory budgeting: Between trivial pursuits and best practices* (pp. 63–87). Palgrave Macmillan.

Sobis, I. (2023). The alleged culprit of poor coordination of integration of health and social care services for very ill older persons in Sweden, 2000–2022. *The NISPAcee Journal of Public Administration and Policy, 16*(2), https://doi.org/10.2478/nispa-2023-0019

Statens Offentliga Utredningar—SOU. (2017:35) (State Public Investigations). *Samling för skolan. Nationell strategi för kunskap och likvärdighet*. https://filedn.com/ljdBas5OJsrLJOq6KhtBYC4/forarbeten/sou/2017/sou-2017-35.pdf. (October 16, 2024).

Statens Offentliga Utredningar—SOU. (2018:47) (State Public Investigations). *Med tillit växer handlingsutrymmet*. https://filedn.com/ljdBas5OJsrLJOq6KhtBYC4/forarbeten/sou/2018/sou-2018-47.pdf. (October 16, 2024).

Statskontoret/Swedish Agency for Public Management. (2016:24). *Statens styrning av kommunerna*. https://www.statskontoret.se/siteassets/publikationer/2016/201624.pdf. (October 11, 2024).

Statskontoret/Swedish Agency for Public Management. (2017). *Utveckling av den statliga styrningen av kommuner och landsting 2017*. https://www.statskontoret.se/siteassets/rapporter-pdf/2018/utveckling-av-den-statliga-styrningen-av-kommuner-och-landsting-2017.pdf. (October 11, 2024).

Statskontoret/Swedish Agency for Public Management. (2018). Utveckling av den statliga styrningen av kommuner och landsting 2018. https://www.statskontoret.se/siteassets/rapporter-pdf/2019/statens_styrning_kommuner-landsting_2018.pdf. (October 11, 2024).

Statskontoret/Swedish Agency for Public Management. (2023, May 29). *Utvecklingen av den statliga styrningen av kommuner och regioner 2022*. Regeringen. Finansdepartementet. https://www.statskontoret.se/siteassets/rapporter-pdf/2023/utvecklingen-av-den-statliga-styrningen-av-kommuner-och-regioner-2022-alla-bilagor---utskriftsversion-1.2.pdf. (September 9, 2024).

Statskontoret/Swedish Agency for Public Management. (2024, June 5). *Statens styrning med statsbidrag till kommuner och regioner 2023. Antal, omfattning och innehåll*. Regeringen. Finansdepartementet. https://www.statskontoret.se/publicerat/publikationer/publikationer-2024/statens-styrning-med-statsbidrag-till-kommuner-och-regioner-2023--antal-omfattning-och-innehall/. (October 11, 2024).

Sveriges Kommuner och Landsting—SKL /Swedish Association of Local Authorities and Regions—SALAR. (2018a). *Ekonomirapporten*. https://skr.se/download/18.45167e4317e2b341b24ae5a5/1642690582341/7585-541-7.pdf.

Sveriges Kommuner och Landsting—SKL /Swedish Association of Local Authorities and Regions—SALAR. (2018b). *Ekonomirapporten*. https://skr.se/download/18.583b3b0c17e40e30384682be/1642690514863/7585-545-5.pdf

Sveriges Kommuner och Regioner—SKR /Swedish Association of Local Authorities and Regions—SALAR. (2024). *Kommungruppsindelning*. https://skr.se/en/skr/tjanster/kommunerochregioner/faktakommunerochregioner/kommungruppsindelning.2051.html

Sveriges Kommuner och Regioner. (2023). *310 val: 2022 års kommun- och regionval*. https://skr.se/skr/tjanster/rapporterochskrifter/publikationer/310val2022arskommunochregionval.69670.html

Sweden—Fiscal Powers (April 2020). (Online) Available from: https://portal.cor.europa.eu/divisionpowers/Pages/Sweden-Fiscal-Powers.aspx. (September 9, 2024).

Szebehely, M. (2006). Omsorgsvardag under skiftande organisatoriska villkor: En jämförande studie av den nordiska hemtjänsten. *Tidskrift För Arbejdsliv, 8*(1), 49–66.

Vallagen. (2005:837)/Electoral Act (2005: 837). (Online) Available from: https://www.riksdagen.se/sv/dokument-och-lagar/dokument/svensk-forfattningssamling/vallag-2005837_sfs-2005-837/. (February 9, 2024).

World Population Review. (2024). *Stockholm*. https://worldpopulationreview.com/cities/sweden/stockholm

CHAPTER 12

Uganda

John-Mary Kauzya

12.1 Introduction

Uganda is an East African country that gained independence from the British in October 1962. It was ruled by highly centralised and dictatorial governments, including military governments, until around 1992, when a decentralisation policy was implemented. Later, it was given a legal and constitutional foundation, which made decentralisation and local governance an important feature of Uganda's governance system.

Uganda is a unitary state and has been since 1967, when the 1962 constitution, which had given the country a semi-federal system of governance, was replaced. Successive governments, including the military governments of 1971–1979 and July 1985–January 1986, were highly centralised if not personalised, which changed in 1992 when decentralised governance was introduced, which was constitutionalised in a new National constitution of 1995.

In effect since 1992, decentralised governance structured around Districts (Local Council 5), Sub-counties (Local Council 3), and lower local councils (Local Council 2 or Parishes and Local Council 1 or

J.-M. Kauzya (✉)
Stellenbosch University, Stellenbosch, South Africa
e-mail: jKauzya@hotmail.com

J. Nemec et al. (eds.), *Local Government and Fiscal Transfers*,
Governance and Public Management,
https://doi.org/10.1007/978-3-031-95674-4_12

Villages) has been a central feature of Uganda's governance. The decentralised governance structure in urban areas is organised as city councils, municipal councils, divisions, and villages. Since 1992, when the decentralisation policy was launched, decentralisation has been an ongoing process. For example, 1991, when the decentralisation policy was being formulated and discussed, the country was divided into 34 districts. As of 2024, the number of districts in the country had grown to 146. Currently, the Uganda Bureau of Statistics (UBOS) gives the following as the number of administrative divisions of the country:

- Cities 10
- Districts 146
- Counties 322
- Municipalities 39
- Sub-counties 1,488
- Parishes 7,553
- Villages 58,197

Increasing local governments and lower administrative units brings government and services closer to the grass-roots people (Mitchinson, 2003). It provides an institutionalised structural arrangement that enables the people to participate and engage in their governance, including demand for accountability from their leaders. Since political leaders of the local governments and lower administrative units (i.e. Chairpersons and members of executive committees as well as Councillors) are elected, the structural arrangement also provides a fertile field in which the people get to exercise their democratic rights through electing their local leaders.

In 1997, an Act of Parliament (the Local Governments Act 1997) led to the decentralisation and devolution of functions, powers, and services in conformity with the constitution. It provided for decentralisation at all levels of local governments to ensure good governance and democratic participation in and control of decision-making by the people. It also provided for revenue, the political and administrative setup of local governments, and the election of local councils.

Such an extensive decentralisation endeavour must involve transferring the requisite resources, including funds, to the areas where powers, functions, and service delivery have been devolved. This means that decentralised governance, as conceived in the constitution and the law, can be effectively implemented when public management values and societal values are effectively promoted and implemented.

12.2 Fiscal Federalism

12.2.1 Local Government Revenues and Expenditures

The ability of local governments to effectively deliver services and engineer local socio-economic development mandates depends on the financial revenues and other resources at their disposal and their efficient and effective deployment and utilisation. Revenue inflows for local governments in Uganda's local governance system include the following: (i) central government grant transfers, (ii) locally raised revenues through taxation, fees, and levies, and (iii) direct grants, donations, and transfers from development partners.

Under the local government law, lower local governments are mandated to assess and collect local revenues. Funding from central to Local Governments has increased over time from "Uganda shillings 0.35 trillion in Financial Year 1993/94 (in Uganda shillings 2016 terms) to Uganda shillings 2.73 trillion in Financial Year 2017/18" (1000 UGX–0.26 EUR). Comprehensive central data showing total local government revenue and expenditure are unavailable; thus, we illustrate below.

Looking at the revenue performance and plans for Mbarara district local government as an example (for 2016/2017 and 2017/2018), it is clear that the expected and received revenues are way below budget, and this affects service delivery. Moreover, the most significant part of local government revenues comes from central government transfers (discretionary and conditional), implying that local governments still depend heavily on central government financing even under decentralisation. The data also suggest that local governments are weak in mobilising their revenues (Table 12.1).

The interplay of approved revenue budgets determines local government expenditures, approved projected spending, actual revenue receipts, and responsible accountability in delivering goods and services. They do not have freedom in spending, especially with conditional government transfers, which constitute the most significant part of local government's revenues. They have to spend the money on the earmarked services. Where the local governments have discretion in expenditure (i.e. discretionary government transfers), the revenues are very low compared to

Table 12.1 Mbarara local government planned and received revenues for the first quarter of 2016/2017 (Uganda shillings 000's)

Approved budget	
Locally raised revenues	1,837,857
Discretionary government transfers	2,789,852
Conditional Government transfers	27,242,192
Other government transfers	343,762
Donor funding	846,452
Total	33,060,116
Real revenues during the given period	
Locally raised revenues	372,380
Discretionary government transfers	697,463
Conditional government transfers	7,131,218
Other government transfers	0
Donor funding	0
Total	8,201,061

Source Author, based on data from the municipality (2025)

conditional government transfers. In effect, the central government still has a strong hold on local government expenditure.

12.2.2 *Financial Transfers from Central to Local Governments*

It is important to note that in addition to central government transfers in the form of grants (conditional, unconditional, and equalisation grants), Local Governments benefit from funds appropriated under Central Government institutions, which finance important development activities at the local level. These include the following: (i) National Medical Stores for delivery of medicines and medical equipment, (ii) National Agricultural Advisory Service, which provides agricultural inputs, (iii) Uganda Road Fund for road maintenance, (iv) Social Assistance Grants for Empowerment (SAGE), (v) Uganda Women's Entrepreneurship Programme (UWEP) and Youth Livelihood Programmes. All these add to the central government's overall contribution to local governments. The picture of central government financial transfers to local governments would be incomplete if these were to be excluded. These funds that are appropriated under central government institutions have been an important factor in promoting the societal values of poverty reduction, social welfare, gender empowerment, youth empowerment, and social equity.

The constitutional basis for transfers from central to local governments is that the 1995 constitution, in article 193, requires the Central Government to provide grants to Local Governments (unconditional, conditional, and equalisation grants), which enable local governments to deliver services to the people. The Equalisation Grant provided for in the Constitution contributes to addressing imbalances in the development of different local governments in the country. Thus, both in concept and in practice, if well applied, the equalisation grants ensure equity in development and respect for diversity and local interest.

There is a noticeable and regrettable trend of decline in the central government's financial transfers to local governments. For example, from 2020/2021 to 2021/2022, the transfers decreased from a total of 940.7 billion Uganda shillings to 768.4 billion, representing a decrease of 18.3%.

Several studies have highlighted reduced financial transfers from central to local governments. First, the percentage of the national budget earmarked for local governments declined from 23% to around 12% during the financial year 2019/2020. Then, eventually, it dropped to 11% for the financial year 2020/2021, which was due to the re-centralisation of functions and funds even though, by law, these functions and funds are mandated to be implemented by local governments. The above has negatively impacted local government service delivery, accountability, and citizen empowerment. Also, it has made local governments depend more and more on the central government for financing.

Among the consequences of the decline in finances is that, as various scorecard reports have established, citizens have limited consultation during the planning and budgeting processes conducted at the local government level. Local governments report that they lack the resources to conduct extensive consultations. Besides, there is limited downward accountability where the duty bearers provide information on planned services and available resources for each locality and pick issues from the citizens (ACODE, 2020).

If it persists, the reduction in financial transfers from central to local governments will likely lead to a reduction in democracy, participation, and accountability. Local government leaders' claims that limitations in financing inhibit consultations with local people and service delivery need to be taken seriously (Ahmad et al., 2005).

12.3 Case Study: Discretionary Development Equalisation Grant

In terms of inter-governmental financial transfers from central government to local governments, there is room to examine the system and practice of financial transfers from central government to local governments to have some insight as to whether and to what extent the system promotes societal and public management values of transparency, accountability, participation, equity, inclusion, empowerment, local autonomy, valuing diversity, poverty alleviation, and socio-economic transformation. In doing this, it is possible to assess the socio-economic impact of the financial transfers in local governments and make policy recommendations.

The main objectives of the Discretionary Development Equalisation Grant are to enable local governments to allocate funds to priority local development needs that are with their mandates and are consistent with national priorities by the provision of discretionary development funding, to provide development financing which caters for the differing development needs of rural and urban areas; to provide local governments with equitable access to development financing ensuring that more disadvantaged local governments receive additional funding to enable them to catch up with the rest of the country, and improve local governments' capacities and systems for provision of quality services by rewarding good performance and sanctioning poor performance.

The Discretionary Development Equalisation Grants are structured into two portions: (i) The District Discretionary Development Equalisation Grant and (ii) the urban discretionary development equalisation grant. They aim to address rural and urban areas' development needs and imbalances, respectively, thus promoting the societal values of equity and respect for diversity.

The Discretionary Development Equalisation Grant is a consolidation of the Equalisation Grant, Local Government Management Service Delivery Programme (LGMSD), Peace Recovery and Development Plan (PRDP), Luwero-Rwenzori Development Programme (LRDP), and Uganda Support to Municipal Infrastructure Development (USMID) and it is allocated in such a way that Local Governments lagging behind national average indicators per the Constitution Article 193 are enabled to improve and catch up with the rest. Without going into the details of the Discretionary Development Equalisation Grants calculations, Table 12.2

shows the basics of the formula used in allocating District and Urban Discretionary Development Equalisation Grants.

The allocation formula intends to be objective, simple, and easy to understand; be (politically) acceptable; and use reliable information from official sources. It is clear from the above table that when allocating these grants, the government intends to make every local government in rural and urban areas able to address critical issues of infrastructure development, service delivery, conflict, equity, environment, and health/epidemics. However, many reports indicate that this form of transfer also has negative consequences for local democracy and local financial management. For example, Ahmad et al. (2005, p. 23) states: "A politically driven and ambitious decentralisation programme implemented by the authorities since the late 1990s has had mixed results in

Table 12.2 Formula for allocation of district and urban discretionary development equalisation grants 2003/2024

Variable name	*Weights in percentage District Urban*	*Justification*
Constant (fixed allocation for Higher/Lower local governments)	20 17.5	Ensure that Higher and Lower Local Governments have minimum allocations for the construction and completion of a meaningful infrastructure
Rural Population/ Urban Population	30 60	Provide for demand/scale of delivering services
Rural poverty headcount/Urban poverty head county	40 15	Equalising variables—to allocate greater resources to districts that lag behind as per article 193 (4) of the Constitution
Conflict	5 3	Allocate more resources to Local Governments severely affected by conflict
Environmental risk index	2.5 2	Ensure that Higher and Lower Local Governments have allocations for addressing environmental risks both in Rural and Urban setting
Population in high epidemiological risk	2.5 2.5	Ensure that Higher and Lower Local Governments have allocations for addressing COVID-19, Ebola, and other epidemiological risks

Source Author, based on data from the Ministry of Local Government (2025)

enhancing service delivery. Paradoxically, concerns with service delivery results, partially driven by donors' requirements, have resulted in a deconcentrated system relying on conditional grants and unfunded mandates. This has reduced the incentives, responsibility, and ownership for local authorities to improve service delivery. Crucially, for functions where the local authorities have had full responsibility, better service quality has resulted than in those areas in which there are overlapping responsibilities between the center and the local authorities".

12.4 Conclusions

In the context of Uganda's history, with highly centralised undemocratic public governance and little government accountability to the people, decentralisation has been an innovative politico-administrative and socio-economic undertaking of high value. Decentralised governance, conceived for the empowerment of local communities' democratisation, participation, equitable service delivery, accountability, and effectiveness, has sustained the promise of making local communities masters of their development.

However, the success of decentralised governance in these terms depends mainly on the effectiveness of the financial transfers from central to local governments. While the financial transfers (conditional, unconditional, and equalisation grants) have been instrumental in pushing forward the purpose of decentralisation, recently, there has been a trend of these transfers declining to the detriment of enhancement of public and societal values pursued through local governments. Reviving progress in these values requires the central government to increase the financial transfers and reverse the trend of decentralisation by, among other things, restraining central government departments from withholding funds that are required by law to be transferred to local governments to support transferred responsibilities and functions, including the delivery of services. This will help avoid unfunded mandates, which jeopardise service delivery, participation of grassroots people in decision-making, inclusion, and accountability.

The sustainability of local participatory democracy strongly depends on how local government financing mechanisms empower local people to be masters of their development processes and outcomes. Much depends on the central government respecting the provisions of the constitution and the law to sustain the financial transfers to local governments and enable them to fulfil their legal mandates, promote public management and societal values, and effectively deliver critical services that enable grassroots people to enjoy human rights.

Annex: Country Profile: Uganda

See Table 12.3.

Promoting democracy has been one of Uganda's ambitions and fundamentals of decentralisation and local governance. It is important to remember that the objectives of the country's decentralisation policy contained a mix of public management values of effectiveness

Table 12.3 Municipal political power structures

Criteria	*Results*
The level of autonomy of municipal governments over their functional mandates: the question of whether municipal governance institutions can only perform mandated tasks or can choose from a predefined scope of tasks Indicator: yes, partly, no	Partly
The level of freedom of municipal governments to decide their own political organisation and electoral system (can they, for example, determine their own electoral districts, number of seats, electoral system, etc.) Indicator: yes, partly, no	No
The constitutional or legal mechanisms to assert the autonomy of municipal governments. Examples of specific constitutional or legal mechanisms that allow municipal governments to assert their autonomy include (a) constitutional clauses or other statutory regulations protecting local self-government; (b) recourse to the judicial system through constitutional courts to settle disputes with higher authorities; or (c) other constitutional or legal protections of municipal autonomy exist (e.g. higher-level governments are prevented from forcing municipal governments to merge) Indicator: yes, partly, no	Partly
Municipal governments' right to use the legal system against higher-level government (de jure and de facto—do they use such right?) Indicator yes (both de jure and de facto), partly, no	Yes
The level to which decisions made by municipal governance institutions are subject to administrative supervision for their responsibilities and if higher-level approval is needed to act in their own matters Indicator yes, no	Partly
Does the higher-level have the right to remove local executives [or other local officials] without judicial intervention? Indicator yes, no	Yes

Source Author, based on own research (2025)

and efficiency in service delivery and the societal values of democracy, participation, people empowerment, and accountability.

Introduced by the decentralisation policy of 1992, the fundamentals of decentralisation in Uganda are currently provided in the national constitution of 1995 in the following terms underpinning subsidiarity, coordination, participation, democracy, and financial autonomy, among other things:

i. "The state shall be guided by the principle of decentralisation and devolution of governmental functions and powers to the people at appropriate levels where they can best manage and direct their own affairs.
ii. The system shall be such as to ensure that functions, powers and responsibilities are devolved and transferred to local government units in a coordinated manner.
iii. Decentralisation shall be a principle applying to all levels of local government and in particular, from higher to lower local government units to ensure people's participation and democratic control in decision-making.
iv. The system shall be such as to ensure the full realisation of democratic governance at all local government levels.
v. There shall be established for each local government unit a sound financial base with reliable sources of revenue.
vi. Appropriate measures shall be taken to enable local government units to plan, initiate and execute policies in respect of all matters affecting the people within their jurisdiction.
vii. Persons in the service of local government shall be employed by the local governments.
viii. The local governments shall oversee the performance of persons employed by the government to provide services in their areas and monitor the provision of government services or the implementation of projects in their areas".

In that way, the 1995 constitution entrenches the financial autonomy of local governments, local democracy, participation in decision-making by grassroots people, and subsidiarity (Tables 12.4, 12.5 and 12.6).

A whole range of services are devolved to be delivered by local governments. They include education (nursery, primary, secondary, and

Table 12.4 Structure and quality of subnational electoral systems

Criteria	*Results*
How are municipal councillors elected? Indicator—election mode	Universal suffrage. Voting age is 18 years and above. Secret ballot and sometimes voters line behind preferred candidates
For what term are municipal councils elected (years)? Indicator—years of mandate	Five years. But they can continue presenting themselves for re-election. There is no limit
What is the level of citizen participation in municipal elections? Indicator: Low—("Normal") voter turnout is below 35% of eligible (registered) voters Average—Voter turnout is between 35 and 60% of eligible (registered) voters High—Voter turnout is over 60% of eligible (registered) voters	Besides media news pointing out that there was low turn out in the 2021 local council elections without figures, we have found no statistics on voter turn out in Municipal elections. Focus is generally on Presidential and Parliamentary elections

Source Author, based on own research (2025)

Table 12.5 Nature of subnational political party systems

Criteria	*Results*
Which subjects can run in municipal elections? Indicator—define who can participate	Citizen of Uganda, Residents in municipality, of voting age (18 years) and registered as voter For chairperson, one must have a minimum of "A" level education (high school)
How are party candidates for municipal council elections selected? Indicator—selected by party, elected by party, self-nomination, other	Sometimes selected and sometimes elected by parties In cases of independent candidates, they are self-nominated
Are there established rules for financing municipal political campaigns? Indicator—yes, no	No
Does the ruling national party have a dominant position in municipal elections? Indicator—yes, no	Yes

Source Author, based on own research (2025)

Table 12.6 Subnational political participation and accountability

Criteria	*Results*
Are all council meetings (required to be) open to the public? Indicator—yes, no	Yes
Are municipal records and documents (required to be) available to the public? Indicator—yes, no	Yes
Is the council (required to) engage in an open, participatory planning process? Indicator—yes, no	Yes
Are alternative participatory mechanisms, such as referendums or participatory budgeting, used? Indicator—yes, partly, no	Partly

Source Author, based on own research (2025)

technical); health services, including most hospitals and health centres; maternity and child welfare; communicable diseases; HIV/AIDS; public and environmental health; water; and most roads. While local governments are mandated primarily to provide such basic services, the central government provides guidance through sector policies, standards, sector budget guidelines, technical supervision, and support. More than delivering such services, devolution is intended to transfer the essentials of governance to the grassroots level, thus enhancing societal values such as equity, participation, inclusion, accountability, and local democracy. The organisational structures of local governments and administrative units are such that they provide a structural framework for promoting societal values and public management values such as effectiveness and efficiency. So, at least conceptually and by design and aspirational intent, decentralisation in Uganda has been an innovative and transformational strategic policy to transform the governance and administration of the country from the highly centralised bureaucracy inherited from colonial administration to an outcome and value-based governance focused on the people, public management values as well as societal values which values can be promoted through appropriate structures established through the decentralised governance as provided in the law. The most important aspect of Uganda's decentralisation is the existence of local councils from the village up to the district level. The political significance of this is that decentralisation was conceived essentially to promote the participation of the people in decision-making and in shaping their development. The Councils are elected, and so are the leaders who chair them and those who serve on executive committees.

Internally, within each local government as a unit, promoting and sustaining the following public management values is expected: accountability, value for money, efficiency in the utilisation of resources, effectiveness in achieving the set service delivery objectives, communication, and participatory decision-making processes that involve and engage the people in determining their needs. However, paying attention only to such public management values would only be inward-looking and self-serving on the part of managers of local governments. Local governments have the prime purpose of servicing the people in the context of participatory, value, and results-based governance. Therefore, local governments are very much expected to provide services effectively and efficiently with societal values of equity, inclusion, ethical leadership and integrity, respect for diversity, and particular attention to local socio-economic development interests and empowerment. Such societal values will make local government leadership respected and credible in the communities. In contrast, the public management values will make local government leadership internally sound, enabling them to serve the people optimally.

The delivery of services and the creation and sustainability of public management and societal values depend, to a large extent, on the availability and utilisation of financial and other resources as well as adherence to and application of the principles that underpin the performance of local governments in serving the people.

References

ACODE. (2020). *Memorandum on local government issues and policy recommendations*. Kampala: Advocates Coalition for Development and Environment.

Ahmad, E., Brosio, G., & Gonzalez, M. (2005). *Uganda: Managing more decentralization*. IMF Working Paper. Washington: IMF.

Mitchinson, R. (2003). Devolution in Uganda: An experiment in local service delivery. *Public Administration and Development, 23*, 241–248. https://doi.org/10.1002/pad.265

Uganda Bureau of Statistics. (2022, February). *Quarterly government finance bulletin*. Uganda Bureau of Statistics.

CHAPTER 13

Transfers and Local Democracy: A Comparative Global Perspective

Juraj Nemec, Michal Plaček, and Purshottama Sivanarain Reddy

13.1 Introduction

This book aims to document, through the selected national case studies, how fiscal transfers to local governments impact local democracy. The eleven country chapters selected and highlighted in the book explore the global effects of transfers in different political and institutional contexts. It also serves as a critique and provides a valuable source of information on

J. Nemec (✉)
Department of Public Economics, Masaryk University, Brno, Czech Republic
e-mail: juraj.nemec@umb.sk

M. Plaček
Department of Public and Social Policy, Charles University, Prague, Czech Republic
e-mail: MichalPlacek@seznam.cz

P. Sivanarain Reddy
University of Kwa Zulu-Natal, Durban, South Africa
e-mail: Reddyp1@ukzn.ac.za

J. Nemec et al. (eds.), *Local Government and Fiscal Transfers*, Governance and Public Management,
https://doi.org/10.1007/978-3-031-95674-4_13

different forms of impacts of transfers from higher levels of government to local self-government and ultimately on local democracy internationally.

Some of the authors argue that transfers may have a positive impact at the local level, as they may serve as a tool that promotes local democracy, empowerment, and the participation of local communities. The selected country chapters indicate that such assumptions may indeed materialise. The chapter on Indonesia, by way of example, states that a newly designed system of transfers improves resource utilisation and encourages and promotes transparency. The chapter on the Philippines presents the most comprehensive research on this topic. In this chapter, the original research of the respective authors highlights the effects of transfers on, inter alia, strengthening good governance and politics at the local level, using the quantitative analysis of data.

However, most studies tend also to emphasise the negative impacts of transfers and mention more specifically the following three directions, in which these effects have over the years manifested themselves, that is:

- Transfers are heavily influenced by political incentives offered to national and local legislators and policymakers.
- Transfers may make local self-government fiscally dependent, and in this regard, they may pursue central goals and priorities more than the local needs of the citizen.
- Transfers have (quite often unintended) impacts on local public financial management's quality, independence, and fairness.

The relevant country chapters document and interrogate all the critical areas of the potential effects of transfers on local democracy in their specific forms. The key findings are summarised and synthesised below.

13.2 Documented Effects of Transfers on Local Democracy

13.2.1 Transfers and Politics

The relevant texts of the country chapters clearly point out that with the help of national grants, the central government pushes its priorities, regardless of the needs of the local communities, making it impossible to plan and manage strategically at the local level. At the same time, it increases inequality, as only the desired projects are supported and implemented. The transfers are frequently used to support the ruling party-related policies; discretionary transfers, like funding after an earthquake (or other disasters), or even equalisation funds, are provided to local governments who have the same political allegiances or to reward the local citizenry for/motivate ex-ante for "positive" voting (deemed as political corruption). Attention, by way of example, is invited to the Albanian chapter, which alludes to this and states that:

> Transfers are often associated with a lack of transparency and risk of misuse, creating spaces for political preferences and use of funds for non-strategic purposes

The Albanian chapter also deals with the specific transfer mechanism—the interventions of the central government in the repayment of arrears of the local governments. This kind of transfer has quite often raised concerns regarding the political influence on the allocation of funds. There have been cases where the distribution of funds has been perceived as favouring the local governments run by the political party in power, raising questions about the transparency and objectivity of the national fund allocation process. In this context, the relevant chapter states that:

> The distribution of funds from the RDF is neither predictable nor transparent, which leaves room for political intervention by giving more access to municipalities with mayors from the political force of most of the central Government.
> During the election campaigns in Albania (March-April 2021 for the parliamentary elections and April-May 2023 for the local elections), a significant increase in the distribution of individual grants for the reconstruction of housing damaged by the November 2019 earthquake was observed.

The "precondition" for politicisation of transfers is the lack of transparency related to the system of allocation of transfers. This issue is mentioned in several chapters (the Czech Republic, Uganda, and Sweden). Non-transparency is the problem, as transparency and predictability are critical pillars of good governance. The Swedish chapter calls for greater transparency and states in this regard that:

> The system of targeted grants decreases the transparency of local government and sectoral finance. The lack of a uniform framework for information and statistical data on state financial transfers necessitates a new policy approach.

13.2.2 Transfers and Voting Participation

The Czech Republic chapter documents a particular issue: the negative impact of low fiscal autonomy on electoral competition. The authors found that Czech municipalities with uncontested elections in 2022 operated with a significantly higher share of expenditure financed from targeted transfers (uncontested elections are electoral races in which citizens are unable to choose among political alternatives, and their vote makes no difference to the outcome because there is only one list of candidates, or the number of candidates equals the number of council seats). Uncontested elections present a very concerning challenge to democracy, and the Czech data confirmed a strong negative effect of uncontested elections on the turnout and the general interest in the elections. It is indeed a matter of grave concern where there is no political competition at the local level for the competing political spaces. It also implies that the best political candidates are not coming forward, and, more importantly, there will be limited diversity relative to local political representation.

13.2.3 Transfers and Fiscal Dependency of Local Governments

The fact that local governments heavily—and excessively—rely on transfers is visible, especially in the sample of less decentralised countries globally. High dependence on non-targeted transfers, which local governments can freely use, may look like a less critical problem; however, this is an underestimation. The fact that the European Charter of Local Self-Government (p. 3) requires that:

> The financial systems on which resources available to local authorities are based shall be sufficiently diversified and buoyant to enable them to keep pace as far as practically possible with the real evolution of the cost of carrying out their tasks.

The above suggests that too much dependence on resources from higher government levels is inappropriate and creates many risks. More specifically, it creates financial dependency, limits local government autonomy, and creates tensions.

A high dependence on targeted transfers represents an even more critical problem. It is directly in contradiction to the principles of the European Charter of Local Self-Government (p. 3), stating that:

> Local authorities shall be entitled, within national economic policy, to adequate financial resources of their own, of which they may dispose freely within the framework of their powers.

A high dependence on transfers directly jeopardises local democracy and limits the sustainability of local public finance. In our sample, transfers represent approximately 50% of local government revenue in Albania. In Uganda, the transfers may represent about 90% of local government revenue (exact data are unavailable). Moreover, most transfer resources are delivered in the form of conditional grants. Even the Discretionary Development Equalization Grant, which is formally a non-targeted transfer, has in its rules that its function is to enable local governments to allocate funds to priority local development needs that are with their mandates and are consistent with national priorities.

The Swedish chapter might be a surprise for many readers. Sweden is generally accepted as a fully decentralised country; however, the country chapter documents that municipal financial resources from targeted state grants have recently increased faster than general grants. The Swedish chapter states:

> The main problem is that targeted grants in the analysed sectors "tell local governments which tasks and activities should be prioritised, force local governments to realise activities financed by the central government and no other services, which might be more important in a concrete territory, and motivate municipalities to undertake tasks prioritised by the central government".

The Indian chapter also heavily stresses the problem of a too-high dependence of local governments on transfers:

> Dependence on one source of revenue restricts their ability to generate diverse revenue streams and limits their capacity to address increasing

> infrastructure demands. Hence, dependence on the transfer of funds from higher levels of government becomes predominant. The absence of an enhanced range of revenue sources and lack of efficiency in revenue collection have led to the municipalities' ineffective management of the funds. This phenomenon is reflected in low spending by the municipalities to provide basic urban services and support growth, productivity, and quality of life.

The Indonesian chapter also deals with this issue:

> Focusing on planned performance indicators also raises regional and local autonomy concerns. Local governments often feel compelled to prioritise initiatives that align with national targets, potentially sidelining specific local and regional needs. For example, prioritising education improvements to meet central performance criteria can divert resources from addressing other pressing local issues, such as access to clean water, basic education, or disaster mitigation efforts. This condition suggests that there are still obstacles in adjusting the achievement of national accountability goals and maintaining the flexibility needed for local governance.

It means that national priorities will take precedence over local needs, which will undoubtedly be challenging if it happens continuously. In many countries, there is a considerable overlap between national and local priorities as they generally revolve around basic needs or related matters. This is a challenge when a wide divergence exists between local needs and national goals and priorities.

The chapter on Japan is another, mentioning pervasive effects of the dependence on transfers regarding free decision-making at the local government level:

> As so-called subsidised projects, central government subsidies (categorical grants) significantly influence local governments' project choices. It is customary for local governments to be able to commercialise a project only after it has been selected for a central government subsidy project.

As pointed out above, this does stifle independent thinking and democratic decision-making at the local level, thereby impacting the quality of local governance.

13.2.4 Transfers and Local Financial Management

Under this heading, several different forms of fiscal transfers' (mostly non-intended) impacts on local financial management are included.

13.2.4.1 Underfinancing of Delegated Responsibilities

Several chapters of this book stress that the state is expected to pay the full costs of delegated responsibilities executed by local governments on behalf of the state/provincial and central governments. However, their local government revenues cover a particular part of these costs. Such a situation undermines local democracy, as the freedom of local bodies to manage local matters is limited by shifting part of the resources towards duties realised on behalf of the state. The Lithuanian chapter highlights this issue more directly:

> As a result, municipalities must use their own budget funds, reducing financing for other activities accordingly.

The objective purpose of problems related to the underfinancing of delegated responsibilities is the fact that the full costs of the execution of delegated responsibilities are unknown. The Albanian chapter states:

> A main challenge for municipalities is the accurate measurement of the implementation costs of delegated responsibilities and the determination of financial needs. ... about 35% of municipalities do not have structured mechanisms for analysing and reporting expenditures, leading to underestimation or overestimation of costs.

The Slovak chapter even suggests that neither the central government nor municipalities are interested in knowing the actual costs of delegated responsibilities. The authors' direct research of the Slovak chapter documented that municipalities do not know the actual costs of delegated responsibilities and that their opinions on the level of cost coverage significantly differ. In one case, the municipality claimed that only 1% of costs are covered; the other extreme is the opinion that 100% of costs are covered—such results represent a curiosity. The authors also stress that they were surprised by such a minimal willingness of municipalities to calculate exact costs, even among larger municipalities.

13.2.4.2 *Unclear Division Between Competences*

The chapter on Lithuania documents that the unclear border between original and delegated responsibilities, or even their overlap, undoubtedly creates (fiscal and political) tension between the entities sharing them. Moreover, such a situation may negatively impact municipalities' motivation to achieve better performance results.

The chapter on South Africa provides a very concrete example where the borders between state and local government competences are unclear, as follows:

> The transportation mandate is typical of functional fragmentation, with the national government responsible for national roads while provinces are responsible for arterials, main roads, and district-level roads, and municipalities are responsible for local roads. However, as towns and cities have grown and the boundaries of municipalities have expanded, many of these main roads have become routes that only service the local municipal area and should have been reclassified and allocated to municipalities to manage. Instead, due to the budget tied to a road (fixed asset), the provincial government has neglected to hand over such assets to the local government. The result is that towns and cities have become a maze of roads which are managed by different entities, each with their own norms and standard of development and maintenance.

The above-mentioned state of affairs presents a governance challenge, not to mention the confusion among the local communities regarding which sphere of government is responsible for a particular road. The above can be seen against the backdrop that many of the roads in South Africa, be they local, provincial, or national, urgently need repair.

13.2.4.3 *Transfers and Equalisation*

One generally accepted transfer function is to support equalisation—to help local governments with a limited revenue base and/or excessive expenditure needs. The chapters allude to the fact that the transfers may not be well designed to fulfil this function. The Slovak chapter states:

> The existing transfer system insufficiently reflects the well-known factors causing fiscal imbalances. The degree of vertical fiscal imbalance varies considerably across local governments in the Slovak Republic, as it results from a combination of several economic and non-economic factors specific to a given local government and insufficient capacity of the transfer

> system to deliver its equalisation function. Too high financial inequalities between municipalities undoubtfully negatively influence local democracy in Slovakia.

The Indonesian chapter also mentions transfers' limited capacity to deliver their equalisation function—it calls for more targeted central government support for less developed regions of the country.

The chapter on Japan documents other problems connected with the equalisation function of transfers—that the equalisation system is excessive and tries to deliver "equality". More specifically, the chapter states:

> In other words, the local fiscal adjustment system under the Local Allocation Tax Law tends to keep local governments at a standardised level. For example, in the calculation of the local allocation tax, if a local government increases its tax revenue, the local allocation tax is reduced by a corresponding percentage. Even if local governments strive to increase their revenues through voluntary efforts, there will be pressure to level the playing field.

The South African chapter also has a similar response and states that:

> The appropriateness of the allocation methodology is questionable in the extent to which it adequately considers differing socioeconomic contexts and the abilities to utilise funds efficiently. The criteria used to distribute funds do not adequately address different municipalities' varying needs and capacities.

The question mark placed on the allocation methodology for grants also alludes to the fact that a "one-size-fits-all" approach or policy is being adopted, with limited consideration given to socioeconomic circumstances, requisite capacities and capabilities, and the urban/rural divide.

13.2.4.4 Transfers, Administrative, and Compliance Costs

This fact that transfers may generate compliance costs on the side of local governments is rarely investigated in the academic literature on fiscal transfers globally. However, the Swedish chapter brings it up by pointing out that:

> The transfers complicate current planning within municipalities and create additional administrative burdens. … The final important negative impact of this system of targeted grants relates to the fact that municipalities must actively apply for state-targeted grants. Such a system creates the risk that unnecessary inequalities in service access between citizens of different municipalities may occur. Even in cases where the service is financed from such a grant is needed, a municipality may not apply, nor to bear the administrative burden of the application and reporting processes.

The chapter on Indonesia raises the same concern—the authors state that around a fifth of all local governments have never been eligible for a Performance Challenge Fund grant. The Indonesian chapter also deals with the capacity of local governments to "receive" grants. It documents that regions with high natural resource capacity, such as Kalimantan and Papua, show more significant potential to adjust to performance criteria for distributing transfers.

The Indian chapter indirectly mentions the issue of administrative costs. This chapter shows that higher levels of government need to establish structures which administer and manage the transfer system. The existence of such bodies means extra costs for the public fiancé system, and these bodies may not function well, as highlighted in the Indian case study. The Indian chapter states, alluding to some of the challenges:

> The Constitution mandates that after every five years, the state government shall establish a State Finance Commission (SFC) in the State. Like the Central Finance Commission, SFCs play a crucial role in allocating State resources to the local governments, including the municipalities. However, timely constitution and effective functioning of SFCs have been a significant challenge in many States.

13.2.4.5 Delayed Transfers

The Indian, and more specifically, the Ugandan chapter, stresses this issue. If transfers from the higher level do not arrive within the stipulated time period and are not in the requisite amount, the local government's capacity to deliver its functions, especially in less decentralised countries, is endangered, negatively impacting local governance and service delivery.

13.3 Conclusions

The selected country chapters documented both the positive and negative impacts of transfers on local democracy in a global context. Although the sample selected is not fully representative globally, some general conclusions can be derived from its contents.

It can be hypothesised that transfers can also positively affect local democracy. The sample selected and the existing literature on the subject, which documents the positive effects and impact of transfers on local democracy (like Dinh Thanh et al., 2023), suggest that in the case of less developed local democracies, less experienced local governments, the central rules and regulations, applied via the transfer mechanisms, may enhance local development. These central rules and regulations may, for example, necessitate greater transparency or accountability at the local level. It is very disputable if transfers can also help to enhance spending patterns, as expecting that the central level knows more about local needs is rather problematic (however, the example of Uganda demonstrates that transfers may have this ambition).

The most important lesson that has emerged is that transfers, if not well designed, may create "problems" and "challenges" in all countries if the process is not well managed. A highly decentralised country like Sweden, which was introduced in the equation as part of the sample, documents several negative aspects of transfers for local social services. It points out quite clearly that even in most democratic and decentralised countries, the pervasive effects of transfers can still be visible.

To conclude, one can emphasise that the above-quoted principles from the European Charter of Local Self-Government are not defined without justification. The role of transfers (especially targeted transfers) in local public finance should be as limited as possible. In the specific case, when transfers are used to finance delegated responsibilities, which is "correct", the predictable and transparent rules for their calculation should exist, requiring the change from cash accounting (the practice at the local level in very many countries) to activity-based accounting. Activity-based accounting is the only mechanism that can determine the actual costs of public services. Without knowing these costs, all disputes about commensurate resources are just non-informed political discussions.

References

Dinh Thanh, S., Nguyen, C. P., Duy-Tung, B., Binh, N. Q., & Van, D. T. B. (2023). Spatial spillover effects of fiscal decentralization on governance and public administration quality. *Regional Studies, 57*(3), 478–496. https://doi.org/10.1080/00343404.2022.2078801

European Charter of Local Self-Government. Council of Europe.

Index

J. Nemec et al. (eds.), *Local Government and Fiscal Transfers*, Governance and Public Management,
https://doi.org/10.1007/978-3-031-95674-4

Kolibri 360 GmbH
Ferdinand-Jühlke-Straße 7
99095 Erfurt, Deutschland
produktsicherheit@kolibri360.de